Introduction to

Ancient
Philosophy

Introduction to
Ancient
Philosophy

Don E. Marietta Jr.

M.E. Sharpe
Armonk, New York
London, England

Library of Congress Cataloging-in-Publication Data

Marietta, Don E.
Introduction to ancient philosophy / Don E. Marietta, Jr.
p.   cm.
Includes bibliographical references and index.
ISBN 0–7656–0215–6 (hardcover : alk. paper). —
ISBN 0–7656–0216–4 (pbk. : alk. paper)
1. Philosophy, Ancient.   I. Title.
B162.9.M34   1998
180—dc21   97–46373
CIP

Printed in the United States of America

The paper used in this publication meets the minimum requirements of
American National Standard for Information Sciences—
Permanence of Paper for Printed Library Materials,
ANSI Z 39.48-1984.

EB (c)   10   9   8   7   6   5   4   3   2   1
EB (p)   10   9   8   7   6   5   4   3   2   1

To Lester Embree

valued friend and colleague

CONTENTS

INTRODUCTION

This book is designed to assist in introducing students to philosophy by letting them see the questions, creative answers, and methods through which philosophy began. There are other ways to introduce students to philosophy; a popular approach is a course in philosophical issues, such as the question of freedom, the nature of knowledge, and the mind/body issue. This approach has the advantage of dealing with matters that most students will recognize immediately as philosophical. If the course explores contemporary issues in social ethics, the students will see the relevance of philosophical issues to individual lives and to society. There will be no question of why the class is studying the subject matter.

With the obvious advantages of the issues approach to philosophy, why take the route of using Greek and Roman philosophy? What are the advantages? One advantage is the systematic exposure to the thought of widely recognized philosophers such as Plato, Aristotle, and Augustine. The student who continues to study philosophy will keep running into the great thinkers who are the pioneers of Western philosophy and should know what they did, not merely recognize that they are considered important.

In addition, learning about the philosophers of Greece and Rome, the student will be exposed to the main issues of philosophy. Very few philosophical issues went unexamined. Most *were* examined, usually in a creative way that led to increasingly sophisticated treatment in later centuries. Some philosophers think that all important issues were explored by the Greek and Roman pioneers of philosophy. Alfred North Whitehead, for example, said that all philosophy is a footnote to Plato. This may be an exaggeration, but one with a core of truth; students meet the main issues of philosophy in a study of the Greek and Roman philosophers.

To accomplish the most in a study of the earliest philosophers, it is important to pay attention to cultural and historical background. To study the individual philosophers in isolation from their cultural backgrounds and without showing their relationships to their predecessors will fail to give adequate knowledge of them. They should not be examined the way one might investigate unrelated old pieces of furniture in an antique shop. These great thinkers did not enter our intellectual world like comets from outer space. They were not visitors, but members of their culture, who were influenced by its values, its beliefs, and even its myths. The teacher of early philosophy should not seek an "Oh! Wow!" response. The purpose is not just to show what a "great mind" the person was. The student should admire, but not the way a tourist who knows little of art or Italian culture might admire a statue in Florence.

We should seek to understand the philosophers' minds within the context of their culture, for not only did most thinkers respond to the ideas of earlier philosophers, but they also were influenced by aspects of the culture that we would not consider philosophical. Even myths and folklore influenced the expression, and in many cases the content of thought, of philosophers, who used these aspects of their culture in their individual ways. Basic ideas about the nature of the world and its processes, first expressed as myth or folklore, as seen, for example, in Homer and Hesiod, reappear in the philosophies as philosophical or proto-scientific concepts. Knowing the cultural background of early philosophers will make what they say much more intelligible, as well as show their creativity. These philosophers were unusual and impressive people, but we must not let our study approach them so individually that we do not see them in a social, political, and intellectual context.

Much of the value of a study of Greek and Roman philosophers is lost if we look only at their declarations and fail to see the creativity and insight involved in their questions. In some cases, the questions show the genius. The lasting contributions to philosophy can lie in its questions, even when the answers are not very exciting. For example, the genius of Thales lay in looking for one underlying explanation of matter, not in the speculation that all matter was water. Often, the questions kept the practice of philosophy moving ahead generation after generation.

After years of teaching Greek and Roman philosophy, I want to produce a textbook that is not so difficult that it discourages part of the class. At the same time, it should be critically and historically sound. It should not be sketchy in reporting and explaining the thought of the philosophers, and it needs to go beyond the common notions about them, which were developed before the critical historical studies of recent years. We now know that some of the stories about these thinkers are not historically sound. I believe a student should realize that historical study does make progress, even when the progress creates uncertainty about some favorite stories.

I do not suggest that a philosophy class should consist simply of debunking older notions from intellectual history. We need to remember that even stories and explanations that are not supportable historically are important to know about. Common perceptions often had great impact on subsequent developments in philosophy. The mistaken notions among European scholars about the teaching of Averroes, the great interpreter of Aristotle, produced some of the most important philosophy of the Middle Ages. There may not be equally striking examples from the Greeks and Romans, but the common notions about Socrates, which do not have a sound historical basis, have influenced thinking for two thousand years. I believe a student should know that the popular picture of Socrates found in the early dialogues of Plato was only assumed to be historically correct. Xenophon gives a different picture of Socrates' philosophical interests. Aristotle, who generally supports the Platonic picture, is not a completely reliable source, since he did not know Socrates and must have accepted the popular picture on the authority of Plato. There would be little point, however, for the student merely to be negative about the picture of Socrates that has influenced many generations of thinkers. There are times when the perception is more important in some respects than the reality, and the popular picture of Socrates inspired generations of philosophers.

A philosophy textbook should not be so loaded with Greek words that students become discouraged, but an important aspect of learning Greek philosophy is knowing that it was Greek. There are mythological and philosophical terms that do not have suitable English equivalents. I encourage students to learn the Greek terms. Some students respond to this with such enthusiasm that they want to learn the terms in Greek letters, and I do not discourage this; it has led some students to a study of Greek. For most students, however, knowing the transliterated terms is as far as they want to venture. *Ataraxía, ápeiron, diánoia,* and a few other terms are not too difficult to learn, and it is better to learn them than to read into Greek philosophy notions that were not part of the thought of the Greek thinkers. Greek words in this text will be supplied along with English translations for the students who are interesting in learning some Greek. This does not get in the way of the reading, and I think it will be appreciated by some students.

This study of Greek philosophy will begin with the Presocratics, the earliest Greek thinkers who can reasonably be considered philosophers. Their interests and ideas were quite different from those of Plato and Aristotle, but they have considerable interest for contemporary philosophers and may be seen as raising heuristic questions, that is, their inquiries led to significant methods of study and theorizing in later years.

Socrates and the Sophists show a new emphasis in philosophy, which developed in Athens during the fifth century B.C., largely replacing the Presocratics' interest in nature with concern for cultural and social matters. Plato and Aristotle left a literary record of systematic philosophy dealing with a full range of interests, from metaphysics to ethics and aesthetics. Plato showed little interest in natural science, but Aristotle was engaged in research and writing on all the scientific areas known in his time.

The period after Aristotle, following the death of Alexander the Great, saw another change in the style and interests of philosophy. This came about in response to the needs of people who had lost much of their sense of security and who longed for answers to their personal unrest and confusion and for help in living their lives, in this world or in a life to come. The Epicureans taught a way of life, grounded in the metaphysics of Democritus, that aimed at achieving *ataraxia,* an inner sense of serenity. The Stoics used the metaphysics of Heraclitus to justify a way of life that freed the wise person from anxiety about those things that are beyond the control of the individual. The Skeptics found relief from philosophical anxiety in acknowledging that certain knowledge is impossible and in living by probability.

Much of the philosophy of the Graeco-Roman period cannot be separated from religion. The basic premises are religious, as is the goal of aiming for release from the burden of an ages-long series of reincarnations. The role of philosophy was understood as providing guidance in eventually reuniting the soul with the divine realm from which it came. Two developments in philosophy during the Roman period profoundly influenced the philosophy of the Middle Ages and later; Neo-Platonism and the Christian philosophy of Augustine bring the ancient period to a close and lay the foundation for a thousand years of Western thought.

To facilitate student reading of the philosophers themselves, not only the commentary, translations of the philosophers' writings are cited in the appropriate chapters as well as in the bibliography. Sources of the fragments of the writings of the Presocratics are discussed in chapter 2. English translations of the works of Plato and Aristotle should be available in college libraries, and selections of their writings are available in inexpensive paperbacks. Scholars usually have their favored translations, but the choice of translation should not be of great importance for the undergraduate college student. Augustine's works are also readily available, and there are inexpensive paper editions of the *Confessions.* Works of other ancient philosophers will be difficult to find outside a college library, but most college libraries will have works like Reginald E. Allen's *Greek Philosophy: Thales to Aristotle* and *Readings in Ancient Western Philosophy,* edited by George F. McLean and Patrick J. Aspell. For the period after Aristotle, see Rosamond Kent Sprague's book on the older Sophists, Whitney J. Oates's book on Stoic and Epicurean philosophers, Jason L. Saunders's *Greek and Roman Philosophy after Aristotle,* and *The Hellenistic Philosophers,* edited by A.A. Long and D.N. Sedley. With help from the course instructor, the student can make a selection of useful passages to read.

Introduction to

Ancient Philosophy

1 GREEK CULTURAL BACKGROUND

Greek philosophy shows the influence of ideas current in early Greek culture. Myths and religious beliefs and beliefs, about the nature of the world, were not the same in all parts of the Greek civilization, however. The ideas that had the most profound influence on the development of philosophy are associated with the mainland of Greece and with Ionia, and these two areas differed markedly in some respects. The people who settled Greece came there at different times and from different places, and these different backgrounds are reflected in various words in the Greek language and in other cultural differences. The topography of Greece also, among other factors, led to the development of separate city-states, with laws and customs peculiar to each state.

Beginning in the eighth century B.C., the Greeks established colonies in the area of the Mediterranean, including parts of Italy and North Africa. The cultures of the colonies reflected the beliefs and practices of the city-states that founded them. Many of the philosophers we will study came from such colonies.

The people living on islands in the Aegean Sea and on the coast of what is now Turkey, an area known then as Ionia, contributed to the development of philosophy in ways mainland Greeks could not, but ideas from the mainland made their own way into philosophical thinking. We will look at the different ways these two divisions of Greek culture influenced developing philosophy.

Ionia

The origin of the Ionian culture is an interesting topic that we cannot go into deeply here. It seems to have had roots in the Minoan culture of Crete and in the culture of the early Dorian invaders, who brought ideas and language that we call Indo-European. We know this culture from the works of Homer and Hesiod. Even though the familiar pantheon of gods and goddesses is a part of the Homeric tradition, however, the Ionian worldview did not include some of the aspects of religion with which Western societies are familiar. There was no religious organization or clergy. There was no body of dogma and no concept of heresy. The religion, if we want to call it that, was largely a matter of civic ceremony, not of personal piety, inwardness, religious feeling, or involvement. John Burnet has described the culture as "secular."[1] W.K.C. Guthrie says the Ionians' "interests lay in this world," and explanations of the origin and nature of the world in terms of the actions of divinities were no longer acceptable.[2] This allowed great freedom of religious thought and freedom for speculation about the nature of the world. The intellectual openness of Ionia stands in contrast to the more restrictive approach of Athens, which banished people for "wrong" religious beliefs, as was done to several philosophers.

The attitude of Homeric religion was optimistic, not oriented toward fear and guilt. It can be described as "this-worldly." There was little concern for an afterlife. There is reference in Homer to Hades, but this does not indicate belief in a meaningful immortality as the reward of living a righteous life. Hades seems to have been a place were "shades" of the dead gradually fade away. The attitude toward it can be seen in Achilles' speech to Odysseus, in which he says that any life on earth is better than being in Hades.[3]

What were the gods and goddesses of the Homeric epics, that they did not give rise to the familiar features of religion? According to the Ionic mythology, the Olympian deities were not the creators of the world. They evolved, along with humans and the world, from a primitive chaos. They were immortal (in the sense of being very long-lived), but were not eternal, not beings who had always existed. There were stories of their interacting with mortals on occasion, but they were not the protectors of humanity.[4]

The Ionian culture contributed significantly to philosophy through providing the freedom and openness in which scientific speculation and metaphysical thought could develop. The freedom to speculate about the origin and nature of the world enabled ideas to develop that might have been suppressed in a different culture. Even though no one seems to have denied that the gods existed, it was not dangerous to interpret them as forces of nature or as having their origin in stories of heroes of times past. Some philosophers freely criticized the moral weaknesses of the gods that were reported in myth and legend.

The Ionians also held some significant ideas about life and the world that influenced the development of philosophical beliefs. In particular, notions that were related to the mythology or folklore of Ionia influenced philosophical views.

One of these notions is the belief that all things have an allotted portion (*moira*) in the scheme of things. Not only humans, but gods and natural forces as well have a role from which they must not deviate. Moera was the goddess of fate, but each thing's allotted place, its *moira,* was not a god, not a personal being, but an impersonal restriction on everything. We might think of it as a force of nature, but using the concept of a "force" might be reading into the concept our modern way of thinking about nature. We should not think of a thing having a given place as "fate," either, for we tend to associate fate with what lies in store for an individual person as an individual, rather than what one has in common with all humans. Even though the goddess Moera was replaced in Hesiod's epics by the Fates, three female beings who determine such aspects of a person's life as the time of death, we miss the depth of the concept of *moira* if we think of it as personal fate. What the early concept involved was a cosmic order affecting all beings and keeping everything in place.[5]

To depart from the allotted place is an act of *hubris,* a transgression that will bring punishment as the offending person, god, or natural element is forced back into its place. The enforcement of the restrictions of *moira* is variously personified as the work of the avenging deities, the Furies or Erinyes or Eumenides. Jean-Paul Sartre employs this theme in his work *The Flies,* in which the avenging force is pictured as flies that torment the offender.

The concept of *moira* can be seen in the way some early Greek philosophers describe the forces of nature. The ideas of order and balance in the world and in human life might be influenced by the notion of *moira,* a mythological concept that is thus restated in early philosophical and scientific doctrines.

Another influential idea is hylozoism, also called panpsychism, the belief that matter is in some sense alive.[6] In most modern thought, with some significant exceptions, matter is treated as inert, dead stuff. If it moves, grows, changes, or is involved with mental activity, some explanation is sought in something outside matter itself. People have not always thought of matter as dead stuff, however. A firm distinction between matter on one hand, and life and thought on the other, is just one way of thinking. With contemporary developments in physics, it appears that those philosophers who did not think of matter as lifeless stuff (and they were not limited to the Ionians or to ancient times) might have had a keener insight into the nature of the world than those who thought that matter is dead until something else acts upon it.

Exactly what the Ionians, and some other philosophers, meant by attributing motion and aspects of mentality to matter is difficult to explain. They did not think that rocks sat about contemplating things or reminiscing about people who had passed them by, but they thought that matter inherently has some aspects of life and is by its nature closely involved with that which we consider mental. This means that some questions that seem very important to those who rigidly separate matter from life and mentality are not problems at all for those who do not accept the firm separation. That some matter displays life and thought is simply what one should expect.

The Greek Mainland

The worldly and optimistic approach of the Ionians was not common to all of Greece. Outside of Ionia, mainly among the poor, and especially in times of grave crisis, people found hope and solace in different kinds of religion, such as worship of household gods or gods associated with special places, and cults based on the nature cycle: the alternation of the growing season, warm in Europe and wet in Egypt, and the dormant season, when crops did not grow and domestic animals did not reproduce.

Philosophy was influenced by the religions based on the nature cycle, referred to as mystery cults because they kept their rites and ceremonies only for the eyes of the initiated. This secrecy was breached by a few writers, such as Apuleius, who described the Isis–Osiris cult of Egypt in his *Metamorphoses*. We now know that most of the popular cults were based on the myth of a divine lord who was killed, and the grief of his consort, a goddess on whom certain crops depended, who failed to attend to the growth of the crops until her lord was restored to life and returned to her. These myths of a dying–rising lord took a number of forms. Some told of a divine being killed by wicked mythological creatures such as the Titans, while others told of emasculation or other evil done to the lord that made him unavailable to his female consort.

One mystery religion with a story suitable for children was the Eleusinian cult, which included a myth of the goddess of grain, Ceres, who is also known as Demeter and by other names. It was not the loss of a lover that made Ceres neglect her task of protecting the growing of grain. Her daughter Proserpine, or Persephone, was kidnapped and taken to Hades by Pluto, god of the underworld. Ceres finally found her daughter but could not keep her except during part of the year, because Proserpine had eaten some of a pomegranate in Hades and therefore had to spend part of every year with Pluto. When Ceres had her daughter with her, she made the grain grow, but when Proserpine was in Hades Ceres grieved and neglected her agricultural duties. A point of the religion was the ceremonies in which the worshipers identified with Ceres, and by acting out aspects of the myth ensured the return of the season in which grain grew.[7]

I learned the story of Ceres and her daughter in grade school but did not then learn of its religious significance. It was just a sweet story of motherly love. The other mystery cult myths would not have been thought suitable for the schoolboy's ears, since they dealt with interruptions in the sexual bliss of a divine couple who had a role to play in the growth of food or making of wine or the fertility of farm animals. The basic pattern of identification with the suffering of the divine pair and use of ceremonies to bring them back together for the sake of a new growing season appears in all of the mystery cults.

It was not in their original, often crude or barbaric, form that the mystery cults influenced philosophy, but as the reformed version of the cult of Dionysus (Bacchus in the Latin pantheon). The legendary Thrasian bard and religious reformer Orpheus reinterpreted the myth of the original cult of Dionysus to make it apply not to the season of wine growing but to spiritual growth. The original cult was popular with the lower classes, especially women, who behaved disgracefully by running in a frenzy through the woods, in which they caught, tore apart, and ate hapless small animals that fell into their clutches. This crude behavior was a reenactment of the death of Dionysus, who was killed and eaten by evil mythical beings known as the Titans.[8]

The reformed cult, known as Orphism, intellectualized the myth, building on the story that Zeus (Jupiter in the Roman pantheon) ate the heart of Dionysus, the only part the Titans had not eaten, and gave birth to a renewed Dionysus. (How he did this is not explained in clear detail.) Zeus also killed the Titans, burned their bodies, and created humanity from the ashes. The Orphic interpretation is that humans are made from evil material, except for the remains of Dionysus, whom the Titans had eaten. This divine material in humans is associated with our one good part, the mind or soul, which must be kept pure so that it can be reincarnated in a better body than the one it occupies at present. The point of the Orphic religion was the progressive purification of the mind so that eventually, after thousands of years and many incarnations, it would be pure enough to escape embodiment and exist as pure intellect.[9]

The Pythagoreans based their communal life on beliefs that were similar to those of the Orphic religion. They influenced Plato, who taught that the goal of life is tending the soul. Plato stressed the distinction between mind or soul and body, and he used Orphic symbols in his writings. How committed he was to Orphism is not known, but through later philosophical schools, especially that of the Neo-Platonists, the influence of Orphism was carried into medieval and Renaissance thought. The continuing influence of Orphism can be seen in philosophies that hold that the mind and body are radically distinct.

We now see that philosophy was influenced by both the Ionic culture and the Orphic religion. The freedom of Ionia facilitated the development of scientific curiosity and philosophy, and ideas of the Ionian culture were often expressed, in less mythological ways, in subsequent philosophies. The concepts of Orphism greatly influenced the Pythagoreans and Plato, and through them centuries of thought. Greek philosophy clearly grew out of the fertile ground of early Greek culture.

2 THE PRIMARY STUFF AND STRUCTURE OF THE WORLD

THE MILESIANS AND PYTHAGOREANS

When most people think of Greek philosophers, they think of Athens; but before there was a native-born Athenian philosopher, a group of philosophers were contemplating metaphysical issues related to the nature of the world. They are called the Presocratics. This chapter will explore the thought of the Milesians and Pythagoreans, who dealt with the basic nature and structure of matter. Then we will examine the ideas of Heraclitus, who held that the world is in the process of orderly change, and the Eleatics, who argued that change is impossible. In chapter 4, we will look at efforts to reconcile the obvious change and multiplicity in the world with the Eleatic claim—which had been supported with logical argument—that there is no change.

Studying the Presocratics is difficult because either they did not write, or their writings have been lost except for reports of their thought and quotations in other ancient writers. These are referred to as fragments. Plato and Aristotle, especially the latter, preserved some of the sayings of the Presocratics and commented on their philosophies. Some of the quotations and reports of the Presocratics in writers from the second century A.D. on are considered accurate, while others are in expanded or corrupt form. Some later writers who used early sources may be more accurate than some earlier writers. The reports of Simplicius, for example, in the sixth century, are considered reliable. Some second- and third-century writers based their reports on those of earlier writers. Sextus Empiricus, for example, relied on the work of Aenesidemus, who was writing two centuries earlier. Diogenes Laertius relied on works from the

Hellenistic era for his *Lives of Eminent Philosophers,* probably written in the third century A.D.

The most often used source of the fragments of the Presocratics, Hermann Diels's *Fragmenta der Presocraticer,* will not be useful to students who do not read German, but there are translations, such as Kathleen Freeman's *Ancilla to the Pre-Socratic Philosophers,* but Freeman does not identify or index the passages translated, so they are not easy to approach except through Diels's book. More useful is G.S. Kirk and J.E. Raven, *The Presocratic Philosophers.* It provides an extensive survey of fragments and identifies the ancient writers. Translations of the fragments are in footnotes. Kirk and Raven present the fragments in thematic order instead of in the order used by Hermann Diels, but the index (starting on page 451) greatly facilitates looking up passages identified by Diels's numbers. *Readings in Ancient Western Philosophy,* edited by George F. McLean and Patrick J. Aspell should prove useful, as will Reginald E. Allen's *Greek Philosophy: Thales to Aristotle.*

The Milesian Philosophers

The earliest group of Greek philosophers is called the Milesians, named for their city of Miletus. In the seventh and sixth centuries B.C. Miletus was an important cosmopolitan trading center on the coast of what is now Turkey. Milesian philosophy was concerned mainly with the nature of the world—what it is underneath its surface appearances. The thought of the Milesians can be seen as the beginning of Western scientific speculation as well as the beginning of Western philosophy.

The first known Greek philosopher was Thales, who lived in the seventh century. Several ancient writers report on his life and accomplishments.[1] He is reported to have been interested in scientific matters, especially mathematics and astronomy. He predicted the eclipse of 585 B.C., even though he did not know the cause of eclipses. He used a Babylonian system based on the observation that eclipses occurred at eighteen-year, eleven-day intervals. He also studied the Nile flood seasons and taught navigation.

Two stories told about Thales show the common attitudes toward the thinker. Aristotle reports that he was successful in business because of his knowledge. From his knowledge of weather he predicted a good year for olives and cornered the olive oil market by leasing all the oil presses.[2] Another story reveals a common attitude toward all philosophers. Plato tells of a serving maid who reported that an absent-minded Thales fell into a well while contemplating the sky.[3]

Thales left no writings; it is doubtful that he ever wrote.[4] The two treatises cited by Diogenes Laertius are probably spurious; Thales is known only by report.

The metaphysics of Thales is important for the questions he raised. He thought there must be one substance underlying all the various things in the world. This was not an obvious idea; traditionally, Greek thinkers had held that the basic elements were earth, air, fire, and water, and this seems to have satisfied their curiosity. Thales speculated that earth, air, fire, and water were not ultimate, but that there was a primal substance underlying those four elements and thus all the diverse things in the world.

Thales' answer to his queries is not as interesting as his question itself. He is thought to have held that water is the primal element. This is based on Aristotle's report that Thales had observed the connection between life and moisture.[5] Aristotle also reported that Thales described the earth as floating on water.[6]

Thales is reported to have said, "All things are full of gods."[7] This is probably an expression of hylozoism, the Ionic concept of matter as containing within itself the principle of life. The most creative aspect of Thales' teaching is the concept of unity underlying obvious diversity. Looking for this unity sets the course of scientific speculation up to modern times. (The use of "god" instead of "God" is deliberate and careful. The concept of divinity in most Greek thought was so unlike that now attached to the term "God" that use of the capital "G" invites confusion.)

The second Milesian philosopher was Anaximander, born about 610 B.C. His life and accomplishments are also reported by several ancient writers.[8] Anaximander is known as the first Greek prose writer and also as the first writer of philosophy, but references to specific titles are questionable.[9] Any writings were lost at an early date, so we know Anaximander only by report. He appears to have been a person of scientific curiosity. He is said to have been the first person to make a map.[10] This was apparently a primitive map, but the concept of a map is a signal intellectual achievement.

The metaphysical speculation of Anaximander consists of an interesting answer to the same question Thales faced. Anaximander held that the primal substance, the basic world stuff, is *ápeiron*, an infinite, unbounded substance from which earth, air, fire, and water separate out.[11] It has been described by scholars as an indeterminate, boundless, infinite, eternal something. Exactly what Anaximander meant by *ápeiron* is uncertain. Earlier historians of philosophy, such as F.M. Cornford, thought he meant that *ápeiron* was indeterminate and unqualified; not having any qualities of its own but able to become various sorts of things. This would make it internally unbounded as well as spatially unbounded. Careful reading of the sources does not clearly support this interpretation, however.[12] Anaximander may have meant only that *ápeiron* is unmeasurable because it is infinite in space.

How does *ápeiron* become the various things in the world? Pairs of opposites (hot–cold, wet–dry, and so on) are continuously generated and destroyed, yielding to a sort of cosmic equity, which ordains for each pair its time of existence. (Note the similarity to the concept of *moira*.) The universe is formed from the separation of opposites.[13] The hot and dry enclose the cold and wet, which form cylinders of water, earth, and air. The hot and dry form the luminaries. The heavenly bodies are made of fire. Anaximander described them as circles of fire, with breathing holes that we see as lights in the sky. The earth is held in equilibrium by being equidistant from all heavenly bodies.[14]

Anaximander held that life on earth is the result of the sun's action upon moist earth.[15] Humans evolved from a fish-like being. This claim is based on the long period over which humans need nurturing, which would not have been possible in the primitive stages of the earth. Anaximander held that species and individuals change and evolve.[16]

The value of Anaximander's speculations lies in the concept of one underlying source of all material, which is not itself a visible element. This view was heuristic; that is, it led to further scientific development.

The third Milesian philosopher was Anaximenes, a pupil of Anaximander.[17] His dates are uncertain, but he had to have lived before 494 B.C., when Miletus was destroyed by the Persians after an Ionian revolt. Only small fragments of his writing are extant.

Anaximenes held that the world stuff is vapor or air (whether he meant this literally or not is unknown). Other elements were formed by condensation and rarefaction of this primal element. He held that the earth is a slab of excessively condensed air floating in an atmosphere. Rarefied vapors from the earth form the sun, moon, and planets. Fixed stars are like nails in the vault of the heavens. The heavenly bodies move horizontally around the earth; the sun is hidden at night by distance and the high parts of the earth.[18]

Anaximenes's view might seem like a disappointment after Anaximander's creative speculation about *ápeiron*. Even though we do not know if Anaximenes realized it, however, his concept of condensation and rarefaction of one primal element, quantitative changes that cause the qualitative differences we perceive in the world, is important. It anticipates one of the important principles in the development of scientific explanation, the use of quantitative factors and movement in space explaining qualitative differences in appearances.

The value of the Milesian philosophers lies in their asking some of the right questions and trying to give naturalistic answers instead of mythological explanations. This was a humanistic approach, which kept the questions alive and led eventually to scientific investigation of the nature of matter.

The Pythagoreans

The Pythagoreans were an influential group of philosophers named for Pythagoras, who was born at Samos, an island just north of Miletus, in the sixth century B.C. Pythagoras may have been acquainted with the philosophy of Anaximander, but any association with Anaximander is not well attested. There were many legends about Pythagoras, including his being a son of Apollo and a worker of miracles,[19] but he was an actual person about whom we have some reasonably grounded knowledge. He moved to Croton, a Greek colony in southern Italy, at forty years of age and founded a religious community based in part on ideas common to the Orphic mysteries. His connection with Orphism, if there was any, however, is not clear. He died in Metapontum, one of the cities to which the Pythagoreans went after their expulsion from Croton. Herodotus mentions his reputation as a philosopher. Diogenes Laertius cites titles of several books written by Pythagoras.[20]

Women were admitted as members of the Pythagorean community, on equal standing with men. One woman, Theano, is reported by name and said to have been well known in the community.[21] Such a public role for women was uncommon in ancient Greece. The acceptance of women might have been the result of a strong idea of human unity, based on the belief in reincarnation.

The religious approach of the Pythagorean community was based on belief in reincarnation of the human soul or mind.[22] The ultimate goal was escape from the cycle of birth and rebirth and reunion with the divine, or a state of pure, unembodied intellect. The life a person is living now determines the form in which they will be embodied next time. To make progress from one incarnation to another a person must keep the mind directed to intellectual matters rather than to worldly concerns. The Pythagoreans practiced a life designed to avoid contamination by the world, encourage intellectual pursuits, and enable them to make progress toward freedom from embodiment with each incarnation. Iamblicus reports that the Pythagoreans had rules prescribing behaviors that have little significance for us and seem to be religious practices with no clear philosophical significance. For example, a person had to wipe away the impress of the body from their bed upon arising, wearing of rings was forbidden, and the eating of beans was avoided. There are indications that eating of meat was forbidden also. Diogenes Laertius also wrote that eating of beans and certain other foods was against the Pythagorean rules.[23]

A more positive side of Pythagorean life was engagement in the study of mathematics and disciplines related to mathematics. Proclus reported that Pythagoras was credited with discovery of the theorem that the square on the hypotenuse of a right-angle triangle is equal to the squares on the sides that make the right angle.[24]

Mathematics was an ideal intellectual pursuit for the religious community because it is a formal discipline that allows a certain detachment from material and mundane matters. The Pythagoreans were also interested in the sciences that are closely connected to mathematics, such as the theory of musical harmonies,[25] the study of which was conducive to purification of the soul. Music played a significant role in the Pythagorean community but not the role it has played in many other religious groups. Music was used to study order and harmony, as an intellectual aid to keeping the soul pure. The relationship between musical harmonies and the fretting of a sounding string was discovered. A string fretted half way gives a note an octave above that of the open string. Other fretting of the string will give a sound that can be determined mathematically.

The study of medicine by Pythagoreans was based on the concept of bodily harmony. Alcmaeon, a Pythagorean who maintained that the senses are connected with the brain,[26] was noted for his interest in medicine. He interpreted health as a balance of the powers of the body. The concept of harmony was also significant in Pythagorean cosmological, ontological, and ethical beliefs.[27]

The ontological belief of the Pythagoreans was that everything is number. Interpreting the meaning of this is complex, as there are several ways it can be interpreted. The discovery that the length of a sounding string determines the musical note it makes would indicate that some physical phenomena, such as sounds, are related to each other mathematically. More important, the Pythagoreans associated physical shapes with numbers. Points, lines, planes, and solids can be interpreted mathematically. Number is the limiting, qualifying characteristic of things that makes them distinctive and knowable; it gives matter form and structure.

There is, however, a more complicated aspect of this idea. Aristotle reported that the Pythagoreans not only interpreted numbers as giving structure to things, but that they held number to have spatial magnitude, so that numbers provide the material as well as the formal aspect of things, a view that Aristotle held was both contrary to that of all other thinkers and had impossible consequences.[28] Let us look first at the role of numbers in giving form and structure to things in the world; then we will deal with the view that things are made out of numbers.

The Pythagoreans identified shapes with numbers. They recognized square and oblong or rectangular numbers, which they probably demonstrated with the arrangement of small counters, such as pebbles. The square numbers were not simply the product of multiplying a number by itself; the square form was the logical shape in which the counters used in studying numbers should be arranged. Four, nine, sixteen, and twenty-five, as well as larger square numbers, show this square shape. Square numbers produce a gnomon, a figure that retains its shape as it is increased in size. In the three figures that follow Xs stand for the counters used in demonstrating the shape of numbers. With square numbers the gnomon starts with one, to which are added successive odd numbers (Figure 2.1).[29]

With rectangular numbers, the gnomon begins with two, to which are added successive even numbers (Figure 2.2). The number ten was held to be of special importance. It was symbolized as the *tetractys,* a triangle composed of the first four numbers (Figure 2.3).[30] The Pythagoreans also attached significance to odd and even numbers. Even numbers, which can be bisected, represent the unlimited or

Figure 2.1. **Square Numbers**

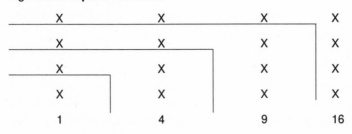

X	X	X	X
X	X	X	X
X	X	X	X
X	X	X	X
1	4	9	16

Figure 2.2. **Rectangular Numbers**

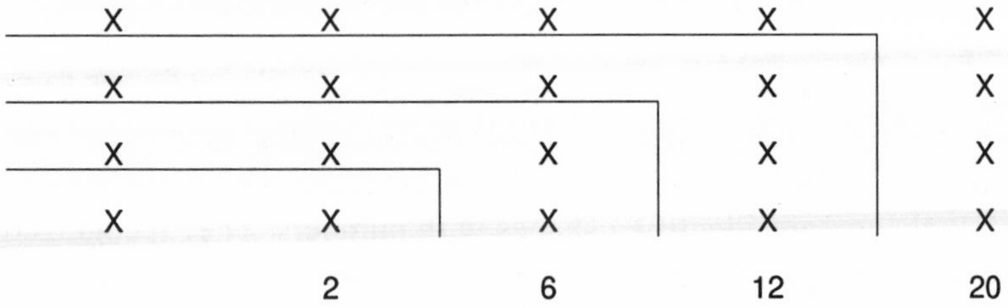

X	X	X	X	X
X	X	X	X	X
X	X	X	X	X
X	X	X	X	X
	2	6	12	20

Figure 2.3. **The Tetractys**

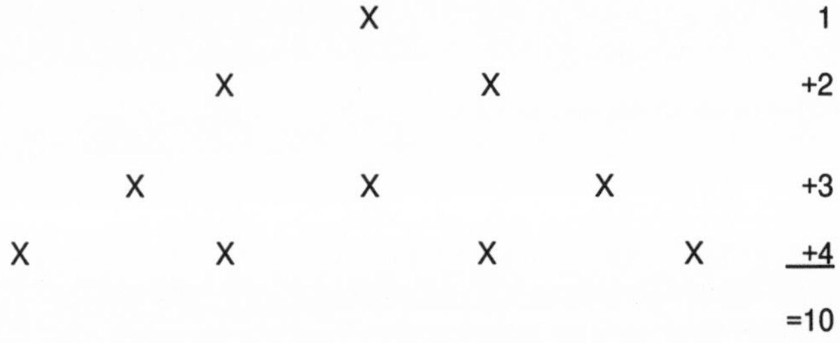

```
                    X                        1
              X           X                 +2

          X        X         X              +3
      X        X         X        X          +4

                                            =10
```

boundless; their lack of defense against bisection indicates a lack of strength and a lack of fixed and determined quality. This lack of firm limits makes a number less knowable than a number that cannot be changed into two or more smaller numbers. Odd numbers represent limit or determinate quality. The Greeks favored the limited or qualified over the unlimited. Limit represented to them definiteness or fixed quality, which they associated with clarity and intelligibility. This may seem strange to us, since we use the term "infinite" as praise, but to the Greeks the infinite was the disordered, the chaotic. The *ápeiron,* the infinite and unlimited, could be nothing significant without measure, by which it was limited and given structure by number.[31] The *ápeiron* was thought to be divisible infinitely into mathematical units. (In his famous paradoxes, which we examine in the next chapter, Zeno the Eleatic attacked the view that space is infinitely divisible.)

The role of numbers as measure, placing limit or structure on things in the world, is not a difficult concept to grasp. It is compatible with the idea of numbers as abstract and immaterial. Aristotle, however, brought up a matter of some difficulty. He said that the Pythagoreans, in the time of Alcmaeon or later, interpreted arithmetical numbers not as abstract and separate from the matter of the world, but as the material principle of things, the matter of which things are formed, as well as the principle of their modification. Aristotle saw this view as contrary to the commonly accepted notion of numbers, which is that numbers are abstract units, and he held that it is impossible that bodies should consist of numbers.[32] If the Pythagoreans held the view that Aristotle attributes to them and considered the point to be the first unit of magnitude, it is difficult to give a reasonable explanation of their position. Later Pythagoreans carried the theory of numbers to extremes, finding the "number" of moral qualities, social institutions, and so on; marriage, for example, was five, the joining of the lowest even number and odd number.[33] The use of numbers and numerology in later Pythagoreanism should not, however, detract from the mathematical contributions of the Pythagoreans.

The Pythagoreans held that the earth is a sphere, with tubes of fire revolving around it. The movement of these tubes creates musical sounds, chords. Later Pythagoreans thought the earth not central and stationary, but revolving (along with a counter-earth and the sun and planets) around a central fire. The heat and light of the sun were believed to reflect this central fire.[34]

According to the Pythagorean epistemology, thought is better than sense experience and intellectual intuition is better than observation. The Pythagoreans, as interested observers of life and the world, favored a certain detachment from life. They used an analogy of the types of people who attend a festival: lovers of gain (peddlers), lovers of honor (contestants), and lovers of wisdom (spectators).[35]

The Pythagorean order became politically powerful in Croton; finally the Pythagoreans were overthrown in a revolt (in the late fifth century), and the adherents of the philosophy were expelled and scattered to other colonies in Italy, Metapontum, Tarentum, and other places. This, however, only increased the influence of the Pythagorean order. It was in Tarentum that Plato became familiar with Pythagoreanism, under the influence of his friend Archytas.

The Pythagoreans approached the question of the underlying nature of the world, the question the Milesians were attempting to answer, but instead of seeking to explain the order of the world in terms of an underlying matter, they explained it in terms of the structure of mathematics and principles such as the contrast between the odd and the even and the unlimited and the limited. They were the first philosophers to hold that it is through reason that knowledge of reality can be acquired, an approach that became known as rationalism, which has been one of the major movements in philosophy.

3 CHANGE, STABILITY, AND PERMANENCE

HERACLITUS AND THE ELEATICS

The Milesians and Pythagoreans did not question the reality of the changes and multiplicity perceived in ordinary experience or provide a philosophical explanation for permanence in the "world process." Heraclitus and the Eleatic philosophers developed metaphysical doctrines regarding change and the unity and permanence of reality.

Heraclitus

Heraclitus, who lived from about 544 to 484 B.C., was an aristocratic citizen of Ephesus in Ionia.[1] He is sometimes called a "mystic," but this can be misleading. He did have a religious philosophy, but his religion was not based on a transcendent god who is separate from the world itself. The divine element in his philosophy was immanent, a part of nature. His religious approach is similar to that of Xenophanes, discussed below, with whose philosophy he was familiar. His deity was the divine element of mind, identified with the fire that he saw as the basic material substance of the world. It is this divine mind that gives unity to the opposites of which the constantly changing world is composed. The world order is eternal, and Heraclitus treats it as divine. He described the process of change in the world as an "Upward and Downward Way." He may also have called the world order the *logos,* a term that came to have great significance for several philosophers in later generations, or he may have used the term to refer to knowledge of the orderly working of the world process. In spite of some obscurities in the fragmentary remains of Heraclitus's writing, it is clear that his religion was based on an immanent power in the world. Heraclitus was critical of religious practices common in his day.[2]

Heraclitus wrote in aphorisms, short pithy statements that were figurative, laconic, and often quite obscure. Some later writers accused Heraclitus of being haughty and supercilious, even misanthropic, but these criticisms seem to be based on sayings of his that these writers resented or failed to understand. Kirk and Raven refer to these negative reports of Heraclitus as "biographical fiction." Heraclitus may have contributed to his reputation by deliberately being obscure. We no longer have any of his writings; he is reported to have written a book entitled *On Nature,* but we know him only from quotations in later writers.[3]

Heraclitus's ontology stressed the significance of orderly change. He held that the entire cosmos is in flux so rapid that the senses cannot keep up with it. He said, "You would not step twice into the same river," for fresh waters are ever flowing in. It would be a mistake to see Heraclitus's philosophy only as emphasizing change, however. Change is obvious, often occurring so rapidly that the motion of change can escape the senses, and Heraclitus recognized its importance; but the main thrust of his philosophy is the unity and order that underlie change. Change occurs according to a pattern, the Upward and Downward Way. The Upward and Downward motion are one, a unity in difference, one and the same. The process does not change; everything changes except this law of orderly change.[4]

This concept Heraclitus considered beyond the understanding of most people. The unity of all things throughout the changes to which they are subject is not obvious and is difficult to grasp. It depends upon a balance of opposites, even an identity of opposites, for the opposites are also a unity. Hippolytus described the view of Heraclitus this way: "God is day night, winter summer, war peace, satiety hunger [all the opposites, this is the meaning]; he understands alteration in the way that fire, when it is mixed with spices, is named according to the scent of each of them."[5]

Heraclitus considered fire the primal element. He may have meant this literally, but the idea is richly symbolic. The primal element must be something that is never static. Fire is always in a process of change, so it is a fitting element to be the world stuff. It is much more than this, however, since Heraclitus considered the fire to be divine reason.

Heraclitus was not doing what Thales and Anaximenes had done, selecting one of the traditional elements to be the primal stuff. The divine fire is not only the fire that exists by consuming fuel; it is a fire that produces rather than one that consumes. The significant contribution of Heraclitus, and his idea that has been the basis of several philosophies, such as that of Giordano Bruno, was the identification of an immanent aspect of the world with reason and with deity. Calling it "fire," or identifying the purest fire with the *aether* that surrounds the cosmos and is the substance of human souls, was not a new idea but had been established philosophical tradition since the time of Anaximenes.[6]

The world comes about as the divine fire builds up pairs of opposites, which change identities from one to the other. As we have seen, Heraclitus stressed the identity of opposites, relating this to the deity. In changes, such as winter into summer, dry into wet, dense into rarefied, both opposites are present at the moment of the change, making the change a transformation, not a substitution of one quality for another. Heraclitus held that the traditional four elements of earth, air, fire, and water exist in balanced quantities. They are all transformations of fire.[7] There is a fixed amount of fire, a central fire that never dies. As a fire is kindled an equal amount is extinguished. Note this concept of cosmic justice; it may reflect the early mythological notion of the *moira,* the allotted place given each thing, that keeps all things in a balanced order.

Friction or tension, which Heraclitus spoke of symbolically as war, enables objects to persist in spite of the ceaseless change. Strife, he held, is necessary. He is reported to have rebuked those who wished for an end of strife. He said, "War is the father of all and the king of all."[8]

Heraclitus's cosmology is obscure and undeveloped. The sun, moon, and stars are bowls of fire, upside down. Eclipses are caused by tilting of the bowls. He said that the sun is new each day; the sun is described as being limited in its powers, another view that seems to reflect the concept of an allotted place. "Sun will not overstep his measures; otherwise the Erinyes, ministers of Justice, will find him out."[9]

Heraclitus's theory of knowledge is not based on sense experience but on reason. He held that because of the rapid changing of everything we experience, the senses cannot record events as they occur. They cannot give us certain knowledge of what things are at the moment. Reason, however, can see through the flux to the law of change. Through reason we can have reliable knowledge of the world, but most people, as we have seen, do not understand the *logos,* do not grasp the unity of all things. Heraclitus, then, is another early philosopher who did not think that we can know through sense experience; our knowledge comes through reason.[10]

Heraclitus's psychological doctrine was that the soul, or mind, is pure fire or *aether,* akin to the divine reason and the fire that is the primal substance. His psychology was moralistic. He held that the "dry" soul is wisest and best. Souls, however, prefer the Downward Way, toward the dense, cold, and wet, to the Upward Way, toward the dry, rarefied, and hot, and the intellectual. Wetness, he believed, deteriorates the soul, but souls like to get wet. He considered drunkenness to be, literally, wetness of the soul.[11]

The Eleatics

The Eleatics are named for the colony of Elea (or Velia) in southern Italy. They flourished in the fifth century B.C. Their approach to the question of change was very different from that of Heraclitus; they held that the appearance of change is an illusion. This claim greatly influenced subsequent philosophers because they did not simply proclaim but argued their case.

Xenophanes

Xenophanes of Colophon, who lived about 570–475 B.C., is considered the first of the Eleatics. He is reported to have been the teacher of Parmenides and possibly of Zeno, although Parmenides did not become his follower. He traveled widely, settled in Elea, and lived a long life.[12]

Perhaps it would be best to consider Xenophanes a precursor of the influential Eleatic school; his thought did not develop the distinctive aspects of the Eleatic metaphysical approach. The only metaphysical concept that Xenophanes shared with Parmenides and the later Eleatics is the belief that all things are one. He held that the One is god.[13]

Xenophanes is best known for his concept of god and his criticism of anthropomorphic concepts of god. He was critical of Homer and Hesiod for their stories of the poor behavior of the gods. He seemed to be scornful of Pythagoras's belief in the transmigration of souls from humans to other animals. Perhaps he was the first thinker to notice that people create their gods in their own image, giving them clothes, speech, and bodies like their own; the Ethiopians had snub-nosed and black gods, while the Thrasian gods had light blue eyes and red hair. He speculated that if cattle and horses could draw, they would give their gods cattle or horse bodies.[14]

Xenophanes held that there is one god, who is in no way similar to humans in body or in thought. God rules the world without putting forth motion or effort: "Without toil he shapes all things by the thought of his mind." God does not have separate parts or organs: "All of him sees, all thinks, all hears."[15] Xenophanes' concept of deity was a hylozoistic or pantheistic view, which does not see the divinity as a being apart from the world but as the vital aspect of the world. It is similar to the approach of Heraclitus.

Xenophanes was doubtful of the possibility of final knowledge; he held that no one will ever know the complete truth. This was an element of skepticism that we have not seen in earlier philosophers. Opinion can resemble the truth, however. Even though the gods have not revealed all things to humans, by seeking, people "find out better in time."[16]

Xenophanes thought all living things originated from earth and water. He was impressed by fossils of sea creatures found on land and on mountains. He saw this as an indication that living creatures originated in mud while at one time the seas covered the earth.[17]

Parmenides

The developer of the Eleaticism that influenced the Pluralists and many thinkers after them was Parmenides, who was born in Elea of a rich and politically influential family about 515 B.C. He was held in high regard. He was a pupil of Xenophanes, but became a follower of the Pythagorean Ameinias. Plato reports in a dialogue given his name that Parmenides visited Socrates when he was sixty-five and Socrates was a young man.[18]

Parmenides' writings are in the form of a poem in hexametric verse entitled "On Nature." The proem pictures Parmenides in a chariot drawn by steeds, conveyed by the daughters of the sun. A goddess, Avenging Justice, welcomes him and says he will learn all things, the heart of well-rounded truth. True belief is not in the opinions of mortals; Parmenides will learn of the false opinions, the way of seeming, as well as the truth. The poem has two parts, "The Way of Truth" and "The Way of Opinion." The latter describes the false view of the world that is derived from sense experience. The first part of the poem gives Parmenides' own view that nothing changes, nothing comes into being or passes out of being, and there is no multiplicity of things. Reality is one, eternal, changeless.[19]

Why was such a view, clearly not supported by observation of the world, widely accepted? It was accepted and had great influence on subsequent philosophy because Parmenides was the first philosopher to defend his theories with logical argument. He held that reason is the ultimate judge of truth, and when sense experience conflicts with reason, its evidence is false. He showed logically that belief in change and multiplicity is self-contradictory and cannot be true. The logic with which he argued was primitive and employed only two basic principles, the principles of identity and contradiction. His logical proofs were convincing until it was demonstrated that these two principles, as correct as they are, are not enough for reasoning to valid conclusions. By the time Plato, then Aristotle, had laid the foundation for a more adequate logic, however, the Eleatic concept of reality as unchanging and unified had been widely accepted.

Parmenides held that one cannot think what is not or even utter it. The same principle holds for being and for thought. The Way of Truth begins with the simple logic that "it is or it is not," *estin* or *ouk estin.* This is ambiguous, since it is not clear what the "it" refers to. It is not clear whether *estin,* "it is," is used in the existential or predicative sense: is "it" referring to matters that exist or to what can be logically said about reality? Parmenides thought that what is and what can be predicated were the same. That which can be spoken or thought must be. Nothingness cannot be, and it cannot be thought. There can be no proof that nothingness exists. One should follow logic and not be misled by sense experience.[20] The significance of there being no void, no nothingness, is that without any empty space in which it could happen there can be no movement or change, there can be no multiplicity without space between things, and expansion and shrinking cannot occur.

What Eleatic logic proved is that what is must be entire, immovable, and without end. It is eternal; never did it come into being, for nothing can come from nothing. Anything must "be" completely or not be. Coming into being or perishing are not imaginable. This also means that the passage of time is an illusion. It would be coming into and going out of existence, which is not possible. What exists is not divisible, and it is all alike, not existing more in one place and less in another. Existence is full, a plenum throughout. Necessity keeps it within bounds; it cannot be limited by having perceptible qualities. Parmenides thought of it as a well-rounded sphere, alike at all points.[21]

The part of the poem that describes The Way of Seeming, the beliefs that rest on sense experience, has been interpreted as a survey of popular beliefs of the time and as a criticism of Pythagorean teaching. In this part of the poem Parmenides rejects the views of earlier philosophers, who seem to be Heraclitus and the Milesians, although they are not specifically named. He says that popular opinion, in complying with sense experience, posits two causes and two first principles, and he speaks of the two sensible opposites, light and darkness or night. He writes of the ongoing argument about perception, between Empedocles and Anaxagoras, whether perception involves like perceiving like or opposite perceiving opposite. According to Theophrastus, he treats perception and thought as the same thing. Parmenides' astronomical observations are not clear, and they are included in The Way of Seeming.[22]

We need to remember that in writing about The Way of Seeming, Parmenides is describing beliefs that he thinks are illogical. The positive part of the poem, The Way of Truth, presents the Eleatic concepts that had a significant influence on the Pluralists and on Plato, and later influenced, probably through the influence of Plato, the concept of reality and perfection held by many thinkers: the view that reality is one, eternal, and unchanging.

Zeno of Elea

Zeno of Elea was born between 490 and 485 B.C. He was originally a Pythagorean, then a pupil of Parmenides or possibly Xenophanes.[23]

Zeno wrote in opposition to those who believed in plurality. He may have been attacking the Pythagorean belief that space is infinitely divisible mathematically. He uses a type of logical argument, the *reductio ad absurdum,* that first assumes the view of the opponent, then shows that this position is self-contradictory or leads to absurdities. He argued that if there is a plurality, things must be both great and small, either infinite or of no size at all. If they have size, they must have parts, and that would make them collections of things, not units. If they do not have size, they would be nothing at all, so that if added to another thing, they would not make it larger. Being either great or small creates an absurdity. He argued also that if there is a plurality, things that are must be limited, no more or less than the number they are; but they must also be infinite, for to be separate things there must be other things between them and others between them, making the number of things infinite.[24]

Zeno is best known for his four paradoxes of motion. The race course or stadium paradox is based on the necessity of a runner having to cross an infinite number of half-way points before reaching the goal. The paradox of Achilles and the tortoise is similar, except that the fast runner (Achilles) would have to cross the point half-way from where the tortoise, given a fair head start, began his slow trek; then he would have to cross an infinite number of half-way points reached by the tortoise as he continued along the way.[25]

The paradox of the flying arrow holds that it would be impossible for an arrow to reach its target, since before then it would have to be in many places between the archer and the target. (Zeno's argument rests on the assumption that time is composed of moments, so that being in a place means being at rest in that place. A series of rests does not add up to motion, hence the paradox.) The paradox of the moving rows envisions a stationary row of objects and two more rows moving in opposite directions. Aristotle's description of the paradox is somewhat complex, and Kirk and Raven think he misunderstood it.[26]

The stadium paradox and the Achilles and tortoise paradox attack the Pythagorean belief that space is infinitely divisible. The moving arrow paradox was intended for the same purpose; it does not rest simply on the Pythagorean concept of space, however, but also on an interpretation of what it means to be in a space. The paradox of the moving blocks is a paradox only if the relativity of motion is not acknowledged. It is only in relation to each other that rows of objects are moving at different speeds at the same time. In relation to the surrounding space, each row is stationary or moving at one rate of speed. These paradoxes have interested philosophers into the present time. Many essays have been written dealing with them and expressing various views about what they mean and how they might be resolved.

Melissus of Samos

Melissus of Samos was the third Eleatic defender of the concept of reality as one and unchanging. He was an honored citizen of Samos, who won fame as the admiral who defeated the Athenian fleet under Pericles in 441 B.C. He was reported to be a pupil of Parmenides. He supported Parmenides' view that reality did not come into being but always existed and will exist and that reality is homogeneous and has no space in it. Real things do not change. He disagreed with Parmenides, however, in holding that reality must be infinite in magnitude. This contradicts Parmenides' view that reality is a finite sphere. Also, Simplicius reported that Melissus held that what exists is incorporeal.[27]

The Eleatic philosophers had a significant influence on the Pluralists and the Atomists, who attempted to reconcile the Eleatic view of reality with the obvious change and diversity in the world. The Eleatic view of reality also influenced Plato's belief that what is real must be unified and eternal.

4 RECONCILIATION OF ELEATICISM AND EXPERIENCE

THE PLURALISTS AND ATOMISTS

The Pluralists and Atomists did not deny the Eleatic concept of reality as an unchanging unity; the Eleatic philosophers had demonstrated that this view of reality was the only logical one. At the same time, the new thinkers were not willing to dismiss the evidence of the senses, which revealed a world of many things that did seem to come into being, pass out of being, and change along the way. What they attempted was a compromise that acknowledged the special importance of an unchanging basic reality but recognized the world of ordinary experience as also real in its way.

The Pluralists

That both Empedocles and Anaxagoras are called Pluralists does not indicate that either was a follower of the other, or that they were members of the same school of thought. They are grouped together because both accepted the Eleatic view of reality as unchanging while trying to reconcile this changeless reality with the obvious change and diversity we experience. Their approaches to the same problem were quite different.

Empedocles

Empedocles was born in Agrigentum (Akragas) in Sicily, probably around the middle of the fifth century B.C. Dating his life is difficult; Aristotle reported that he was slightly younger than Anaxagoras but began his philosophical inquiry earlier. Simplicius quotes Theophrastus's claim that Empedocles was an associate and admirer of Parmenides but an even greater admirer of the Pythagoreans. He was probably active in public life, but stories about him preserved by Diogenes Laertius are questionable. He was acclaimed as a physician.[1]

Empedocles had strong religious interests of the kind associated with the Pythagoreans and Orphics. He believed in reincarnation and thought of himself as a soul wandering from life to life for a thousand years. He objected to anthropomorphic concepts of deity, holding a view that might reflect the influence of Xenophanes.[2]

In his poem, "Purifications," he described an early golden age when Aphrodite (Kupris) alone reigned over an age of peace and love. Under the reign of Ares and other gods there followed a period of strife, marked by bloodshed and the eating of meat.[3] This idea seems to be based on Orphic mythology, and it parallels Empedocles' view of stages in the world process (see below).

In addition to "Purifications," Empedocles wrote another long poem, "On Nature," which was mainly an explanation of the physical universe, and a prose work on medicine.[4]

The influence of Parmenides on the metaphysical doctrines of Empedocles can be seen in his belief that nothing comes from what is not and nothing passes out of being. He held that reality is a plenum with no void. He described reality in one of its world stages as a harmonious sphere. He held that the world is composed of the traditional four elements; he called earth, air, fire, and water the eternal roots of all things.[5] Individual things are made by the separation and mingling of these roots by love and strife, but these four roots are eternal and inert, as demanded by Eleatic logic. The four elements and love and strife gave Empedocles his six First Principles. It is not clear whether Empedocles conceived of love and strife as material or as nonmaterial forces. John Burnet claims that they were thought of as corporeal, since the concept of incorporeal forces had not been conceived. Eduard Zeller seems to resist the idea that they were simply corporeal; he refers to them as "half material, half mystical."[6]

Love and strife power an unending world process of four stages. In one stage Love dominates, and the four roots are completely mingled. This may be thought of as a Parmenidean sphere. This stage is followed by an intermediate stage, in which strife begins the separation of elements out of the homogeneous stage. Air and fire tend to be borne upwards to the highest regions, but this does not always happen: "as it may chance." In the next stage strife has triumphed, and the four roots are entirely aggregated as earth, air, fire, and water. In the following stage love begins a process of mixing, with a chance joining of parts of creatures, creating some complete creatures who survive, but some incomplete creatures who do not survive. There are monstrosities, such as ox-faced humans and human-faced oxen. This suggests an evolutionary view, in which the well-adapted survive and the ill-adapted perish. Aristotle, who believed in the fixity of species according to their essence and rejected any concept of evolution, ridiculed Empedocles's "man-faced ox-progeny."[7]

The world can exist only in an intermediate stage. Aristotle claimed that Empedocles said the world occurred in a period in which strife is gaining dominance, following a period in which love was dominant.[8] He argues that bodies could not be combined from a state of separation by the power of love, since a previous state of unity and combination must be supposed, which seems to reflect his essentialism. I do not find Aristotle's argument convincing, especially in the face of Diels' fragments 35 and 36, cited by Simplicius and Stobaeus, that describe the dominance of love in the stage in which separated things came together.[9] Kirk and Raven point out the fragments are "vague in outline and obscure in detail," and see Empedocles' use of the cosmic cycles with love and strife changing positions of influence, instead of reaching a state of equilibrium, as an unnecessary difficulty that probably was inspired by the cosmogony of the poem "Purifications."[10]

Some fragments (Diels) of Empedocles' works show an interest in aspects of biology and physiology. He had some fanciful views about human reproduction, but he also held the view that both the male and female contribute to the makeup of a child, a view not popular in his time or upheld by Aristotle. He held that plants and animals are developed in four stages—development of separate limbs, joining of the limbs, the generation of whole-natured forms, and finally the capability of sexual reproduction. This might have involved a crude notion of evolution. Human blood and bones are composed of the four traditional elements.[11]

Empedocles gave a physiological explanation of perception and consciousness. Perception occurs when outside stimuli cause movement in the pores of the skin. He accepted the Eleatic view that there is no void, but he held that movement is possible without a void. An example of such movement is that of air and blood in the pores of the body, which he believed were tubes leading into the body. The pores were filled with air and blood, but as the levels of both changed, perception occurred. The pores were, however, never empty, since air was not thought of as a void but as a corporeal substance. He saw this principle demonstrated with a child's toy, the *klepsydra*.[12] This is simply a tube; if it is held in water and the hand placed over the upper end when it is lifted from the water, it will carry the water that remains inside it until the hand is removed from the end of the tube. Empedocles pointed out that the tube is never empty but always has water or air in it, just as the bodily pores have blood and air in them.

Empedocles did not share Parmenides' distrust of sense experience. He saw sight and hearing as paths for understanding. His epistemology was based on the theory that like perceives like. Humans perceive properties akin to properties in themselves in sense perception, which he believed takes place through the pores in the skin, as effluences from objects fit into the pores. He believed that consciousness has a physical basis in the blood, which is composed of the four elements plus love and strife.[13]

Empedocles also held views on cosmology and astronomy; he thought the sun reflected the light of terrestrial fire, but he understood the cause of eclipses and day and night.[14]

Some aspects of Empedocles' metaphysics clearly show the influence of Parmenides' philosophy. The description of the four roots as inert, unchanging, and eternal were efforts to meet the Eleatic standard of reality. The absence of a void is in keeping with Eleatic thought. The stage in which love is dominant is like Parmenides' description of reality as a homogeneous and transparent sphere. Empedocles preserved these Eleatic views, but he could not reconcile the monism of Parmenides with the world known through sense experience. His doctrine of permanent and unchanging reality was understood in pluralistic terms.

Anaxagoras

Anaxagoras was born in Clazomenae in what is now Turkey, probably about the year 500 B.C. He became a philosopher in Athens at age twenty and taught there for thirty years. He was a prominent person and became an associate, perhaps a teacher, of Pericles in Athens.[15] His pupils included Archelaus the natural philosopher and Euripides the dramatist. He is said to have written one book. Fragments are extant of his work, *On Nature.* Anaxagoras was critical of the popular religions. He was tried for impiety, based on his astronomical views, which denied the popular view that the heavenly bodies were intelligences; he held they were made of hot metal or rocks. He was banished and fled to Lampsacus, where he was held in high honor. He died there, probably about 428 B.C.[16]

Anaxagoras may have been the first full-time philosopher. He was not involved in business or politics. He was interested in science and studied astronomy, meteorites, and other scientific matters. He is credited with solving the problem of the cause of Nile floods. Herodotus cited three explanations for the summer rise of the Nile, and the third, that it is caused by melting snow in Ethiopia, is generally attributed to Anaxagoras.[17]

Anaxagoras accepted the Eleatic definition of the real, but he divided reality into many "seeds," with different but indestructible and unalterable characteristics. He explained movement and alteration as combinations and rearrangements of these particles. The seeds are too small to be individually perceptible; the objects that are conglomerates of the same kinds of seeds are perceptible. Seeds of everything are in some measure present in all objects, so that everything includes a portion of all things. Anaxagoras seemed to reason that nothing comes from what does not exist and like things come from like things. One application of this is seen in his observations on nutrition and growth, that foods such as bread and water nourish and produce blood, bone, and sinew. This meant that those elements were in bread and water, even if in amounts too minute to be observed.[18]

Some scholars try to reconcile Anaxagoras' concept of the seeds as homoeomeries, substances composed of parts qualitatively like the whole and like each other, and the view that the seeds contain a portion of everything. Kirk and Raven acknowledge that Anaxagoras is not easy to understand, and what might be a problem for later philosophers might not have been one for him. Kirk and Raven make the reasonable suggestion that he probably meant what he said rather than something he did not say but could have, and hold that his statements must be seen in relation to the views of Parmenides, Zeno, and other Presocratics. Anaxagoras might not have used the terms designating homoeomereity to designate his seeds, for these terms are used by Aristotle and Aetius in talking about his views but do not appear in fragments of Anaxagoras' own expression.[19]

Mind is not mixed, but is "infinite and self-ruling and is mixed with no Thing, but is alone by itself." It is described as "the finest of all Things and the purest."[20] Scholars have disagreed about what Anaxagoras meant by the "finest and purest." John Burnet thinks that mind was thought of as corporeal. Zeller acknowledges that Anaxagoras did not explicitly call it incorporeal but believes that is what he was trying to express.[21]

Anaxagoras held that originally all things were together in a colorless mixture, which sounds like Parmenides' transparent sphere, except that it was a mixture of countless seeds of things. The view that all things were in the original mixture enabled him to deny that things came into being or perished, but claim rather that change can be seen as mixing and separating.[22]

The separating of things from the original mixture was done by a rotation caused by mind, the one thing that was not mixed with anything else. The heavenly bodies were separated out, then the opposites, hot and cold, light and dark, and dry and moist. Anaxagoras said that mind began and controlled the rotation.[23] Plato accused Anaxagoras of making inadequate use of mind in explaining the origin of the world, a complaint raised also by Aristotle, who said mind was not treated as teleological, that is, acting with purpose.[24] Kirk and Raven say that mind played a less direct role, as secondary causes governed the continuing development of the world.[25]

The rotation started by mind first separated off air and aether (fire), as the dense, moist, and cold came together at the center where the earth now is. The hot, dry, and rarefied went to the outside. The earth was solidified, water was separated from the clouds, and the cold solidified stones from the soil.[26] The two guiding principles at work are: (1) heavy bodies occupy a lower position, while light bodies take the higher, and (2) things of a like kind tend to go together.[27]

The world that was formed by the rotation begun by mind was described as flat and suspended on air because of its size, the lack of a void, and the strength of the air. The sea came from the waters in the earth, which was hollow and contained water in its hollows, and from the rivers that flowed into it. Rivers received their waters from the rain and from the waters in the earth. The sun, moon, and stars are red-hot rocks carried in the rotation of the aether. Other bodies, invisible to us, are carried around with the sun and moon. Anaxagoras held that the light of the moon comes from the sun. The luminaries pass under the earth in their revolutions. Eclipses of the moon are caused by its being screened by the earth or one of the invisible bodies beneath the moon. Eclipses of the sun are caused by screening by the new moon.[28]

Anaxagoras did not believe that separation of opposites, the sort of separation that formed the earth, happened only here. He held that there are other worlds, with animals and people who grow crops and build houses as we do.[29]

Anaxagoras also held that sense perception occurs through opposites. In seeing, an image is cast on the pupil of the eye; but the image is not of the color seen, however, but of a different color. He also believed that hearing involves the brain. Anaxagoras believed that knowledge of the world comes through sense perception, but he realized that the senses give inadequate information. Only reason gives true knowledge.[30]

Anaxagoras believed that animal life originated in moisture. Plants, he thought, came from seeds in the air, which come down with the rain.[31]

Elements of Anaxagoras' metaphysics show the influence of Eleatic philosophy. He claimed that the seeds are unchanging and indestructible. He held that there is no void, which he equated with nonbeing, as Eleatic logic had interpreted it, and held that air is not a void. (Aristotle criticized Anaxagoras and Empedocles for not disproving what people really mean when they claim that a void exists.[32]) Anaxagoras seems to have held that there was an original mixture in which nothing stood out separately. Things were separated out of this original oneness. This idea would be similar to Empedocles' description of the world stage in which love in dominant. Like Empedocles, however, Anaxagoras preserved parts of Parmenides' view of reality but could not maintain the unity of an unchanging reality.

The Atomists

The first of the Atomists was Leucippus. Little is known of his life, even his place of birth, which may have been Elea or Miletus. The dates of his life are also uncertain, but apparently he lived in the same era as Empedocles and Anaxagoras. Some ancients doubted his historical existence.[33] Knowledge of Leucippus is derived from comments of other writers. He is always associated with his pupil Democritus. Two writings are attributed to Leucippus: Theophrastus says that he wrote *The Great World-system,* which others attribute to Democritus, and *On*

Mind, from which comes the only extant fragment apparently from Leucippus himself (quoted by Aetius) and which may be a section of *The Great World-system.* These works have been lost, except that parts of the former work may be incorporated in the writings of Democritus.[34]

Democritus was born about 460 B.C. in Abdera in Thrace. He was a young contemporary of the aged Anaxagoras. He was rich and well traveled. Democritus wrote much about a wide variety of subjects. His literary output was second only to that of Aristotle, according to Diogenes Laertius. He had a good literary style. His chief literary work was *The Lesser World-system.* His whole literary corpus has been lost; only doubtful fragments remain. He is known from comments and quotations in other writers. He taught, developed a group of disciples, and was held in high repute in Graeco-Roman times.[35]

The ideas of Leucippus and Democritus must be seen as a single system. There does not seem to be any dependable way to distinguish the contributions of Leucippus from those of Democritus.

The Atomists accepted the Eleatic teaching that the real must be homogeneous, uncreated, unalterable, indestructible. Like the Pluralists, they observed the ceaseless changes of things in the world, so they divided Parmenides' reality into small parts and added another view, that there is a void in which changes occur.[36]

Atomism held that reality exists in an infinite number of minute elements, or atoms. Each atom is a plenum, with no empty space within it. The atoms are the same in their material but differ from one another in shape and size. Mind and fire atoms are spherical, the shape associated with greatest mobility. Movement and rearrangement of atoms cause the changes perceived by the senses.[37]

The world was formed from a group of atoms in the void that formed a vortex. Within this whirling mass, atoms attached themselves to other like forms, as animate and inanimate things tend to do. Finer atoms went to the outside, and others stayed at the center and became entangled, forming a sphere. The world was enveloped in a membrane formed from atoms hooked together. Other atoms were drawn into the membrane. Some that were originally moist dried out and ignited, forming material for the heavenly bodies.[38] All of this happened of necessity and was caused by the vortex. This is a mechanical explanation of formation of the world. Aetius described it as happening through "the resistance and movement and blows of matter."[39] Others held that the formation of the world happened by chance, but it not clear what this means, only that the means for it were not mechanical.[40]

Leucippus and Democritus believed, as did Anaxagoras, that many worlds came about the same way our world did. Democritus said that they differ in size, in whether they have luminaries, and in whether they are occupied by living beings.[41]

Compound bodies, according to the Atomists, come into being when atoms, which differ in their shapes, sizes, positions, and arrangements, collide with each other, become intertwined, and stay together.[42]

Aristotle rebukes the Atomists for not specifying the motion natural to atoms in the void, apparently meaning their original motion. Kirk and Raven think this is not a very important question. Since the atoms have existed always and have been colliding with each other, this derived motion would have long since replaced any original motion.[43] Aetius held that Democritus said all motion results from vibration, but he is thought to be reading an Epicurean idea into Democritus.[44] As we will see in the chapter on the Hellenistic philosophers, Epicurus based an unfortunate argument for freedom of the will on his view of original atomic motion as a swerving fall through space.

Aristotle held that atoms have weight according to their bulk or size. Democritus attributed more weight to compound bodies containing less void, and lightness to those bodies with more void, which is not the same as attributing weight to the atoms themselves. Aetius in probably correct in holding that Democritus attributed only size and shape to atoms, but Epicurus added the concept of atoms having weight. This issue is still being discussed and will be treated in the chapter dealing with Epicureanism.[45]

Democritus held that perception occurs as a result of effluences in the form of small "images" coming from objects in the world and striking a sense organ. Sight results from images the same shape as the object seen when the images strike the eye, or when air shaped by an image strikes the eye. Perception is not exact because it is affected by the state of the body and things that impinge upon the movement of the images through space. Also, some of our judgments of the quality of things are governed by convention or usage. This gives an obscurity to sense impressions. In an incomplete fragment, he claims that we have a finer tool that enables us to escape the distortion of transmission through space, providing for genuine knowledge.[46] Our "tool for distinguishing more finely" must be reason, not another type of perception. Still, it is not clear how strong a claim is meant for genuine knowledge. Part of fragment 125 (Diels), following a reference to color, sweet, and bitter being conventional, is considered a defensive reply of the senses to the intellect; it says, "Miserable Mind, you get your evidence from us, and do you try to overthrow us?" Kirk and Raven think this might have been an addition to the fragment by a later critic, who was trying to correct the skeptical implications of the reference to conventionality in perception. They think Democritus' real opinion is expressed in fragment 117, which says, "We know nothing in reality; for truth lies in the abyss." Fragments 7 and 8 deny that humans can have more than opinion about the nature of things. In view of the difficulties with knowing that Democritus mentions, this might be the most honest thing for him to say.[47]

There is no indication that Democritus developed an ethical theory, but many fragments give pithy moral advice, most of it common sense, along with advice on friendship and handling one's relationships with other people. Some of his comments would now be considered sexist. A few of his ethical admonitions rise above commonplace wisdom; he urges refraining from crime not through fear but through duty, and he sounds like Plato when he says that the wrongdoer is more unfortunate than the man wronged.[48]

From the perspective of the development of natural science, the Atomists' metaphysics make what can be seen as basic advances over the teaching of the Pluralists, Empedocles and Anaxagoras. The atoms have no secondary qualities, such as color or taste; every atom is alike in substance and differs from other atoms only in size and shape. Each atom is a plenum; it is solid, with no emptiness in it. Atoms have spatial magnitude, hence are divisible in mathematical theory; but they cannot be divided actually, hence the name *a-tome,* "not cut." Note that each atom is like a small Eleatic reality.

The significances of this advance are as follows. (1) Qualitative differences are explained as quantitative differences, which is a basic principle of the modern scientific method. Sensible qualitative differences are the results of differing shapes and sizes of atoms and of differing spatial positions and arrangements of atoms in the things composed of a conglomerate of atoms. (2) The Atomists did not retain the Eleatic position that there is no void or empty space. They held that empty space is infinite, and atoms move in it. This avoided any complicated discussion of whether a void is a nothingness or some other kind of place. (3) Atoms are seen as inherently in motion. No outside principle (such as mind or love and strife) is needed to account for change. The motion of atoms is uncreated and indestructible. (4) Atomic movements are mechanical in nature. Objects produce effects on others only through impact or pressure. When this is done from a distance, as in magnetism or vision, the effect was believed to be caused by effluences. The atomic system is deterministic; the antecedent situation determines the motions and arrangements of atoms. The determinism governing movement of atoms affected several aspects of Democritus' philosophy, especially his biological and psychological doctrines.

The Atomists held that the human is a microcosm of the universe, which is an idea that played a significant role in philosophical thought in later periods.[49] One thing the microcosm notion meant for Democritus is that the working of the bodies of living things, including humans, follows the same principles as in the cosmos, one of which is that all bodily actions are determined and governed by mechanical principles.

The atomic nature of the soul and the lack of a personal immortality were made part of the Epicurean philosophy, which saw these points as advantages since they took away the fear of what might happen to a person's soul after death.

The atomic theory of Leucippus and Democritus influenced many philosophers in subsequent periods. One value of Atomism was that it was heuristic, that is, it led to continued speculation and research. Even though it is quite different from the atomic theories current today, it deserves credit for starting an important line of inquiry.

5 THE SOPHISTS

The term "sophist" was used to designate a diverse number of people in ancient Greece. The word did not have a clear meaning, except that it was related to the word for wisdom. Solon, Pythagoras, the Seven Wise Men, and even Socrates were called Sophists, without any reproach intended. Lysias called Plato a Sophist, possibly as a term of reproach.[1]

The group of teachers we now refer to as the Sophists were scorned by Plato especially, and by Aristotle and Xenophon. Plato accused the Sophists of being mercenary sellers of knowledge and masters of eristic, the art of verbal combat, in which winning in a dispute could replace the pursuit of truth.[2] Aristotle derided the Sophists as moneymakers and said that their wisdom was apparent, not real.[3] Xenophon compared the Sophists—who sold wisdom for money—to prostitutes. He denied that they were wise and accused them of deception.[4] Was Plato's distinction between Sophism and philosophy justified? Who were the Sophists?

Who Were the Sophists?

The Sophists represent a changed emphasis in philosophy, a turning from speculation on the material makeup, structure, and origin of the world to a study of humanity and society. Ethics, law and customs, the origin of religions, and language were now the focus of philosophy. As we will see, these are the issues with which Socrates was concerned, and Plato attended to questions more akin to those of the Sophists than those the Presocratics. His answers to questions about the nature of society and the nature of humans, and proper personal and social behavior, were different from those of most of the Sophists, and this probably had much to do with his condemnation of the Sophists generally.

The Sophists were teachers who came to Athens from other cities and colonies beginning in the middle of the fifth century B.C. They did not have formal schools in which to teach, but they were the professors of their day. They ordinarily gave formal public lectures and taught courses for pay. The Sophists were individuals with their own special interests and academic specializations such as grammar or poetics. Most of them showed little interest in metaphysics; their emphasis was on the human person as an individual and as a social being. They were interested in various aspects of culture; some were specialists in language, literature, ethics, law, or government.

The Sophists differed from the Presocratics not only in subject matter but also in philosophical method and in the purpose of their teaching, which was practical: to teach their pupils how to live, to enable them to better meet their roles in life and society. This was often referred to as teaching virtue, *aretē*. "Virtue" did not mean to Greek thinkers exactly what it means in current English usage. The Greek concept includes strength and ability. Aristotle spoke of moral virtue, but he considered intellectual virtue also very important. Our word "virtue" comes from the Latin *virtus,* which came from *vir,* the word for "man," and referred to courage and strength as well as moral goodness. The meaning of the concept was very clear in the writings of the humanists in the Italian Renaissance. They placed great importance on *virtu,* by which they meant strength and ability. The man or woman of *virtu* was a person of achievement. This is closer to what the Greeks meant by *aretē* than our moralistic concept of virtue. After the Counter-Reformation and the Council of Trent, virtue was contrasted to moral vice, and now we speak of virtue only in a moral sense. Some people use it primarily to refer to chastity. This is not how we should interpret the Greek term *aretē*.

The Sophists' teaching of virtue usually encompassed the elements of a liberal education: mathematics, astronomy, and grammar (to which several of them made great contributions). Study of grammar included interpretation of the poets. Their teaching also emphasized rhetoric, the effective use of speech in political and personal affairs.[5]

The Sophists have been called empiricists or phenomenalists.[6] It is a bit risky to identify ancient thinkers using terms developed for modern schools of thought, but there are aspects of the Sophists' method of acquiring knowledge and their epistemological theories, as we can ascertain them, that make seeing them in terms of empiricism and phenomenalism instructive. When we contrast their approach with that of Parmenides and Plato, we see that the Sophists are far more like the empiricists than the rationalists. They do not seem to have relied on speculation and metaphysical principles, but acquired their knowledge of various cultures through personal experience in their travels and from reports of others.

Sophism was not a school of thought. The thinkers who came to be called Sophists held a wide variety of views on most subjects. Even when we find some common elements in Sophism generally, there are exceptions to most of these generalizations.

What Did the Sophists Teach?

One of the disputed questions among the Sophists and other thinkers was whether laws and customs were based on nature or on convention. Some held that culture is a matter of *nomos,* the laws and conventions, which differ from one city to another and have no basis other than their having been adopted in religion, ethics, law, and so on. Other Sophists held that there is a basis for laws, ethics, and other aspects of culture in *physis,* or nature. The older Sophists, such as Protagoras, Hippias, Prodicus, and Gorgias, recognized an antithesis between nature and convention, as did later Sophists such as Alcidamas and Lycophron.[7] *Nomos* was upheld by such intellectuals as Democritus, Aeschylus, Sophocles, Euripides, Lysias, Pericles, and Isocrates as the source of human progress and the support of what is right and just. Prometheus and Sisyphus are pictured as heroes who helped raise mankind from its pitiful natural state.[8] A high regard for *nomos* is expressed in Protagoras' story of the gods giving humans the skills necessary for civil society, to save them from the perils of statelessness.[9] His notion of humanity rising above a state of nature suggests the view of society later developed by Hobbes, Spinoza, and Locke. Aristotle reported that Lycophron held that civil society is a contract by which the citizens guarantee to one other their just claims.[10]

One question treated by some Sophists is whether social status rests merely on convention or is grounded in nature. Antiphon and Lycophron are reported to have expressed disagreement with the respect and regard society pays to people of "noble" birth.[11] Slavery, a prime case of social status determined by a society, was widely accepted in the Greek world, but Alcidamus, who was a pupil of the noted Sophist

Georgias, was opposed to slavery and held it contrary to nature. He said, "God has set all men free; Nature has made no man a slave."[12] Aristotle reports that Alcidamus was solidly on the side of *physis* and called philosophy "a defense against the laws."[13]

The Sophists who based their views on the concept of laws of nature did not all argue for social equality. Thrasymachus argued that it is nature's way that the strong will rule, and justice is whatever is of advantage to the ruling class.[14] Callicles argued that according to nature the strong should rule over the weak, and he rejected the idea that the strong should practice self-restraint in the satisfaction of their desires.[15] Against the view that the wise person will practice justice, Glaucon held that nature makes all people pursue self-interest.

Related to the *physis/nomos* distinction was the question of unwritten laws. Some Sophists believed there are divine or natural laws apart from the written laws of the state. Customs and local precedents can serve as unwritten laws. Other Sophists considered the recognition of unwritten laws to be dangerous in a democracy.[16]

The Popularity of the Sophists

There was great interest in the skills taught by the Sophists in fifth-century Athens. Several things contributed to their popularity and success. There was growing distrust in the power of humans to attain final knowledge about the issues dealt with by the Presocratic philosophers. Distrust of sense perception had been fostered by Heraclitus, Parmenides, and Anaxagoras, who held that sense experience is an uncertain source of knowledge. Reason also was discredited, by the conflicting speculations of the metaphysicians and by the logical paradoxes of the Eleatics. This disquiet made practical knowledge much more appealing.

A cosmopolitanism was developing in Athens as people became aware of different customs, laws, and religions in the other Greek cities. This awareness led to doubt about the absoluteness or superiority of particular systems of law, ethics, or belief, which stimulated thought about the origin, nature, and value of civilization.

Political conditions in Athens created a need for the skills the Sophists were teaching. The direct democracy practiced in Athens at the time allowed decisions to be made in large assemblies; even juries were open to any citizen who wanted to take part, causing juries numbering in the hundreds in some cases. Ability to speak convincingly became very important and provided opportunity for new leaders to arise. Those who could not speak effectively were at a significant disadvantage in public life.

Four Great Sophists

Four of the early Sophists are generally acknowledged to be among the leaders of Sophism. They reflect the diversity within Sophism. In spite of the difficulty of establishing exactly what they taught, as is the case with many early Greek philosophers, these four should be studied individually. They seem to have been respected, or at least acknowledged to be important thinkers, in their day. Even Plato treats them with a degree of respect. We will now look at the thought of these four creative thinkers, Protagoras, Prodicus of Julis, Gorgias of Leontini, and Hippias of Elis.

Protagoras

The most highly regarded of the Sophists was Protagoras, who was born in Abdera, probably about 490 B.C., and was a pupil of Democritus.[17] He lived in Athens from the middle of the fifth century and is considered the most gifted and original Sophist. He was a friend and confidant of Pericles, who is reported to have taken counsel with him on at least one difficult case and chose him to draw up a constitution for Thurii.[18] He contributed to knowledge of Greek grammar. He distinguished different kinds of sentences. Aristotle credits him with identifying the three genders of nouns and three tenses of verbs.[19] He wrote several books, the titles of which are uncertain, but which are reported as including *Truth and the Rejection* (his most important work), *Original State of Things, The Contradiction, On Personal Qualities,* and *On the Gods.* Diogenes Laertius lists a dozen works that were extant in his time.[20]

Plato treated Protagoras with some deference in the dialogue given his name, probably because of his reputation and advanced years. He is presented as a teacher of virtue, who claimed to make his pupils better citizens. He had an interest in and knowledge of poetry and was a good lecturer and was also good at instruction by question and answer. Much is made, however, of Protagoras' taking a fee for teaching.[21]

Plato is generally critical of Protagoras' teachings in his other dialogues, and much of our knowledge of what Protagoras taught comes from Plato; unfortunately, we have no way of knowing how reliable Plato's reports are.

Protagoras is reported to have been expelled from Athens, and his books burned, for the writing of *On the Gods*. He fled Athens and died in shipwreck, probably about 420 B.C., at the age of ninety (Plato says he was about seventy).[22]

Protagoras was noted for several ideas. He is reported to have said, "Of all things the measure is man, of things that are, that they are, and things that are not, that they are not."[23] Plato, Sextus Empiricus, and others interpreted this as expressing a subjectivist theory of knowledge and value. It is not clear whether Protagoras meant "man" in an individual or collective sense. Mario Untersteiner holds that in some cases he might have meant individual man, while in others he might have meant the general experience of humanity.[24]

The teaching that infuriated the Athenians was in *On the Gods,* which he began by saying, "With regard to the gods I know not whether they exist or not, or what they are like. Many things prevent our knowing: the subject is obscure and brief is the span of our mortal life."[25] This seems to be an expression not just of personal agnosticism, but of belief that knowledge of the gods was not possible.

Protagoras was noted for skill in argument, in which he could take either side. Plato accuses him of claiming that contradiction is not possible and all opinions are true, but Plato was not an unbiased reporter. Aristotle says that he was skilled in making the weaker argument the stronger, of which Aristotle was critical, but this seems to be exactly the skill college debaters are trying to learn.[26]

Protagoras held that humans are by nature social and political, but the particular laws and social systems they adopt are a matter of convention and not based on nature. Laws, customs, and religions arise not by *physis,* but by *nomos,* and were given to humans by the gods.[27] Protagoras seems to have advised a sober life of obedience to local laws, which should be respected for their social value and for the personal advantage and safety of obedience.

Prodicus of Julis

Prodicus of Julis on Ceos (an Aegean island near Corinth) was probably born between 470 and 460 B.C. He was unlike Protagoras in temperament and in his philosophical interests. He is reported to have been of a pessimistic temperament, but it was part of the lore of the time that the people of Julis were dour. Prodicus' teachings were certainly of a serious vein; he wrote *The Hours,* a moralistic treatise built on the myth of Heracles (Hercules in Roman lore) and his choice of difficult virtue over easy vice, but the work does not seem especially pessimistic. Prodicus warned against a soft, easy life and urged following the example of Heracles. He stressed the danger in passions and the worthlessness of riches and possessions.[28]

Plato seems to have admired the morally earnest Prodicus; Socrates referred to himself as a pupil of Prodicus, who in the dialogues is called "a distinguished man of letters," a man "of inspired sagacity," and of a "god-given wisdom." Yet even while acknowledging that Prodicus was admired in Athens for his eloquence, Plato mentions his charging fifty drachmas for his full course and one drachma for a short course and is critical of him for making "an astonishing amount of money" by demonstrating his wisdom, something the "great men of the past" did not do.[29]

Unlike most Sophists, Prodicus was probably interested in natural philosophy. He wrote a work, *On Nature,* which probably included the treatise *On the Nature of Man.* He theorized about the origin of religion in worship of benevolent aspects of nature.[30] (The leaders of Athens had banished Anaxagoras for similar explanations of the origins of religion.)

Prodicus was interested in the study of language and was known for making distinctions between synonyms. Plato disapproved of this attention to words, calling it "playing a game," and Aristotle rejected the distinct meanings of different synonyms.[31]

Gorgias of Leontini

Gorgias of Leontini in Sicily lived between 483 and 375 B.C.; he lived to be over a hundred. He visited Athens in 427 as the ambassador from Leontini. According to tradition, he was a pupil of Empedocles and the teacher of Isocrates and other prominent Athenians. He knew the Eleatic philosophy, but its influence on him was to provoke skepticism.[32]

Gorgias wrote *On Nature or the Nonexistent*; *The Art of Rhetoric*; and model orations, "Praise of Helen" and "Defense of Palamedes;" as well as a famous funeral oration; speeches for the Olympic and Pythian games; and an encomium for the people of Elis. The orations are usually treated as models of the art of rhetoric, but Mario Untersteiner has analyzed the speeches and argues that Gorgias used "Helen" and "Palamedes" as vehicles for discussing serious epistemological issues.[33]

Gorgias stressed the difficulty in determining which ideas correspond to reality and which do not. He held that words for things are mere conventions. His main theses were: (1) nothing exists; (2) if it did it could not be known; (3) if it were known, it could not be communicated. These three theses, however, stated simply as they are here—as they are usually reported—do not give a correct impression. They are the headings of a carefully presented treatise on the problem of knowing what exists and the difficulties in talking about it. Some scholars think *On Nature or the Nonexistent* may have been directed at the Eleatics as a parody of their logical approach, but this would not prevent its being a serious treatise.[34]

Gorgias' skepticism lead him to abandon philosophy. He ceased claiming to teach virtue and said that he taught only rhetoric. He did not claim to possess knowledge but was content with probability. He held that the power of persuasion was stronger than logical argument. In "Helen" he sees the use of persuasion in theories of astronomers, speeches in law courts, and disputes of philosophers.[35]

Gorgias is considered a founder of aesthetics and poetics. His main interest was the use of artistic illusion in speech.[36]

Gorgias apparently looked upon the laws as conventions, with the natural law being that the stronger shall rule, a view held by some of the lesser Sophists. He held that morality varies with age, sex, nationality, and role in society. Gorgias was a strong supporter of pan-Hellenism and was opposed to warfare between Greek cities. Philostratus reports that in a funeral oration he said that victories over barbarians require hymns of celebration, but victories over other Greeks require laments.[37]

Hippias of Elis

Hippias of Elis (in the northwest Peloponnesus) was of a younger generation of Sophists, a contemporary of Socrates. He was often an ambassador from Elis to Athens and Sparta. He was widely traveled and was well-educated in mathematics, grammar, harmonics, history, mythology, and literature. Xenophon called him a polymath, and Plato remarked on his memory and intellectual gifts. His writings on ethical and political subjects were numerous; he wrote histories and speeches as well as literary works such as *Trojan Discourses, Names of People, Register of Victors at Olympia,* and the *Collection,* but most titles of his works are unknown. The *Anonymous Iambilchi* and *Dissoi Logoi* echo his thought, and he is regarded as the author of some sections of both works.[38]

Hippias was a person of ethical concern, as seen in his *Trojan Discourses,* which treated the virtues appropriate to the young. He taught an ethic of self-reliance and independence of other people through being able to meet one's own needs. This independence is the Greek virtue of *autárkeia,* the practice of self-rule. Hippias' emphasis on *autárkeia* did not exclude an individual's concern for the social good, however, which is also good for the individual.[39]

Hippias stressed the difference between conventions and laws of nature. W.K.C. Guthrie says that he held a social contract view of law but did not claim there was a historical contract. Hippias supported *physis,* the unwritten law. Convention, he held, can violate natural law; the law of governments, written law, can do violence against nature, as demonstrated by disagreements and changes in laws and the despotic laws of Sparta. Obeying the written law does not mean justice. The law of nature is not tyrannical and binds humanity together. *Physis* overcomes the barriers that *nomos* erects between people. Untersteiner holds that Hippias reached through the idea of pan-Hellenism a cosmopolitanism that recognized the unity of all humanity. Guthrie says that there is no conclusive evidence that Hippias supported more than pan-Hellenism but thinks it is probable that he viewed all humanity as one family.[40]

Hippias thought that the Sophist must have wide knowledge of "the nature of things." The knowledge of nature involves several aspects, linguistic knowledge, mathematical knowledge, and knowledge of concepts and definitions, such as an understanding of the concept of justice.[41]

Sophism's Bad Name

The word "sophistry" is now a derogatory term, implying the use of clever but specious reasoning. Why did Sophism get its bad name? Part of the negative reaction to the Sophists came from people who did not trust rhetoric and oratorical skill. It was feared that a concern for audience reaction would overshadow the quest for truth. Many people still distrust a speaker who is very polished.

There were other factors at work in the Sophists' reputation. One was the attitude of Plato and Aristotle, who somewhat artificially distinguished between philosophy and Sophism. The view, once generally accepted, that the Sophists were shallow-minded subjectivists is a legacy primarily of Plato's dislike for the Sophists, and it should not be accepted uncritically. Plato was opposed to the Sophists because he saw them as skeptics and moral relativists. This was a one-sided and inaccurate view of the leading Sophists, but it influenced the way philosophers for centuries thought of the Sophists and contributed to the bad name of Sophism. Guthrie holds that Plato was not solely responsible for giving the Sophists a bad reputation,[42] and it is true that Xenophon, and others, had no respect for Sophism; but Plato had the most to say about them and attacked their teaching, where Xenophon attacked them for teaching for money. The influence of Plato and Aristotle was enough to create a general disregard for Sophism, however. Modern philosophers did not question Plato's view of the Sophists until the late eighteenth century, when George Grote stoutly defended them.[43]

In Athens, Plato's criticism of the Sophists fell on sympathetic ears. The conservative people of Athens were uncomfortable with what they saw as the subjectivism and individualism of the Sophists, and they probably took even greater offense at those Sophists who held that class status was contrary to nature. They could be expected to fear that Sophism would break down moral standards, community cohesion, and their position of leadership.

Athens was a very conservative city. There was prejudice against foreigners and against teaching for pay. There could thus easily be considerable animosity against foreign teachers on the part of the hereditary aristocrats, who saw their influence lessened by people more capable of civic leadership than they. On the other hand, those too poor to afford the lessons taught by the Sophists probably resented the rise to influence of people who became leaders in part because they had taken the courses in rhetoric.

The charges brought by Xenophon, Plato, and Aristotle against the Sophists, especially their belaboring of the practice of teaching for pay, indicate social prejudice. Plato was the product of two aristocratic families, and he shared the political views and social values of the class from which he came. He was the strongest opponent of Sophism. There seems to be a strong connection between his background and his disdain for the Sophists.

The morally questionable views of some later and lesser Sophists, for example the individuals Euthydemus and Dionysodorus reported in Plato's *Cratylus* and *Euthydemus,* helped to give Sophism a bad name. It is hardly surprising that some Sophists would be people of limited talent and even morals.

There is little point in condemning or idealizing the Sophists. They were teachers who provided instruction for which there was a need and a demand. They were scholars who made significant contributions in several areas of thought. They did not philosophize in the way of the Presocratics, and their views were not those of Plato and Aristotle, but to deny that they were philosophers was a mistake that we are not likely to continue to make. They were more like philosophers of modern times than were the Presocratics or Plato and Aristotle. They can be seen as the professors of their day, except that they had no academic appointments. They tended to develop special areas of interest, such as ethics, rhetoric, language, or poetry. The subjectivism, relativism, and skepticism for which they were criticized, as well as their concern with language and communication, are commonplace in contemporary philosophy. The undeserved bad name of Sophism will probably fade as more people come to understand who the Sophists were and what they were doing.

6 SOCRATES

Socrates was born in Athens about 470 B.C. and died in 399. He was the first native Athenian philosopher. His father, Sophroniscus, was a sculptor or a stone cutter; his mother, Phaenarete, is referred to as a midwife; she was probably not a professional but a good neighbor who helped younger women give birth. Socrates left no writings; he taught by conversation within the informal circle of his followers. We know him from Plato's dialogues and from Xenophon, especially the *Memorabilia.* Aristophanes' *The Clouds* pictures Socrates, but this is not a serious source.

Plato's Picture of Socrates

Plato used Socrates as his spokesman in most of the dialogues, but it is impossible to tell how accurately Plato portrayed Socrates and his beliefs, or even whether he was intending to present a biographical sketch. Many scholars think that the *Apology,* the *Crito,* and the *Phaedo,* the dialogues using the trial, imprisonment, and death of Socrates as their settings, are efforts to portray Socrates. We do not know whether that is the case. The early dialogues about specific moral virtues, the *Euthyphro,* the *Laches,* the *Charmides,* and the *Hippias major,* are believed by some scholars to present Socrates' teaching, while the later dialogues only use Socrates as a literary device. The early dialogues might also be using Socrates as Plato's spokesman without intending to present the ideas in them as Socrates' teaching. Plato's use of the figure of Socrates in the dialogues was acceptable in his time; it was a tribute, not an effort to misrepresent.

Plato's picture of Socrates in the early dialogues, historical or not, is the one generally known, and it is an inspiring story. Socrates is pictured as civic-minded but not a professional politician. He is shown as a courageous person, who served in battle with valor and fortitude. On several occasions he showed great moral courage. Once, when he was president of the court at the trial of generals who had left the dead unburied after the battle of Arginusae, the angry crowd wanted to try the generals together and, of course, condemn them. The law required separate trials for each general, and Socrates stood up to the crowd and refused to carry out the illegal act the populace was asking for. On another occasion he defied the Thirty Tyrants, who wanted his assistance in framing a man they wanted to get rid of.[1]

Plato pictures Socrates as temperate but not prudish. He was sociable and good company. He experienced trances, some of which lasted for several hours. He also claimed to have an inner voice, a *daimon,* that warned him when he was about to make a mistake. According to Plato's picture, Socrates believed it his duty to the gods to be a gadfly: to expose ignorance and to be a goad to the state. This notion of Socrates' purpose is expressed in his speeches during his trial, as in the following.

> I still go about seeking and searching in obedience to the divine command, if I think that anyone is wise, whether citizen or stranger, and when I think that any person is not wise, I try to help the cause of God by proving that he is not.[2]

> If you put me to death, you will not easily find anyone to take my place. It is literally true, even if it sounds rather comical, that God has specially appointed me to this city, as though it were a large thoroughbred horse which because of its great size is inclined to be lazy and needs the stimulation of some stinging fly. It seems to me that God has attached me to this city to perform the office of such a fly, and all day long I never cease to settle here, there, and everywhere, rousing, persuading, reproving every one of you.[3]

Socrates was pictured as trying to get people to think about life; he thought the unexamined life not worth living. Ignorance should not be covered up but acknowledged. Socrates' attitude is indicated in the story about a friend who asked the Delphic oracle whether Socrates was the wisest of men. When Socrates was told that the oracle had said he was the wisest, he interpreted this to mean that he was the wisest because he readily admitted his own ignorance.[4]

The admission of ignorance is not an end in itself; it is the first step in the realization of truth. Socrates referred to his mother's service as a midwife and claimed to be an intellectual midwife.[5] By the maieutic method, the practice of midwifery, he exposed the ignorance of those with whom he talked and helped them "give birth" to true ideas. The possibility of people giving birth to true ideas as described in the dialogues is based on Plato's belief in innate ideas. Plato held that people know the truth from the time before their souls entered their bodies. The shock of entering a body makes the soul lose its awareness of what it knows, but the practice of dialectic helps the soul remember.[6] Whether Socrates actually believed in innate ideas cannot be determined, but the importance of the concept for Plato is clear.

Plato has Socrates express beliefs about the state and citizenship in the discussions in the *Crito,* in which he explains why he should not escape from prison and leave Athens. Socrates says that the city of Athens has been like a parent to him, and he has received benefits from the city. He believes that he must obey the city, even when it is unjustly planning to execute him. He feels bound by a tacit agreement to obey, as he is under a compact with the state.[7] These views are very conservative and may be compared to beliefs Plato expressed later in the *Laws.*

Socrates' decision not the flee from prison and to accept the death penalty has been seen as a paradigm of ethical reasoning. Socrates gives both practical and moral reasons for his decision. The practical reasons are his age and lack of preparation for life in another city, as well as the welfare of his wife and children. His moral arguments are based primarily on consistency, that is, practicing what he preached, and on the belief that the state, like a parent, is owed a debt of gratitude. An interesting way to look at the reasoning behind Socrates' decision to stay and be executed is to examine the presuppositions on which the arguments rest. Questions regarding the citizen's obligation to the state and the limitations of obligation have been important to many thinkers and continue to bring out differences of opinion. Plato's view of the state, which we will examine later, seems clearly reflected in the *Crito.*

Plato's Socrates asks questions about the definitions of various virtues. The early dialogues explain that it is not simply the things that are virtuous, but the nature of virtue, that is being discussed—Socrates is not asking what things are virtuous but what virtue is.[8] When Socrates discusses the nature of courage with Laches, Laches gives some examples of courage, and Socrates says,

I fear I did not express myself clearly, and therefore you have answered not the question which I intended to ask, but another. . . . I was asking about courage and cowardice in general. And I will begin with courage, and once more ask what is that common quality, which is the same in all these cases and which is called courage?[9]

Euthyphro also fails to understand Socrates' question and gives an example of a holy deed. Socrates says,

. . . bear in mind that what I asked of you was not to tell me one or two out of all the numerous actions that are holy; I wanted you to tell me what is the essential form of holiness which makes all holy actions holy.[10]

The discussions with Laches and Euthyphro clearly imply that the virtues have some permanent, universal meaning, an essence, which is one of Plato's central doctrines.

Interestingly, the dialogues about the virtues all end inconclusively. The reason probably rests on Plato's belief that the virtues form a unity, making it impossible to define one in isolation from the others. This concept is in keeping with the Eleatic standard of reality. We will look at this view in more detail in treating Plato's ethical theory.

Plato presented Socrates as believing in the immortality of the soul and in the possibility of knowledge of unchanging essences, including moral knowledge. These concepts are important aspects of Plato's philosophy and will be examined in our treatment of Plato's thought.

Xenophon's Picture of Socrates

In his *Memorabilia* Xenophon gives a picture of Socrates that is different in some respects from Plato's, although Socrates' character is the same in both reports. He is temperate, frugal, self-disciplined, self-reliant, and courageous, and he possesses great fortitude and takes care of his body.[11]

Xenophon and Plato are also in agreement that Socrates was not interested in metaphysical discussion of natural philosophy and cosmology. He did not speculate about the world and its origins but was interested in human affairs.[12] (Interestingly, human affairs were the concern of most of the Sophists.)

The two pictures of Socrates diverge in that Plato pictures Socrates as discussing such issues as the nature and immortality of the soul, the essences that give a fixed nature to things, and moral knowledge; while Xenophon does not mention such interests. Also, the reports of Socrates' attitude toward virtue differ. Xenophon indicates that Socrates discussed not the essences of the virtues but which things are virtuous.[13] This is very different from the point of the discussions in Plato's dialogues. Asking what things are *x, y,* or *z* is not the same as asking what is the essence of *x, y,* or *z.*

Xenophon gives examples of Socrates' skill in argument. He reports a discussion with Aristippus regarding the good and beautiful:

> Aristippus asked him if he knew anything good, in order that if Socrates mentioned some good thing, such as food, drink, money, health, strength, or daring, he might show that it is sometimes bad. But he, knowing when anything troubles us we need what will put an end to the trouble, gave the best answer: "Are you asking me," he said, "whether I know anything good for a fever?"
> "No, not that."
> "For ophthalmia?"
> "No, nor that."
> "For hunger?"
> "No, not for hunger either."
> "Well, but if you are asking me whether I know of anything good in relation to nothing, I neither know or want to know."[14]

Note that in this argument there is no discussion of a universal definition of the good.

A lack of concern for universal essences of the virtues is even clearer in another argument:

> Again Aristippus asked him whether he knew of anything beautiful:
> "Yes, many things," he replied.
> "Are all like one another?"
> "On the contrary, some are as unlike as they can be."
> "How then can that which is unlike the beautiful be beautiful?"
> "The reason, of course, is that a beautiful wrestler is unlike a beautiful runner, a shield beautiful for defense is unlike a javelin beautiful for swift and powerful hurling."[15]

In other discussions, Socrates argues that wisdom is not always good for a person, and that things such as beauty, wealth, and power, things that usually make people happy, have sometimes brought calamity to their possessors. He argues that good conduct is the best object of study.[16] The purpose of dialogue was not understood by Xenophon to be the remembering of innate knowledge but to develop skill in reasoning. He has Socrates say that it is "the duty of every one . . . to make himself ready in this art, and to study it with the greatest diligence; for that men, by the aid of it, become most accomplished, most able to guide others, and most acute in discussion." [17]

Who gave the more accurate portrayal of Socrates? We do not have the means of determining this. Xenophon was an educated person, a good writer, and an outstanding military leader, but it is possible that he lacked the philosophical sophistication to realize what Socrates was doing. He might have "heard" from Socrates only what he was able to comprehend. On the other hand, it is possible that Plato was simply using Socrates as a literary figure to speak for him in the dialogues. The ideas expressed were certainly Plato's ideas, and Socrates might not have held or taught them.

Socrates and the Sophists

The philosophical approach of Socrates was much like that of a Sophist. His lack of interest in speculation about the origin and nature of the world and his focus on matters of human concern were shared with most of the Sophists. His interest in reasoning, especially Xenophon's interpretation, was similar to the Sophists' teaching of rhetoric. There were, however, two major differences between Socrates and the Sophists: he was a native Athenian, and he did not teach for pay. Since a cosmopolitan background and a teaching for pay are the features the Sophists had in common, Socrates was clearly not a Sophist. He did teach an informal group of followers, but he was not a professional teacher. The widely varying views later espoused by his followers indicates that he was not a dogmatic teacher.

The Death of Socrates

People have long been fascinated by the question of why Socrates was condemned to death. He was charged with impiety and with corrupting the youth, charges that Xenophon considered wholly false. Xenophon says that Socrates improved the character of youths and taught them love of virtue.[18] In the *Apology,* Plato has Socrates explain his teaching as a service to the city, his god-given task of being a gadfly, exposing ignorance and arousing the city from sloth.[19] Some of the speeches in the *Apology* sound arrogant; Socrates may have provoked the jury to declare him guilty. Instead of accepting their verdict with penitence and agreeing to pay a large fine, Socrates offered to pay an absurdly small fine and then said that he should instead be rewarded as richly as the best athletes. During the sentencing of Socrates, the jury voted for death, with more voting for his execution than had originally voted him guilty.[20]

These facts give a picture of a stubborn and haughty man, who brought on his own death. His own unconventional behavior in the trial might be part of the explanation of the outcome, but an important factor may have been the narrow piety and provincialism of Athens. Socrates did not need to teach radical doctrines to create animosity in the citizenry. His practice of questioning and use of logical reasoning[21] were bound to have angered many citizens.[22] This closed and biased society, which had already banished some of its best minds, was not a safe place for an open-minded and critical thinker. The aliens could be banished, but Socrates, one of their fellow natives, may have offended so greatly that nothing short of death would satisfy the angry Athenians.

The Lesser Socratics

The thinkers who were part of the informal group around Socrates are called the lesser Socratics. They do not form a single school of philosophical thought, as their philosophies were quite varied. Some began lines of thought that were eventually developed by better known philosophers. The main source of information on them is *Lives of Eminent Philosophers* by Diogenes Laertius.

The Megarics were led by Euclid of Megara, a city west of Athens; the school was named after his city. Euclid was trained in the Eleatic philosophy of Parmenides. He stressed the impossibility of plurality, motion, or change. He identified the Eleatic (one and unchanging) real being with the good. He also taught the comforting doctrine that nothing but the good is real, therefore only the good exists. Followers of Euclid, however, resorted to logical hair-splitting and "catch questions," an approach that did not win many followers, and the Megarics faded from the scene.[23]

The Cynic school may have been originated by Antisthenes; a pupil of Socrates, he was born in Athens early in the fourth century B.C. Antisthenes was a fiercely independent and uncouth man, who ignored social amenities, dressing as a beggar. He had his own followers after the death of Socrates. They met at the school for illegitimate children and the children of foreigners called Cynosarges. The name "Cynics" may have come from the name of the school, although it may have come for the word for "dog," a term that Diogenes, another early Cynic, liked to apply to himself. Antisthenes followed a harsh, rigidly disciplined way of life. He held that government, laws, and religion are conventions (*en nomo*).[24]

The most colorful Cynic was Diogenes of Sinope, a colony on the Black Sea. He died about 324 B.C. Originally a counterfeiter, Diogenes had fled from Sinope, taking refuge in Athens. He was captured by pirates and sold into slavery; he was then bought by a Corinthian, who made him tutor to his children and later gave him his freedom. He taught in Athens and Corinth.

Diogenes was very independent and known for flouting convention. There are some interesting stories about him. He lived in a large tub and called himself "the dog." He held animal behavior to be better than human conduct. He is also reported to have wandered the streets of Corinth with a lantern by day, looking for a worthy man. According to one story, Alexander the Great heard of the strange philosopher and went to visit him. He so impressed Alexander that the great ruler, standing beside the domiciliary tub, offered to do Diogenes any favor he asked. Diogenes' request was, "stand out of my light."[25]

Cynic thought stressed the virtue of *autárkeia,* independence and self-sufficiency. The goal of life was composure in the face of all circumstances; inner serenity was a defense against bad fortune. This approach to life's troubles was later developed more fully and given a metaphysical foundation by the Stoics.

The Cynics developed a philosophy that denied most of what Plato affirmed. Platonic forms (discussed in chapter 7) were denied; Antisthenes said, "I see a horse, but not horseness." The uniqueness of each individual thing was stressed; each is in a class by itself. Synthetic judgments were held to be illogical; the only valid statement about an entity is that it is itself.

Also, each person was held to be a law to himself. All classes, standards, and institutions are artificial. Civilization, being unnatural, causes unhappiness; happiness is found in getting back to nature. Marriage, social position, government, money, property, and religion are all artificial and bad. Pleasure in these things is bad. Even pleasure associated with elemental natural activities interferes with a person's inner serenity and dignity. Antisthenes is reported to have said, "I'd rather be mad than feel pleasure."[26]

The Cyrenaic school was founded by Aristippus, who was born about 435 B.C. in Cyrene in north Africa. Aristippus was a genial, good-natured, and clever young man. He was a wealthy pursuer of pleasure, probably attracted to Socrates' geniality.[27]

After Socrates' death, Aristippus traveled; he visited Dionysius I of Syracuse, whom he wanted for a patron. Dionysius, however, was not pleased with the young philosopher and spat in his face. Aristippus is reported to have taken this calmly and later said that one must expect to get splashed when trying to land a big fish.

Aristippus taught that pleasure is the good. He based this normative principle on his belief in psychological hedonism, that is, took the questionable step of saying what people do is an indication of what they should do. Aristippus's hedonism is wholly unqualified; he held that there is no basis for rating pleasures as higher or lower. He also held that all pleasures are physical. Sensation is caused by movement; gentle movements are pleasurable and rough movements are painful. The morally good is the greatest pleasure of the present moment. Therefore, since gentle movements are most pleasurable, in practice, Aristippus advocated the calmer, more repeatable pleasures. According to Panaetius, Aristippus did not consider pleasure to be only the removal of pain or freedom from discomfort.[28]

Aristippus considered so-called universals to be only superficial similarities. Each individual is in a class alone, a law to itself, and names of classes of things are conventional. This is, of course, a rejection of Platonic forms or any theory of essences. Aristippus carried this nominalism into his theory of knowledge. All a person can know are his sensations, but our impressions of reality (our experiences) cannot be compared: an entity may not appear the same to different viewers. There is, therefore no definable, objective, "public" world. Diogenes Laertius cited a number of books in circulation during Aristippus's time, that were attributed to him and wrote of several of his disciples.[29] Eventually, the Epicureans adopted and developed the hedonism taught by the Cyrenaics.

The lesser Socratics were so called in contrast to Plato, the great Socratic. Whether Socrates held and taught the doctrines developed by Plato or those of some of his other followers we do not know. Socrates must have been a very tolerant teacher, and he might not have placed great store by the teachings of any of his pupils. Nevertheless, Plato came to dominate the philosophical scene, and the complexity and systematic relationship of the several parts of his philosophy show why he deserves to be known as the great Socratic.

7 PLATO

METAPHYSICS AND THEOLOGY

Plato was born in Athens in 427 B.C. of an aristocratic family; through his father he claimed descent from Codrus, the last king of Athens, and through his mother from Solon, the famous lawgiver.[1] On both sides his family was wealthy and prominent in public life. Plato received a good education; his early interests included athletics, painting, and poetry. Aristotle said that he was familiar with the philosophy of Heraclitus through contact with Cratylus, an extreme follower of Heraclitus.[2] He was influenced by Socrates, but his place in the Socratic circle is uncertain. He was present at Socrates' trial but not at his death.[3]

Plato had relatives in government office and had intended to have a political career, but he became disillusioned with the way the Thirty Tyrants governed. He became even more disheartened when Socrates was put to death and decided against a career in government.[4]

Plato traveled after the death of Socrates, possibly first to visit Euclid in Megara. He reports that he visited Italy when he was about forty years old. He became a friend of Archytos, a leader of the Pythagoreans in Tarentum, and of his associate Archedemus. Two of his epistles are addressed to Archytas.[5]

Plato visited Syracuse several times, as reported in his *Epistle VII,* written to friends of Dion, brother-in-law of Dionysius I, the ruler of Syracuse, whom he had hoped to advise politically. He did not, however, have a satisfactory relationship with Dionysius I or his successor, Dionysius II. Plato apparently hoped to help reform the government of Syracuse, but the trips to Syracuse subjected Plato to serious danger and mistreatment. Later Dion, Plato's friend, seized control of Syracuse with aid from members of Plato's Academy. Callipus, a member of the Academy, then overthrew Dion and ruled for a year. This probably did not help the reputation of the Academy.

At about age forty Plato founded a school at his house near a playing field known as Hecademas Park, hence the name Academy.

The Academy was basically a school for aspiring leaders, drawn from prominent families in various Greek cities. The Academy lasted for about a thousand years, even though it underwent a number of changes in its philosophical position.

Plato died in 347 B.C. at age eighty.

Plato was primarily interested in ethics and politics, which are two sides of one concern, that is, human behavior in its personal and social aspects. His metaphysics and epistemology supported his ethical and political views. He defended essentialism, the belief in essences that make things what they are, and believed in the possibility of absolute knowledge. He used essentialism and belief in absolute knowledge to undergird his conservative social views. Plato's thought was systematic, that is, each aspect of his thought is relevant to other aspects. His thought developed throughout his lifetime, and he was able to criticize his early formulations of his beliefs, but he does not seem to have changed his basic positions.

We know Plato's work from his dialogues, and the large number of these gives us more access to Plato's thought than we have to the thought of any earlier philosopher. The dialogues were popular literary works, however, and Plato probably attached less value to the written dialogues than to discussions in the Academy. Unfortunately, we did not have access to these discussions, so we are fortunate in having the dialogues. We should remember, though, that the treatment of a topic in a dialogue might not have been Plato's last word on the subject.

Philosophical Influences on Plato

There were several influences upon the formulation of Plato's philosophy. He used these various schools of thought in different ways in the creation of his own system. He studied under a pupil of Heraclitus, and he used Heraclitean views regarding the changing world in his description of the sensible, material world. He considered the objects of sense experience unreal in that they are in flux, which in the Eleatic concept of reality kept them from being real. The sensible world is a world of things becoming something else. Plato distinguished between becoming and real being.

This does not mean that he denied the existence of the world in an absolute sense, however; it does exist as an object of the senses. He considered it unreal because it does not meet the Eleatic standard of being—eternal, unchanging, and one. Plato accepted Parmenides' definition of real being and held that reality lay in forms that are intelligible but not part of the sensible world. They alone are eternal, unchanging, homogeneous, and one; they alone are what really exists.

The Pythagoreans helped shape Plato's thinking and writing; he was influenced by their emphasis on the significance of mathematics, and, like the Pythagoreans, he was interested in the structure of the world rather than the question of its matter. Also, we see in his philosophy some of the elements associated with Orphism that are found in Pythagoreanism; he used Orphic images and terminology and held a dualistic view of soul and body. We cannot tell how literally Plato believed in some of the images from Orphism, though. In several places he seems to distance himself from some stories and the more mythical elements by saying that he is reporting a story told him, or even by warning us not to take his words literally.[6]

Although he was scornful of Sophism, Plato shared an interest in the questions that occupied most of the Sophists, such as their interest in human concerns. He did not favor speculation about the nature and origin of the natural world, since he believed that there could be no knowledge of changing things. In his one dialogue dealing with cosmology we are warned that what is said is no more than a likely story.[7]

The influence of Socrates upon Plato is hard to determine, although the traditional view is that his emphasis on universals and ethical concerns came from Socrates. Xenophon's picture of Socrates does not show him talking about universals, however, and the rejection of universals by some people in his circle makes it a matter of question whether Socrates taught that universals are the heart of knowledge. Xenophon speaks of Socrates' concern about matters of ethics, but he does not show him seeking universal definitions of the virtues (see chapter 6).

Plato's metaphysics seem to be based on a Heraclitean concept of the material world and an Eleatic concept of real being. Plato held that reality exists not in the matter of which the world is made but in the forms (or "ideas"), which provide the qualities that give limit and structure to the world. The real, the forms, is immaterial and intangible; it is intelligible, however, since it can be known by reason. This distinction between the sensible and the intelligible plays an important role in several aspects of Plato's philosophy.

The Doctrine of the Forms

Plato's reality is referred to as consisting of *ideai* or *eidé,* sometimes *eidos.* This concept is sometimes translated "ideas," but this can be misleading. We think of ideas as psychological entities, something that is thought. That is not what Plato had in mind; he said that reality does not exist through being thought. It was real before it is thought, some parts of it might never have been thought about, and it will be real if no mind continues to think it. *Ideai* and the other terms that are used interchangeably with it can also be translated as "forms." This term is preferable, but it is still not a perfect translation. The problem with calling Plato's reality "forms" is that we tend to think of form primarily in terms of shape, and Plato was talking about much more than shape. The forms provide the aspect of reality in the things of the world, including all the intelligible aspects of the things.

Plato spoke figuratively of the forms as "laid up in heaven" or in "that place beyond the heavens."[8] He must have said this to emphasize that the forms are not part of the earth. Speaking of the form as being in a place does not make any literal sense, since the forms are not material, spatial things.

Plato held that there is a form corresponding to every universal notion; he said a form exists "when we give the same name to many separate things." The form is one entity, a unity.[9] "Beauty" is a single form by which all beautiful things are made beautiful. Plato discussed the question, "Of what things are there forms?" The most easily recognized examples of forms come from mathematics; most people think there is such a thing as a perfect square, even if it is not found on earth. Plato was interested in mathematical realities, but what concerned him most was the idea that there are forms for the virtues. He also thought that there are forms for the essences underlying universal terms, both of natural entities and of artifacts. Plato realized, though, that there are some puzzles concerning the limit of number of things that have forms. He was not sure that there were forms for mud and hair.[10]

The forms are absolute reality; the form is a definite something by which an earthly entity is good, wise, beautiful, and so on.[11] The forms are not averages but perfect ideal prototypes. They are not ideals derived from human experience, as we judge things like horses and show cats. They are known by intellect but not by abstraction from sense experiences.

Reality, according to the Eleatics, must be one, as well as unchanging. Plato held that unity is provided for the forms by the Form of the Good, which is the source of all the other forms and which makes them all intelligible. He compared this form to the sun, which gives earthy things their existence and makes them visible.[12] The exact nature of the unity of the forms, the sense in which they are one, however, is not explained clearly.

In several of the later dialogues Plato dealt with the question of how the forms are related to things in the world. He was not satisfied with some of the terms in which such a relationship could be expressed. Plato examined the concepts of participation in the forms and resemblance of the world to the forms. Both participation and resemblance presented problems because of the way the terms were used in his day. Participation, visualized as things being covered as with a sail, suggested that different things would be differently related to the form, with any thing being related to only a part of the form. The concept of resemblance also posed a problem for Plato, since resemblance seemed to lead to a "third man" regress; that is, resemblance was seen as requiring three things, the two things being compared and the perfect version of the relevant qualities against which they were being measured. The ideas of participation and resemblance are not used in the same way now, but for Plato these problems were serious. Plato also spoke of the difficulty of knowing the forms, which can be known only by a person of exceptional gifts.[13]

Plato's final interpretation of the nature of the forms seems to have been mathematical. He used the concepts of limited and the unlimited in reference to the forms; the *Timaeus* creation story relates the elements to mathematical shapes and says god fashioned them by form and number.[14] Aristotle's reference to Plato's mathematizing of the forms is important evidence in support of the view that Plato came to understand the forms in terms of mathematics.[15] We will see that Aristotle was critical of Plato's turn toward mathematics in interpreting the forms.

Plato may never have been completely satisfied with the way he could describe the relationship between a form and the object in the world of which the form is the essence, but we can say that the form enables a worldly entity to be what it is, to belong to the class of things to which it belongs, and to be something that is knowable.

Plato gave very little ontological status to matter. He referred to matter as *topos,* a place or a space. The nature of matter in itself is not known, for only the real is knowable. We can have a notion of matter only by a kind of spurious reflection.[16] Plato's lack of attention to scientific matters did not reflect simply a lack of interest in the subject; he did not believe that such matters were significant objects for intellectual attention, since they cannot be known.

Plato's Aesthetics

Several aspects of Plato's metaphysics apply to his aesthetic theories. Beauty is cited in several dialogues as having its essential being in a form. It is an especially important form, since beauty and goodness are commonly considered the same in Greek thought, and Plato accepted their equivalence.[17] Plato's view of poetry, painting, and sculpture as being doubly removed from reality (see below) is grounded in his metaphysical belief that reality lies in the forms, including the form "beauty" through which all beautiful things are beautiful.[18]

The Nature of Beauty

In Plato's *Hippias major* Socrates asks what is the essential nature of beauty. This dialogue is like the *Laches,* the *Charmides,* and the *Euthyphro* in that it raises a question, looks critically at some efforts at a definition, and ends without reaching a conclusion. The dialogue portrays Hippias as an unsophisticated, unphilosophical, and foolish braggart (a questionable picture of a respected and noted person), who says that beauty is a beautiful maiden. After he is forced to admit that mares, lyres, and even pots can be beautiful and that a beautiful maiden is ugly compared to the race of the gods, some more general answers to the question of beauty are raised and rejected. That gold and ivory are beautiful, even when appropriately used, is not an acceptable answer, nor is their appropriate use itself. The appropriate use of decoration may only give a false appearance of beauty; some things that sometimes appear beautiful may fail the test of never appearing ugly.[19]

Hippias then gives the answer that beauty consists of having wealth, health, honor; of burying one's parents then being buried by one's children; but he is forced to acknowledge that his definition will not apply to gods and heroes.[20]

Hippias then claims that the beautiful is the useful, but he has to admit that power, which is useful, is not beautiful when put to bad uses. The next definition is that the beautiful is the beneficial, that is, the cause of good, but this runs into the objection that a cause is not the same as its effect, and the beautiful and the good are not separate things.[21]

Finally Hippias and Socrates examine an answer that will seem reasonable to many modern readers, that the beautiful is that which brings pleasure through the senses of hearing and sight. Socrates first suggests that there are beautiful things that are not appreciated through sight and sound, such as the laws, and raises the question of whether pleasure through the other senses can be a form of beauty, but this interesting question is passed over. Socrates next raises what he sees as a critical problem, that of locating beauty in two senses, as the definition does, or in one sense. He goes into a long discussion about the problem of ascribing qualities to himself and Hippias as to single individuals or to a pair. He simply rejects the definition of beauty as pleasure in the senses rather than clarifying the issue.[22]

We should not expect to find Socrates improving the definition of beauty in terms of pleasure through the senses. We know that Plato found the nature of beauty in the form "beauty," and he believed the senses can deceive, making something appear beautiful whether it is really beautiful or not.[23]

The Metaphysical Status of Art

The ancients did not have a concept of "the arts," the collective term for what we call the fine arts. "Art" referred to any making of things, any *techné,* including the manual arts.[24] Plato did have an opinion about the nature of what we know as the fine arts, however, even though he spoke of them individually, as poetry, painting, sculpture, and so on.

The several fine arts were generally understood in the ancient world as imitation (*mimesis*) of nature and human actions. Some thinkers in ancient times (as well as in later times) claimed that the arts could be an important source of learning about reality. Discussions in the *Republic* indicate that Plato did not share this enthusiasm for the fine arts; he questioned the cognitive worth of poetry, sculpture, and painting. He said that painting is twice removed from reality, an imitation of an imitation. It imitates a phantasm, an appearance, which keeps painting from being an important avenue to knowledge of reality.[25]

Plato held that there are two types of imitation (*mimesis*): making likenesses, which are shaped like the natural object, and making semblances, which distort shape to give the proper appearance when viewed from below or a distance. He likened imitation to the claims of the Sophists, whom he called illusionists, to have knowledge. He seems to be saying that the poet or sculptor is telling a lie, in even a more basic sense than in the false stories told by Homer and Hesiod.[26]

In addition to believing they failed as means toward knowledge, Plato criticized the fine arts for their bad effect upon character. He opposed dramatic performances in which men imitated women, especially those behaving badly, or imitated slaves or cowards or profane people. These performances, he felt, teach children the wrong lessons. Also, certain modes of music and certain instruments, such as the flute, lead to weakness of character. The rhythm of poetry and the diction of readers must be seemly. There must be no use of bad language or imitation of animal sounds.[27]

Because of the bad effects he expected from some fine arts, Plato advocated rigorous censorship of drama, poetry, music, even children's stories.[28]

Artistic Ability and Production

Plato's negative assessment of the fine arts as means to acquire knowledge and his fear of unregulated employment of the arts cannot be credited to ignorance of the arts. Plato's dialogues, with a few exceptions, are considered works of art. He wrote poems when he was young, some of which are still extant, although they do not deal with philosophical subjects. Plato knew the works of Homer and Hesiod, the tragic and comic poets, and others. He also grasped the principles of artistic production, explaining that artists and artisans do not select materials at random but seek to give their work a fixed order, in which things fit harmoniously to make an ordered and regulated whole.[29]

Poetry, however, is not a product of craftsmanship, according to Plato. He described the poet as inspired, even possessed, by the muse, who has taken over the poet to be a minister of the gods. The poet is like a mad person, like the priestess of the oracle who does not know what she is saying. Plato likened the poet to the worshipers of Dionysus, who lose themselves in their ecstasy. The poem is not a product of human workmanship but a work of the gods.[30]

Plato described the inspiration of the muses as a contagion, or like the ability of a magnet to both attract and magnetize as the iron rings held by a magnet can attract other rings. Not only the poet, but also the actors or reciters and even the hearers are caught up in the divine frenzy. In the *Ion,* Ion says that Socrates has described his own experience as a reciter of Homer and is pleased to be considered divinely inspired.[31]

Plato's Theology

Speaking of Plato's theology will be misleading if we think of theology in terms of the beliefs, questions, and concerns that have constituted theology in the Common Era of Judaism and Christianity. Plato, like the rest of Greek philosophers, must be seen in terms of the intellectual paganism of ancient Greece. Plato has tended to be a favorite of theologians, with Philo Judaeus at the beginning of the Common Era, Augustine at the end of the Roman period, the Franciscans during the Middle Ages, Marsilio Ficino during the Renaissance, and numerous religious philosophers in modern times finding Plato more compatible with their religion than most of the ancient pagans. Yet Plato is best understood against the background of paganism, a religious approach that included some ideas also found in Judaism and Christianity, to be sure, but which are probably found in almost all religions. Judaism and Christianity built upon ideas found in Greek philosophy, but also are based on ideas from the ancient Hebrew culture. Judaism and Christianity received a great deal from the Greek agora but received at least as much from the Middle Eastern desert.

Plato was not interested in exactly the same questions and did not think in quite the same categories as Christians and Jews, but he was religious. In his dialogues we find many references to god, to the human soul and its immortality, and to duty to god. He talked also about the gods, so we should not expect the term "god" to carry for him the same significance it carries for members of modern Western religions.

In the *Republic* Plato said that god is good; he causes only good, not evil. God does not change, assume disguises, or tell lies, contrary to what poets have written.[32]

Some references to god may be simply formal polite references, like "God bless you," and would not be fruitfully probed for meaning. Other references show more significant beliefs. Plato shared the common belief in a world soul, which he described as a self-moving motion, the original aspect of the world's existence, and the universal cause of all change and motion, good and bad.[33] One world soul is beneficial, but there is at least one other world soul, that is less good and that is capable of doing what is not beneficial.[34]

One reason for Plato's appeal to Christians and Jews is his belief in the creation of the world, even though it is significantly different from the creation out of nothing of Jewish and Christian theology (see chapter 19). In the *Timaeus,* Timaeus argues that the world is perishable, in a state of becoming rather than fixed being; therefore it is a creation, and every creation must have a creator. The creation, however, is more a remodeling than a building anew. The divine creator, the Demiurge, found the visible sphere unordered and inharmonious; from his goodness he gave it order, patterning his reconstruction after the forms. He made the world an ensouled living creature and called it a god. He could not make the world eternal, however, so he made time as a moving image of eternity.[35]

The *Timaeus* is ostensibly a book of natural philosophy, but it is actually a religious book; it is not, however, very satisfactory as a book of theology. It does not explain the nature of the Demiurge but says, rather, that the "father and maker" is past understanding. Also, Plato doubly distanced himself from what is said in the *Timaeus,* first by having Timaeus, rather than the person we expect as a spokesperson for Plato, Socrates, do the telling, and second, by having Timaeus say that what he reports is but a probable tale.[36]

Late in his life Plato wrote the *Laws,* a proposed law code with a strong underpinning of religion. The *Laws* proposes very severe laws against atheists and harsh punishment for the "ungodly," including unbelievers whose lack of religion leads them to bad behavior and those who commit moral and religious offenses. See chapter 9 for more detailed analysis of this proposed law code.[37]

The Immortal Soul

Plato based his concept of justice in the individual person on the concept of a three-part soul. This aspect of his beliefs about the soul is treated in chapter 9. Here, we look at the part of Plato's belief about the soul that is of primarily religious interest. He believed in immortality as reincarnation, which required thousands of years of purification of mind before a soul could escape the repeated rebirths into physical bodies. He gave several arguments for immortality of the soul.

Plato's arguments for immortality of the soul were accepted by succeeding generations of theologians, even though he was not arguing for immortality as Christians understood it. He based his arguments on the unity of the soul, and the nature of the soul as the principle of life.

In the *Phaedo* Socrates argues that souls had to exist in another place before our births because the generation of a thing is from its opposite; so life comes from death and from death comes renewed life.[38] His supporting examples, however, that if a thing becomes bigger it must first have been smaller and a better must have been worse, simply do not support the questionable metaphysical thesis on which the argument rests.

The argument from the doctrine of reminiscence, if it is accepted, would only prove preexistence of the soul, not that it continues to exist following death, as Simmias and Cebes pointed out.[39] (See the explanation of reminiscence in the next chapter.)

The argument that the soul cannot be destroyed because it is a simple, not compounded, substance has been employed by a number of theologians. Socrates argues that the soul, unlike the body, is invisible and invariable. It cannot be dissipated as the body is, even though it can be tainted by the body and be drawn back toward the body. This drawing back is the cause of reincarnation, which only the completely pure and philosophical soul escapes.[40]

Simmias raises the counter-argument that even if the soul cannot be dissipated, the soul might be not a substance but an epiphenomenon, like the sound from a tuned instrument. Cebes argues that the soul, even if not dissipated, may eventually exhaust itself.[41]

In answering Simmias and Cebes, Socrates appeals to the forms and to final causation, leading to the argument that the soul cannot have two contradictory forms, the forms of life and death.[42]

One of Plato's most popular arguments has been that based on the definition of the soul. Socrates says that the soul is self-moving. It is the first principle of motion and life, therefore it must be imperishable. This argument is given in the *Phaedrus* and in the *Laws*.[43]

Plato placed considerable importance on the concept of the tripartite soul and the effect of the three parts upon human behavior, but he does not give a precise account of the ontology of the parts. What are the parts? It would seem to fit Plato's philosophy better if parts are functions or activities rather than substantial units. Treating the parts as substantial units would compromise Plato's concept of the soul as a unity, a simple substance that cannot be dissipated by death. It is difficult to be sure this is the correct interpretation of Plato, however, especially in light of descriptions in the *Timaeus*.

In the *Timaeus* the parts of the soul are said to be in the head (the *logistikon,* the rational part), the breast (the *thumoeides,* the spirited part), and the belly (the *epithumetikon,* the appetitive part). In this dialogue, the *logistikon* is distinguished from the mortal parts of the soul, suggesting that the spirited part and appetite are not immortal. This certainly goes against the argument for the immortality of the soul as it is given in the *Phaedo*.[44]

How can we get around this apparent contradiction? As we have seen, Plato seems to doubly separate himself from the description of the soul in the *Timaeus*. We should not assume that Plato was committed to this description of the soul, which is not given by Socrates, but is in a long speech by Timaeus, a visitor from Crete, who states that what he says is only probable.[45] The belief that the parts of the soul are not all immortal may not be Plato's view at all.

8 PLATO

THEORY OF KNOWLEDGE

Plato's epistemology, that is, his theory about the nature and possibility of knowledge, makes an important distinction between the sensible and the intelligible. In the famous parable of the cave, he illustrated this distinction between the sensible, of which there can be no knowledge but only opinion, and the intelligible, the realm of the real and knowable.[1] People in the cave think they know something because they know images that show up on the wall of the cave and the order in which they appear, but they do not know that they are seeing shadows, not real things. The scene in the cave, dealing with sense experiences, is contrasted with events seen in the sunlight above the cave. We must be careful in interpreting this parable, which uses an analogy, and not take the references to events in the sunlight literally. In Plato's ontology (theory of what is real), sunlit experiences are part of the realm of becoming, the unknowable. The cave experiences stand for ordinary sense experiences, those that the unenlightened consider real. The things seen in sunlight represent ideas known intellectually.

Knowledge and Its Objects

To explain in more detail the difference between knowledge and mere opinion, along with showing the difference between real and unreal things, Plato described a line divided between levels of belief and levels of knowledge.[2] (See the diagram of the divided line on the following page.)

The two sections of the line to the left represent two levels of

Figure 8.1. Plato's Divided Line, Representing Degrees of Knowledge and the Objects of Opinion and Knowledge (*Republic* VI.509d–511e)

	THE SENSIBLE		THE INTELLIGIBLE

DEGREES OF KNOWLEDGE

dóxa (opinion)		*epistē̄mē̄* (knowledge)
Opinion about things in the sensible world		Knowledge of the intelligible world

eikasía (Conjecture)	*pístis* (Belief)	*diánoia* (Understanding)	*nóē̄sis* (Knowledge through dialectic)

LEVELS OF BEING

eikasía	*pístis*	*diánoia*	*nóē̄sis*
Images, shadows, reflections	Actual objects in the world	"Intelligible particulars"	Forms (ideas)
		Mental images	Pure reason: without images. Not hypothetical
		Assumptions	
		"Addible numbers"	"Non-addible numbers"
		Not to be taken as absolutes, but as "footings" or "springboards" (*Republic* VI.511b)	

opinion (*dóxa*) and two levels of the realm of becoming. It is important to see that the divided line diagram combines Plato's ontology—his theory of being, and his epistemology—his theory of knowledge. They are related, of course, since only the real can be known. The lowest level, at the extreme left, is *eikasía*, often translated "conjecture" for lack of a better term. This level deals with opinion about shadows, mirror images, and other images that virtually everyone realizes are not real. The things that most people consider real, objects in the world that we can see, hear, and touch, are also not real according to Plato, and we can have only opinion about them. Plato calls this level *pístis*, or belief.

Knowledge (*epistēmē*) is also on two levels, shown in the two sections of the diagram to the right. First is the level of knowledge about things that are partly real because they are in the realm of the intellect, such as the numbers used in arithmetic. They are not pure reality, however, so thinking about them uses a lower level of knowledge. Plato called this level *diánoia*, sometimes translated "understanding." This level is not the highest knowledge because it involves mental images, which are built upon sense experience. It also is hypothetical, involving conjecture. The imagistic objects of *diánoia* are intelligible, but they are still particulars, while pure knowledge is completely general. One way to contrast the objects of *diánoia* and the objects of pure knowledge, *nóēsis*, is to note the difference between addible numbers, which are in the lower level of knowledge, and non-addible numbers, which are objects of the highest level of knowledge. Addible numbers are those we manipulate in adding, subtracting, multiplying, and dividing. Among them is the 1 that we add to 4 to get 5 and the 8 that we divide by 2 to get 4. The non-addible numbers are pure concepts, such as oneness and duality. While 1 plus 1 equals 2, no such operation can be done with "oneness." Oneness cannot be added to duality to get another number.

Plato considered *diánoia*, the sort of knowledge that most believe to be the highest form of knowledge people can have, to be knowledge only in a limited sense. Most of our scientific knowledge and mathematical knowledge falls within this form of knowledge, but it is still imperfect because it is particular instead of completely general, hypothetical instead of absolutely certain, and tied to sense experience since it contains mental images. Plato thought it was a useful step toward perfect knowledge, however. He called it a springboard or a footing.

How we move from such a footing to pure knowledge, to *nóēsis*, is not clearly spelled out in the dialogues, but Plato indicated that it is not easy, possibly not for everyone, to make this move to perfect knowledge.

Plato's primary interest was in *nóēsis*, the highest level of knowledge, knowledge of what is real, knowledge of the forms. Knowledge of what is real is certain, knowledge that cannot be false under any circumstances. Through *nóēsis*, Plato relates the eternal and unchanging reality to the perfect knowledge of this reality, thereby presenting the apex of his ontology and his theory of knowledge.

Let us note an important aspect of the divided line. In addition to including the concepts of both what is real and the nature of knowledge, the line progresses (from left to right) not only from the sensible to the intelligible, but also from the particular to the general. This point is important in regard to Plato's ontological theories as well as his epistemological theories. Reality, as well as knowledge, is intelligible and general. That which is sensible and that which is particular lack complete reality and are either not knowable or are objects of a lower level of knowledge.

Knowledge of the forms is not a simple matter. In the dialogue *Parmenides*, the old Parmenides gets the young Socrates to agree that the forms are completely different from the world; therefore, only the gods can know them. Then Socrates objects to the implication that the gods do not know or care about the world, and agrees with Parmenides that only an exceptional person can know the forms.[3]

Other dialogues indicate that Plato believed the forms can be known after sufficient dialectic, serious discussion that attends carefully to the meaning of philosophical terms and the differences between ideas. The purpose of dialectic is to remember what is already known, the innate knowledge that has been lost to conscious awareness with the embodiment of the mind.

Reminiscence

The way to recover knowledge of the real is through reminiscence. Plato expressed his doctrine of innate knowledge and reminiscence in mythological terms, basing it on the notion of preexistence of the soul, which had access to knowledge before it was born into a body. Innate knowledge is demonstrated by Socrates with the example of a slave boy whom he involved in dialectical reasoning about a problem in mathematics, about which the boy had not been instructed.[4]

We cannot determine whether Plato had a nonmythological explanation of innate knowledge that he did not give in any of his dialogues. He might have believed literally in the mythology of preexistence of the soul, but we cannot be sure of this. In several places in the dialogues Plato seems to separate himself from mythological notions by presenting them as stories told to him by others, which might be a device that enables him to avoid presenting the material as his own belief. In the *Phaedo*, he warns us against taking literally his explanations about the soul.[5] If Plato did have a nonmythological explanation of innate knowledge, we can only regret that he did not share it with us.

What Is Knowledge?

An important aspect of Plato's epistemology is the definition of knowledge. In the late, critical dialogue, the *Theaetetus*, Plato attempted to answer the question, "What is knowledge?"[6] He rejected three suggested definitions. The definition of knowledge as perception was rejected. This does not surprise us, since we know that Plato considered knowledge an intellectual matter. The difference between one person's perceptions and another's was taken as a logical reason to reject individual perceptions as a basis for knowledge claims. Plato did not consider those perceptions upon which there is wide agreement, what we might call intersubjective verification, as adequate knowledge, either, because for him knowledge was not a matter of the sensible but of the intelligible.

It is next argued that knowledge is not true judgment. The basis for this rejection is that a person can come to a correct opinion by inadequate means. Accurate opinions for which a person cannot adequately account do not deserve to be called knowledge.

Finally, the definition of knowledge as true belief with *logos* was rejected. *Logos*, which means "word," but came to mean an account or explanation, was interpreted as knowledge of why true belief is true. This definition was rejected on the grounds that it is circular, using knowledge as part of the definition of knowledge. Plato did not try to restate the definition so as to avoid the circular use of "knowledge," because he did not believe that any type of opinion is knowledge. As we saw in his divided line, opinion and knowledge are entirely different. The currently popular definition of knowledge as justified true belief, or something similar, seems very close to the third proposed definition in the *Theaetetus*. Plato's concept of knowledge is thus not compatible in several respects with recent definitions of knowledge. For him, and for Aristotle, knowledge had to be not only convincing but infallible; it was unable to be false or mistaken.

How Error Can Occur

A complete epistemology must be able to account for intellectual error. If we have an adequate basis for knowledge, how can intellectual error occur? In the *Theaetetus* Plato examined the analogy of a waxed block that receives an impression, as of a signet ring. The impression can be marred by a flaw in the wax. He rejects this account of false judgment as a misfit between thought and perception.[7] Perception did not for Plato play a role in either knowledge or error. He then used an analogy of an aviary in which a man has all kinds of birds. When he reaches in for a particular bird, he grasps the wrong one. He rejected this explanation of error, by which we are "perpetually driven round in a circle. . . ."[8]

In the *Sophist*, Plato defined error as "thinking what is not." According to Eleatic logic it would be impossible to think what is not, for that would give it a sort of being. In this dialogue, Plato argued that "what is not" must indeed have some sort of being.[9] In explaining how "what is not" can have some being, Plato made a logical point that has been of great importance. Without it, Aristotle's system of logic could not have been developed. The sort of being that "what is not" can have is seen in an analysis of synthetic propositions, those propositions that unite a subject (that which is being described) and a predicate (what is being said about the subject) that are not joined by logical necessity but are seen to be joined in fact. "Round tennis ball" is analytic; that is, by analysis of the terms we see that they are together of logical necessity; but "green tennis ball" is a synthetic idea. It puts together two ideas that are logically distinct. Some tennis balls are green, but others are white. To call a white tennis ball a green ball is to put the wrong subject and predicate together. Thus, Plato explains how error can occur. Also, different predicates can be associated with the same subject, so reality can be both changing and not changing. In explaining error this way, Plato rejected a literal Eleatic view and an extreme Heraclitean view. Things are not always unchanging (the Eleatic view) or everywhere changing (the view of Heraclitus). This allows, for example, for both motion and rest to be present in the world.[10] Plato pointed out that some forms can and some cannot combine, as is the case with letters of the alphabet and with words.[11]

Plato's View of Natural Science

Plato did not believe that knowledge of nature was possible. This is one aspect of his belief that knowledge could only be of the intelligible and the general.[12] The most Plato would say of natural science is that it was likely or probable.[13] The *Timaeus,* which appears to be an exercise in the kind of speculation about the natural world that we saw in the work of the Presocratics, and the only dialogue that talks of such matters, is seen upon closer examination to be more a work of theology than natural history. In it, Plato claims that the divine "father and creator" patterned the world after the forms, making the heavens a "moving image of eternity" and structuring the whole world after mathematical proportions.[14] In having Timaeus say that his talk about the natural world is only a likely story, Plato remained consistent with his belief that knowledge can be only of what is real, that is, that which is one and unchanging. The natural world is not a fit subject for knowledge.

9 PLATO

ETHICS AND POLITICS

Plato's views on ethics, politics, and the soul are not three separate topics grouped in one chapter simply for convenience. Ethics and politics are two aspects of one subject, proper human behavior, including virtuous behavior for the state and individual. The soul was an important part of Plato's ethics; he held that the purpose of life is tending the soul, and he understood justice to be a healthy condition of the soul.

Virtue and Happiness

Plato opposed the view that might makes right, that injustice is better than justice for those who can get away with it. He held that the wise person will not seek power and advantage over other people; they are not the best thing to have. In the *Republic* and the *Gorgias* Plato argued against the view that power is desirable, that law and morality are means by which the weak protect themselves against the strong, that the strong should rule, and related beliefs that he felt were mistaken. In the *Republic,* he has Socrates argue with Thrasymachus, then with Glaucon, and finally with Adimantus, who picks up the argument when Glaucon tires.[1]

In the *Gorgias* Plato argues, against Polus, that the person who does an injustice is worse off than the person who suffers the injustice; it is better to be wronged than to do wrong. To do wrong is harmful to the soul. He claims that the person who does wrong is better off caught and punished, because punishment can lead to reformation of the person who has done wrong. He compares this to the unjust person regaining his health; he compares punishment to surgery.[2] In the *Republic,* Plato tries to make his point by proving the hardest case; he claims that the just person, even if tortured, is happier than the unjust person.[3]

In the *Gorgias,* Callicles accuses Plato (Socrates) of supporting the morality of the weak, who are trying to prevent the rule of the strong who should rule. Callicles is offended by Socrates' asking him whether the strong should rule himself and replies that the strong man should give free rein to his passions and desires.[4] Socrates forces Callicles to admit that the pleasant is not the same as the good, and Callicles finally admits that some pleasures are better than others.[5] Socrates argues that reason must judge the pleasures and decide which are conducive to health and harmony in the soul and in society. Plato was arguing that a virtuous life is good for the person; the value of justice is its good effect on the person, as he argued in the *Republic.* The temperate and disciplined man is the happiest.[6]

When Plato talked of the happiness of the virtuous person, he was referring to *eudaimonia,* which is not a joyful state of the emotions but a state of wholeness and well-being. The virtuous person possesses a happiness that consists of balance and harmony in life, a healthy state of the soul. This state of *eudaimonia* is rewarding in this life, in that one is in a healthy state of being, and in the next incarnation, in which the virtuous soul will be closer to the eventual release from bodily existence. Plato treated tending the soul as the purpose of life.[7] We will examine in more detail the psychic harmony that is the goal of tending the soul when we consider Plato's psychological doctrines.

Opposition to Psychological Hedonism and Egoism

Plato believed that people are free to tend the soul by seeking to live a virtuous life. He opposed the psychological doctrine that people cannot avoid putting their own pleasure and self-interest first, even though most people usually do seek what they expect will give them pleasure and be in their own interest. Glaucon, in arguing that it is lack of power that keeps a just person from doing what is in his interest, that is, being unjust and benefiting from it, held that every creature by its nature pursues self-advantage. He told the story of the ancestor of Gyges who was working as a shepherd when an earthquake opened a chasm in the ground. Among other wonderful things in the chasm, the shepherd found a corpse wearing a gold ring, which he took. He discovered that when the collet of the ring was turned toward his palm he became invisible. He used this power to seduce the queen, murder the king, and take the kingdom. Glaucon argued that if there were two such rings and a just man wore the other, he would of necessity behave no differently than the unjust man.[8] Plato's view was that the just man could refrain from acting unjustly, and he would have ample reason to do so, to tend his soul by being virtuous.

Virtue and the Forms

In keeping with his metaphysical doctrine that held that the real must be unchanging and one, Plato related virtue to the forms as a kind of wisdom and held that the virtues are unified.

Plato believed that in a sense all virtues are one. In the *Protagoras* Socrates asks Protagoras whether virtue is a single whole, with justice and holiness and the other virtues part of it, "or are these latter all names for one and the same thing?" Protagoras answers that virtue is one and virtuous qualities are parts of it, related to each other as the parts of the face are related, but the virtues do not resemble one another. Socrates tries to get him to agree that justice is holy and holiness just, but Protagoras will grant only that they slightly resemble each other. Socrates does get him to agree that he would be ashamed to say that one can be temperate in acting unjustly. After a long discussion of other subjects, Socrates reviews Protagoras' statements, and Protagoras then holds that most virtues resemble one another closely. Courage, however, is different, since a person can be courageous even if unjust, unholy, intemperate, and ignorant. In the discussion of the nature of courage and foolish false courage, Socrates is not able to get Protagoras to equate wisdom and courage.[9] This was an argument between Socrates and a Sophist, who did not accept Plato's belief in the unity of the virtues.

The unity of the virtues may be a large part of the reason that the early dialogues on the virtues (*Charmides, Laches, Euthyphro,* and *Hippias major*) fail to reach acceptable definitions of each virtue; the virtues cannot be defined independently of one another. As we saw in the chapter on Plato's metaphysics, the form of the good gives all of the forms their existence and their intelligibility. This would make it related to all the virtues. The several virtues could not thus be defined without reference to the forms and the form of the good.

Virtue as Innate Knowledge

Plato held that wrongdoing is error; no one knowingly chooses evil. The doers of evil do not really know what they are doing. Goodness is advantageous, and by virtue we receive the advantage, but the good must be pursued with wisdom if it is to bring advantage and not loss, as with foolish courage. Therefore virtue, according to Plato, is a sort of wisdom, and all of the virtues have a common opposite—ignorance.[10]

Plato did not accept the claim of those Sophists who said they could teach virtue. Virtue, he said, is innate, acquired before birth, and it is through recollection of what we already know in the recesses of our minds that we recover knowledge of virtue. The wisdom that is virtue comes through recollection, as do other forms of innate knowledge.[11]

Pleasure Is Not the Good

Plato attacked ethical hedonism in several of his dialogues. He did not deny that pleasure is good, but he did not accept it as *the* good. Intelligent thought, right opinion, and reasoning are better than pleasure. Even in the arts pleasure is not the proper standard of evaluation, and in morality pleasure and the good cannot be wedded. Pleasure can lead to wrongdoing.[12]

Not all pleasures are equal. In a passage that reflects the view that the soul has three parts, Plato held that the pleasures associated with the mind are the sweetest. Not all pleasures are good, however; in fact, pleasure can at times be bad, especially when one seeks pleasure without knowledge. Nevertheless, Plato did not base his morality on seeking the better pleasures. To qualify pleasures, saying that some pleasures are morally better than others, one must go beyond the hedonic standard; it is not as pleasure that some pleasures are better, but because of some more significant factor associated with them. Plato suggested that if we valued pleasure most highly, the greatest good would be scratching, a pure and readily available pleasure.[13]

The philosopher will not seek bodily pleasure. A life dedicated to the enjoyment of pleasure would be like the life of a shellfish, but a life without pleasure is not required. A life that includes wisdom and pleasure is best.[14]

Unlike the Epicureans, Stoics, and others, Plato did not understand pleasure negatively, as merely the absence of pain. He defined pleasure as the restoration of balance, as when a hungry or thirsty person eats or drinks. He argued that pleasure and pain are not opposites, as are good and evil; while a balance is being restored, one experiences pain and pleasure at the same time. Thus, even though Plato rated pleasure about fifth in his scale of values, he was far more positive about pleasure than many other ancient thinkers.[15]

Platonic Love

Plato's views on love are an important part of his ethics. For him, love is not just a sentiment and not just an important motive for doing good things for other people. It is an important part of the tending of the soul. Platonic love leads to a life of intellectual growth. This is, of course, a much stronger concept than the common notion of "platonic love"; it involves much more than abstinence from sex.

Plato talked of love in several dialogues. In the *Symposium* Plato explained that love is a yearning for the good; and understanding what this means explains some important aspects of Plato's ethics.

The *Symposium* (also called the *Banquet*) is one of Plato's most deservedly popular dialogues; it is a literary gem. The setting is a dinner party at which the participants decide to drink only lightly and to entertain themselves with speeches about love. The first resolution is forgotten, but the speeches proceed. The orations begin with talks by Phaedrus and Pausanus in praise of homosexual love, followed by a physician's pedantic thesis.[16]

Aristophanes' humorous myth about our choice of lovers resulting from the gods' splitting apart originally double human creatures, who were sexually self-sufficient in themselves, may anticipate the speech by Socrates. The double creatures, now divided, were no longer free of sexual needs, since they were separated into male-only or female-only beings. In their need they sought the male or female part they had lost. Socrates builds on the concept of need and the seeking of fulfillment. Before Socrates speaks, Agathon the poet talks in praise of the god of love, of his beauty, gentleness, temperance, and general moral excellence. This speech also prepares the way for the speech of Socrates by turning away from the physical aspects of love, of which the earlier speakers talked.[17]

Before his speech, Socrates engages in a dialogue with Agathon, in which they agree that love is desire for what the lover is lacking and that love is the love of beauty and the good. Socrates then relates a myth about the conception of Eros, which was told him by Diotima, a Mantinean woman. Eros was conceived at a party to celebrate the birth of Aphrodite. Poverty managed to get pregnant by Resource, who, having gotten drunk, had gone to a garden to rest. As the child of Poverty and Resource, Eros is always needy and is always seeking. What Love seeks is happiness in the good and the beautiful, which he wants to have forever, so Love's seeking is really a yearning for immortality.[18]

Some people seek immortality in progeny, some in fame, in inventions or literary work (as Homer and Hesiod) or, better, in statesmanship (as Solon and Lycurgus). Plato's belief about what love should be is expressed as a ladder, whereby love leads the lovers from love of a beautiful body to love of many beautiful bodies and then to love of beauty itself in bodies. The ladder then rises to love of beauty in souls and finally to love of the beautiful itself, a path that traces, in effect, the movement from the sensible to the intelligible and from the particular to the general that we saw in the divided line of levels of being and knowledge.[19]

Love between two persons should grow in this way. In the *Phaedrus* Plato wrote of a love relationship that helps the lovers mutually reach the innate knowledge with which they lost touch in the shock of being born, the fall into embodiment from a better condition of unembodied rationality. He described the searching for knowledge as the lovers regaining their lost wings, with which they will soar above the limitations of sensible awareness. The release of the soul from bondage to embodiment takes 3,000 years for the seeker after wisdom, which is shorter than the 10,000 years required for others.[20]

Homosexual Love

Homosexual love was common in the upper classes of Athens. This fact was probably related to the status of women, who were seldom educated or knowledgeable about literary and intellectual matters. Plato did not object to affectional relationships between two men, but he did not speak favorably of physical homosexual acts. In the *Phaedrus* he writes of the disadvantage of the younger person in a physical relationship. In the *Republic* Plato calls the right love a sober and harmonious love of the orderly and beautiful; nothing of madness or license infects it. In the *Symposium* Alcibiades makes a speech that tells of his unsuccessful attempts to seduce Socrates. In the *Laws* Plato condemned homosexual acts.[21] Plato is sometimes listed among supporters of homosexuality, but he seems to have been unable to understand physical same-sex relationships as anything more than indulgence in pleasure; note, however, that he gives no sign of seeing heterosexual physical relationships as anything more either, except that they can produce offspring.

Justice and the Ideal Republic

In the *Republic* Plato integrated his ethical and psychological theories. This book is often taken as a treatise in political science or as Plato's utopia. Either approach fails to understand the nature of the *Republic,* which is a book primarily about ethics; the purpose of the description of an ideal city is clearly stated in Book Two. The subject of the dialogue is the definition of justice in the just person, and the description of the state is an attempt to see the nature of justice more clearly by seeing it "writ large."[22] Plato employed an analogy, using an imaginary city to represent the nature of the just soul. The city described shows a relationship between the classes within the city; this same relationship is that of the three parts of the soul of a just person. The kind of justice about which Plato was concerned was not simply political justice, that which we usually think about when we speak of justice. It was *dikaiosúnē*, the broadest ethical sense of justice, that refers to moral rightness generally. The just state of the soul, which is the healthy state, is explained in psychological terms.

The *Republic* is a large dialogue, and in making its ethical points it treats a number of subjects that Plato saw as related to the righteous life; he dealt with metaphysical, epistemological, educational, religious, and other issues. It is a rich book, without which we would know far less of Plato's philosophy. We will not discuss some of the descriptions of the ideal city that do not throw much light on the main philosophical issues. There is no evidence that Plato ever had in mind presenting his ideal city as a political blueprint for cities to follow. The sex life of the guardians, for example, was probably used to stress the point that they should be focused on their task of ruling and not diverted by family life, as the rational part of the soul should be focused, but there is no indication that Plato was trying to do away with marriage even for those in positions of leadership in actual cities. The importance of gymnastic and music in the education of rulers was of much more significance, since these are important parts of the education of every soul.

In Plato's ideal state there were three classes. The largest class was that of people engaged in the economic life of the city, the consumers and producers. This is usually referred to as the artisan class, but it included many more people than only the artisans. It included all the people engaged in economic activity, such as artisans, tradespeople, farmers, and merchants. It also included entertainers, jewelers, beauticians, nurses, and doctors—all the people who are meeting the needs of the population of the city and maintaining its economic life.[23]

The second class was that of the defenders of the society, the soldiers and the police. This class was referred to as the helpers or auxiliaries, who assist the rulers of the city. The auxiliaries did not engage in economic activity, since learning to do their tasks left them no time to engage in farming, making shoes, or any such other profession. The needs of this class were met by the economic class.[24] Apparently the auxiliaries were given the same education in childhood that the highest class, the rulers, received; in fact, they were not distinguished from the guardians at this time. (In describing the education of auxiliaries and guardians in music and gymnastic, Plato expounds at length on the need for censorship of the arts to which these young minds are exposed.[25])

The highest class, and the one of most interest to Plato, was the highly educated ruling class, the guardians, referred to as "guardians" in the full sense of the word. The guardians did not own property, have families, or engage in any economic activity. They engaged only in ruling the city, and they were given the education to prepare them for this task, first strictly traditional training in gymnastic and music, then training in mathematics, and finally, at age thirty, five years of dialectic.[26]

Membership in the two upper classes was determined by ability. Status was not achieved by birth, and parents of one rank sometimes had children not suited for that rank. The populace was told the "necessary lie" that every person is born of gold, silver, or iron, so that people would accept their assigned class without question. Women with the right personal qualities and abilities could be assigned membership in the auxiliary or guardian classes.[27]

Justice in the imaginary city consisted of members of each class doing the work of that class according to the appropriate virtue of the class and not becoming involved in the activities of any other class.

Guardians must rule; that is their one and only task. Their virtue is wisdom. Auxiliaries must protect the state and not engage in any other business. Their virtue is courage. All classes must be temperate. The economic class had no distinctive virtue of its own.[28]

Justice in the Individual

The concept of justice in the individual was based on Plato's psychological doctrine that the soul has three parts. Justice lies in each of the three parts fulfilling its own role. The city has three parts, which corresponded to the three parts of the soul: the appetitive part of the soul corresponds to the economic class, the spirited part corresponds to the auxiliaries, and the rational part corresponds to the guardians. The parts of the soul have the same virtues as the analogous parts of the city, wisdom for the ruling rational part, courage for the spirited part, and temperance for all parts.[29]

Plato explained justice in the individual as a kind of psychic harmony. He described the three parts graphically in the analogy of a chariot with two horses. One horse is fat and lazy and prone to stop along the roadway to graze. The other is spirited and prone to pull the chariot too swiftly and dangerously. The driver of the chariot keeps the two horses working in harmony, spurring the one that would prefer to eat to greater effort and keeping the other in check. The driver, of course, represents the rational part of the soul, which, like the guardians in the analogy of the city, must rule the other parts. Plato held that justice, a harmonious state of the soul, is like health. Vice is like disease.[30]

Inferior Constitutions and Unjust Persons

Plato held that government constitutions could degenerate from the ideal of balance between the classes, as one class after another dominated, removing the rightful rule from the rational class. People could become corrupt in the same way. The first lapse is timarchy (timocracy), rule by lover of honor, by the spirited class or the spirited part of the soul. In a government, this stage is oligarchy, rule by the wealthy. In a disordered, timocratic soul, the person is ruled by ambition and acts in anger or passion. Rule by the populace is democracy, which Plato saw as a state of disorder, which is vulnerable to tyranny if a despot wins control of the state and rules for his own benefit.[31]

Later Political Views

Late in his life Plato wrote two dialogues on political economy. The *Politicus* ("Statesman") stressed the qualities of a kingly man, one who can provide the kind of monarchical rule that Plato favored. He upheld the advantage of elasticity of laws, to be administered by an enlightened despot. This was not written in support of tyranny, for Plato condemned tyranny in several dialogues. In the *Laws* Plato upheld the value of statesmanship, with the rule of law under a constitution.[32]

Plato rated political structures according to the number of rulers and whether the government was lawful and constitutional as opposed to government by revolution or usurpation. The ideal government is one led by a despot who is skilled in the art and science of statesmanship. In the absence of a real king, a rare phenomenon, the best government is rule by one statesman, that is, a constitutional monarchy. Rule by a small number of rulers has a "middle potency for good or ill." Rule of the many is weakest in every way, not capable of "any real good or serious ill" compared to other forms of government. Among lawful governments, democracy is the worst government, but among lawless types, it is the best.[33]

In the *Statesman* Plato's spokesman, not Socrates but the respected Stranger from Elea who directed the discussion in the *Sophist,* defines the nature of the art of statesmanship or kingship. After examining the idea that the statesman is a type of herdsman and going through long, drawn-out distinctions between various types of herds, the Stranger abandons this idea as applicable only to a divine king and explores the analogy of the king as a weaver, a concept he uses once he has distinguished kingship from other arts, such as generalship, the administration of justice, and the art of public persuasion. The art of kingship is a higher level art, involved in deciding when and how to use coercion or persuasion, how to use the judicial art, and when to use warfare and when to use friendly settlement of disagreements. The king, in short, weaves these arts into the life of the community. He also weaves good but conflicting types of human character, such as being warlike and being peaceful, into the kind of character needed in the state.[34]

The question in the *Laws,* in which the discussion is led by an Athenian, with Socrates never mentioned, was the nature of a good code of laws. The legal code advocated by the Athenian is conservative, austere, and puritanical. It has a strong theological basis. Perhaps the code should be seen as reactionary more than conservative. It stands in opposition to the nonreligious views of "modern men of enlightenment." It calls for laws against atheists, who are viewed as enemies of the state and to be punished by imprisonment in all cases, the degree depending on their kind of impiety. Those who are not vicious but are atheists out of sheer folly receive five years of solitary confinement. The really stubborn atheists are imprisoned for life, and their corpses are finally cast out of the city unburied. Several types of sacrilege are cited, including outrage against the gods through satire or mockery, and behavior that comes from not believing in the gods or in believing that they are powerless or have no concern for humans. The modernistic opinions that Plato opposes are similar to the beliefs that brought banishment to several earlier philosophers, such as those of the astronomers who held that the heavenly bodies are rocks and not intelligences.[35] One method cited for controlling religious thought was to allow no private shrines.

The principle behind the laws is that morals, which are divine goods, should be legislated. All aspects of life are covered by law; sex is for procreation only, and there are severe laws against homosexual behavior. The laws are not to be questioned by the young, and the old must not criticize the laws in the presence of the young.[36]

10 ARISTOTLE

METAPHYSICS

Aristotle was born in 384 B.C. in Stagira (in Thrace) of a middle-class family. His father, Nicomachus, become court physician to King Amyntos II of Macedonia, and Aristotle may have lived much of his childhood in Pella, the new capital of Macedonia. At age seventeen or eighteen, Aristotle enrolled in Plato's Academy, where he stayed for about twenty years. He left the Academy upon the death of Plato, when Speusippus became its head. He traveled to Atarneus and Mytilene. He married Pythias, sister or niece of Hermeias, a friend who had invited him to Atarneus. They had one daughter.[1]

In 343 B.C., Aristotle became tutor to the twelve-year-old son of King Philip of Macedon, Alexander, who was to become the conqueror Alexander the Great. Philip appointed Alexander regent about four years later. Philip was assassinated in 335 B.C., and Alexander took the throne.

Aristotle next returned to Athens and founded his school, called the Lyceum, since it met in buildings in a park dedicated to the Muses and Apollo Lyceus. The school was also called "peripatetic" either from Aristotle's habit of strolling while lecturing or from the covered walkways that were an architectural feature of the buildings.

Pythias died soon after Aristotle's return to Athens; he established a union with Herpyllis, who bore him a son, Nicomachus, for whom the *Nicomachean Ethics* was named.

Aristotle did a tremendous amount of research and writing, covering every known field of inquiry at the time, but especially biology. Most of his writings have been lost; what we are familiar with are remnants of dialogues and edited lecture notes. These do not reflect the fine literary style of most of Aristotle's writing.

Alexander died in 323 B.C. Greece was then in revolt against Macedonia, and because of his connections with Macedonia Aristotle had to flee Athens, saying he would not give the Athenians a chance to sin twice against philosophy. He was referring, of course, to the death of Socrates, but Athens had demonstrated a tendency to deal harshly with other philosophers at whom the city had taken offense, as seen in the treatment of Anaximander and Protagoras.

The death of Alexander might have saved Aristotle from another sort of unpleasantness. If he and Alexander had had a good relationship as pupil and teacher, it did not last. Aristotle disapproved of Alexander's adopting the role of an oriental monarch, marrying a Bactrian and two Persian princesses, and encouraging his troops to intermarry. Aristotle and Alexander became further estranged when Alexander accused Aristotle's nephew of complicity in a plot against him, then had the young man tortured and killed. Later Alexander accused Aristotle and Antipater, the regent in charge of Macedonia, of complicity in the conspiracy.

When Aristotle left Athens, he retired to Chalsis on the island of Euboea, the home of his mother, Phaestis. He died a year later of stomach disease.

Aristotle on the Wise Person

Aristotle believed that wisdom seems much like scientific knowledge, but it is only part of knowledge. Art and science begin in experience, but experience deals with things individually, not with general principles and the causes of things. This makes experience good for practical action, but the practical person only knows that something is the case, not why it is so. Art and science are more truly knowledge than experience. Because wise artists know what they are doing, they can teach more than people who have only experience.[2]

The wise seek knowledge of the exact sciences, which deal with first principles, the most universal principles. These are harder to learn and understand than things of sense experience, which is common to all humans. The sciences farthest from the senses, for example, theoretical mathematics, as contrasted with practical mathematics, are really the most knowable because they involve fewer principles and are more exact. Aristotle called knowledge of first principles, the reasons and causes of things, divine knowledge.[3]

Plato and Aristotle

Aristotle found in Plato a friend and philosophical mentor. He accepted most of Plato's philosophy at first, and his early writings indicate this. Later, he was not uncritical of Plato's views, and he may have left the Academy in part because he did not approve of the mathematical emphasis that may have become stronger in Plato's later philosophy and seems to have dominated the thought of the Academy after Plato's death. He said that with the turn toward mathematics, "the whole inquiry concerning nature has been eliminated."[4]

One difference between Aristotle and Plato was that of temperament. Plato was religious, emotionally involved in issues, and primarily concerned with ethics. Aristotle tended to be calm, inquisitive, and systematic, in some ways more "academic" than Plato. Unlike Plato, Aristotle was interested in physical science. Where Plato was most concerned with philosophy as a way of tending the soul, Aristotle stressed the human desire to know and thought philosophy grew out of wonder. Leisure made possible the search for theoretical knowledge, that is, the sciences that do not aim at giving pleasure or meeting the common needs of life.[5]

Seeing Plato and Aristotle as polar opposites and founders of radically opposed philosophical schools is based on superficial interpretation of both philosophers, however. Even when he disagreed with some of Plato's beliefs, Aristotle considered himself a friend of Plato and his followers. When duty required him to take issue with them, he expressed his regret. He wrote,

> We had perhaps better consider the universal good and discuss thoroughly what is meant by it, although such an inquiry is made an uphill one by the fact the Forms have been introduced by friends of our own. Yet it would perhaps be thought to be better, indeed to be our duty, for the sake of maintaining the truth even to destroy what touches us closely, especially as we are philosophers or lovers of wisdom; for, while both are dear, piety requires us to honor truth above our friends.[6]

Aristotle and Plato are best seen as belonging to one school of thought, but with different interpretations and sharp disagreement on some points. They were both essentialists, holding that things are what they are because of an enduring essence. The most basic difference is not between Plato and Aristotle but between the two of them and other philosophers of their time and later, who did not explain reality in terms of essences.

Aristotle's Criticism of Plato's Metaphysics

When Aristotle first started his studies with Plato, he accepted Plato's interpretation of the essences as forms removed from the sensible world, as well as his religious approach. The *Protrepticus* and *Eudemus* are from this period. In a somewhat later dialogue, *On Philosophy,* he rejected the concepts of a created universe, the Demiurge, and separate forms.

Aristotle's main disagreement with Plato was over Plato's separation of the forms from objects in the world, the entities of our sense experience. Not only did he think that there was no convincing evidence of the existence of forms apart from things in the world, but the notion of separated forms leads to postulating forms for things that we do not believe have forms. He held that Plato's doctrine turned the forms into another group of things, making universals that are general and abstract into particular entities, thereby multiplying the number of forms called for by the theory. In addition to making the forms into a set of particular entities, Plato's theory would require a multiplicity of forms for each sensible object. There would need to be forms for negations, relations, and things that have perished.[7]

If the forms existed independently, they would be powerless to explain the existence of sensible entities and their changing characteristics. As we have seen, Aristotle rejected the identification of the forms with number, and he did not think such an interpretation of forms could explain how forms could be causes.[8]

Aristotle's Concept of Substance

Aristotle held that real being is not in the universals (the forms), but in each particular, concrete, individual thing. The particular object has an essence, of course, but the combination of matter and form is a substance in Aristotle's original and most interesting use of the term "substance." Aristotle recognized several other uses of the term "substance."

In places he uses the term for matter, for the essence, or for the universal, meanings of the term already in use. "Substance" as universal or essence plays an important role in his logical works, to designate the logical primary being, but Aristotle's concept of a concrete primary being is his own metaphysical invention. His concept of substances as concrete primary beings that are form and matter, or formed matter, is called hylomorphism, from the Greek words for form and matter.[9]

Form and matter do not exist apart from each other; there is no formless matter or matterless form. Universals, which are not material, can be substances only in a secondary sense.[10]

Knowledge is of Universals

Knowledge is not of individual entities. Mere acquaintance is not knowledge. Aristotle held that knowledge is of universals. We have a faculty for deriving a knowledge of universals, of classes of things. Without this faculty things would be perceived, but there would be no conception of what they are. There could be no definitions or logical demonstrations about sensible things. Scientific knowledge would not be possible, because definition and scientific knowledge rest on what is necessary. Opinion can concern of that which is not necessary and subject to change, but logical definition and argument cannot.[11]

This view of knowledge, which holds that knowledge is of what is unchanging and necessarily true, agrees with Plato's concept of knowledge. This is another demonstration that Plato and Aristotle belong to the same school of philosophy.

Perspectives on Form and Matter

Objects can be seen from two perspectives, one relative to their being the actualization of a form and one relative to their being matter that is potential for actualizing another form. Every object is both (1) the actualization of a form, having used previously existing objects as the matter from which it is made, and (2) potential matter for other forms. Aristotle thought of matter as potentiality to receive form, not just the inert, extended, solid stuff we usually think of as matter. For him, matter is matter in relation to a form. This relativity of form and matter makes change in worldly objects possible.[12]

Four Kinds of Causation

Aristotle thought that his predecessors gave incomplete explanations of change; they considered only part of the causation of change. He held that four factors must be taken into account, and he referred to them as four kinds of causation. First is the *material cause,* that which is changed from one form to another. That which brings about the change is the *efficient cause.* Change takes place according to a pattern, the *formal cause,* and it happens for a purpose, the *final cause.*

He gave the example of making a sculpture, in which the material cause is the marble, the efficient cause is the action of the sculptor, the formal cause is the particular type of sculpture desired, such as a bust of a famous person, and the final cause is the sculptor's desire for fame or money. This example suggests, however, a too narrow concept of final cause as only human desire. Final causation is to be found in natural occurrences when human desire is not involved. Consider a rock rolling down a hill; the final cause is the nature of unsupported objects to come to rest at the point at which they are supported. This idea is often expressed figuratively, as in the saying that water seeks its lowest level. Aristotle thought of nature as having purposes in this sense, as we will see. These four elements of causation are present in every change, even when they overlap in a particular case, as when the efficient cause of an explosion also determines the form of the explosive event.[13]

The final cause (and the actuality) are prior to potentiality and efficient cause in several ways. In terms of being, the human person is prior to the seed, the adult to the child. The actual is prior causally; the reason for or knowledge of the actual must be present before the potential can be known. In one sense, actuality is prior in time; an actual person or plant is already active while its materials are still merely potential, and when something potential becomes actual it does so by the agency of something already actual. Aristotle held that just as people learn to build in order to build, they have vision in order to see. They do not see in order to have vision. The most significant way in which actually is prior, however, is that the actual is eternal. This shows how mistaken it is to say that Aristotle rejected Platonic forms. He did not think the forms were separated from things in the world, but the eternal and unchanging forms show up in various parts of Aristotle's philosophy, as they clearly do here.[14]

Aristotle's Teleological View of Nature

Aristotle's philosophy is called "teleological," from the Greek word *telos,* for "end" or "purpose." Aristotle thought that nature is purposive. He said nothing happens by accident or chance. In nature, as in human actions, everything happens for a purpose. Nature makes nothing in vain; changes in nature do not occur because of necessary conditions. Necessity is not related to circumstances but to ends. This view is an important aspect of Aristotle's rejection of the idea of evolution of species. He scorned the idea of Empedocles' ox-faced progeny that did not survive because they were ill-adapted to their environment. Monsters, he thought, are not a product of chance but the result of a corrupt principle in nature; they are not good things, but they are not accidents.[15]

Thus, there are no real chance occurrences. The events that seem to us to be chance occurrences are the result of incidental causes. We run into someone we want to see and consider the meeting a lucky chance, but each of us was in the place of meeting for a reason although neither of us anticipated the meeting.[16]

The Defining Form: Entelechy

Aristotle held that the real nature of a thing is that into which it grows, and what it grows into is determined by its essential nature. Aristotle recognized a difference between the form that a thing may have at a given moment and its final or mature form. The *entelechy* is the final, complete form that gives a thing its identity. The growth of an organism is a progress toward what it really is. Some things, such as a lump of lead, have the same form they will always have; the concept of entelechy has more importance for things that develop. It is important to see that the entelechy of a thing is determined by that thing's own nature; human interest in a thing or incidental uses of a thing do not determine its entelechy. Being cut down and sawed into lumber is not the entelechy of a tree. Its entelechy is to grow into a mature tree. The entelechy of a pig is not to be pork but to be a parent to litters of piglets.[17]

Levels of Actualization

Aristotle believed in different kinds of entelechies, related to others and graded according to their level of actualization. This can be seen as a kind of hierarchy. Things that have a high level of potentiality but a low level of actuality are toward the bottom of the hierarchy of entelechies. They are part of the material causation of things higher on the hierarchy, and their functions and abilities are more fully realized in the higher level entelechy. Werner Jaeger says that it is the "fundamental principle of Aristotle's teleology" that at every level of actualization the functions of the lower are in the higher.[18] Highly actualized things are at the top of the hierarchy. Each level is related to lower levels of the hierarchy through actualizing the potentialities of those levels, which are in turn potentiality for a higher level.

The lowest level of actualization contains the five elements of traditional Greek physics, earth, air, fire, water, and aether (which does not appear on the earth, but is the material of heavenly bodies). These elements have a high level of potentiality, since all things are composed of them. Nothing exists on a less actualized level than the basic four earth elements. Aristotle did not believe that prime matter, matter without form, exists. A higher level of actualization contains inorganic bodies composed of the four terrestrial elements. This level has more actualization than the base level, since it actualizes the potentialities of the basic elements, but it is not highly actualized. It provides the potentiality for living things, which Aristotle called souls. (In his mature philosophy he abandoned the Platonic concept of the soul as a substance and used the term "soul" for the entelechy of an organic body.)

The lowest level of living things contains organic bodies with the functions of nutrition and reproduction. Aristotle refers to them as vegetative souls; this is the level of plant life. The next level is that of sensitive soul. On this level are animals with at least one of the senses and animals with all five senses and consciousness, but not reason or self-consciousness. Organisms on this level actualize the potentiality of vegetative souls. On the highest level are rational souls, who actualize the potentialities in sensation and all the other life functions of the levels below. These levels of life are described more fully in chapter 11.

The Prime Mover

Aristotle believed that there must be a primary cause of motion or change for the existence of the world to make sense. An infinite regress of explanations would in effect leave the world unexplained, and nothing would be knowable. He does not bring the regress of explanations to an end with a first material cause or a first efficient cause, however. He believed that matter, time, and change have always been. There has always been the primary kind of change, locomotion, occurring as circular motion, the primary kind of locomotion, in the eternal primary heavens or the area of the fixed stars. This circular motion is eternal and necessary. Since there is no movement apart from things, there must be an eternal substance.[19] But the matter and motion that have always been do not provide Aristotle with the sufficient explanation of reality he sought.

The primary cause must be an unmoved mover; only final causation avoids an eternal regress. The eternal power that produces eternal motion must itself be non-material, a primary source of motion that impels movement without itself being moved. This prime mover must be completely actualized and not material, "an unmoved mover, being eternal, primary, and in act," that is, completely actualized. An unmoved mover cannot be the primary cause of movement by being an efficient cause, for efficient causes cause movement by moving.[20]

What is this unmoved mover that Aristotle calls divine? It is eternal, unmovable, and separate from sensible things. It does not have magnitude and is indivisible and without parts. It is not subject to change of any sort, or it would not be the primary cause. It is not involved in any process of becoming, any process of actualizing; it is completely separate from change. This means that it is not a form and does not depend for its actuality on the potentiality of any other substance. It is not the potentiality for any form. The prime mover is self-existent, self-sustaining. It is not an object in the sensible world but is intelligible.[21]

The prime mover not only causes motion without exerting force, it causes motion without having volition (will). How then does it cause motion? The primary cause moves the intelligences that govern the heavenly bodies by being desirable, "an object of love." Thus it is as final cause that the unmoved mover causes the circular motion in the primary heavens.[22]

This object of desire, that which is the highest good and the most beautiful, is mind. It is the thing that Aristotle calls god, the divine reason, but Aristotle's god is not at all like the Judeo-Christian deity. Aristotle does not say that the prime mover knows about or loves human beings; people do not love it and are not moved directly by it. It is attractive, an object of love, to the intelligences governing the heavenly bodies because the prime mover is the highest kind of intellect, pure reason (*nóēsis*). It is contemplation, not practical problem solving or discursive reasoning. As the highest kind of reason, it thinks what is best. What is the best, the highest, the most beautiful? It is the unmoved mover itself, pure contemplation; hence the prime mover is the object of its own contemplation. *Nóēsis,* the highest contemplative reason, contemplates contemplation.[23]

The purely actualized prime mover does not exist by actualizing the potentiality of any other entelechy. It is not a continuation of the gradations in the hierarchy of entelechies. The prime mover is distant in a sense from anything in our sensible world. Only the celestial intelligences in their bodies of aether move from love of the prime mover. The ordinary souls, even the rational souls, of this world are not moved by love of this most excellent of beings. Aristotle did not think, however, that the prime mover is completely unrelated to the gradations of being in worldly entelechies. In a fragment of his book *On Philosophy,* preserved in Simplicius, *De caelo,* he wrote, ". . . where there is a better there is a best. Since, then, among existing things one is better than another, there is also something that is best, which will be the divine."[24]

Jaeger points out that an argument from grades of being was used by the Christian scholastics to prove the existence of God. It is also used by Boethius in *The Consolation of Philosophy.*[25]

Philosophy of Art

Aristotle's aesthetic theory in the *Poetics* is primarily addressed to poetry; some of his generalizations about dramatic poetry are too narrow to apply to all the fine art forms, but some general aspects of aesthetic theory can be found in his books. Remember that the concept of fine arts was not developed in classical times. Talk of art was talk of craftsmanship, but the fine arts as we know them were talked about individually.

Aristotle, like Plato and other classical thinkers generally, thought of poetry, sculpture, and painting as cognitive, that is, in terms of knowledge. Can these arts convey significant truth?

In the classical period, the arts that came to be known as fine arts were thought of as an imitation of nature, which for Plato made art of little value as a source of knowledge (see chapter 7). Aristotle did not view art as a copy of a copy, as Plato seems to have done. Poetry, he held, may reveal the "essence" more truly than do natural objects. Poetry and drama are more scientific than history, that is, they are a better source of knowledge. He was thinking of history as chronicle that reports particular events as they occurred. Poetry may alter the particulars to reveal more sharply the real significance of the events. It is important for poetry to reveal a possible event, however, an event that reveals a general truth about human life.[26]

Aristotle talked about the emotive role of drama. He did not see this as a bad thing, as Plato did. He held that drama can quiet or purify the emotions; it is a catharsis. The term translated "catharsis" is not often used in Greek literature, so it is difficult for us to know exactly how to interpret it. Some interpreters have held that drama serves as a purgation. Others think of it as a purification of the emotions. In the *Nicomachean Ethics* Aristotle says that emotions must be experienced to the right degree, toward the right objects, and in the right way. Aristotle might have thought that drama assists in achieving this balance and right direction in the emotions.[27]

Aristotle also says that imitation in poetry gives pleasure, which is a legitimate aspect of drama and poetry. People enjoy imitation from childhood. It is a method of learning and taking pleasure in learning. Imitation, along with rhythm and harmony, are given us by nature.[28]

Aristotle is still valued for his ideas on the principles of dramatic construction, including the several elements in a drama or dramatic poem and the requirements of different types of drama and poetry. The *Poetics* is still a first textbook for the student of drama and literature.

Unlike Plato, who held that the poet was only a conduit for the muse (see chapter 7), Aristotle does not hold that the poet does not know what he or she does and thus cannot teach. Aristotle says that art is more truly knowledge than is experience; the artist can teach, while a manual worker cannot, because the person who understands the principles of an activity knows, unlike the laborer, what they are doing. Aristotle was talking about master workers in all crafts, but there is no indication that he did not mean to include poets, painters, sculptors, and musicians in what he said.[29]

11 ARISTOTLE

PHYSICS, BIOLOGY, AND PSYCHOLOGY

Aristotle's writings on scientific subjects were extensive. Biology was one of his main interests, and his writings indicate that he did some biological research. Much of his writing on scientific subjects is of little philosophical interest, but some of it is philosophically important and helps to clarify aspects of his metaphysics.

Aristotle's Physics

Aristotle's views on physics and astronomy were influential, especially before the late Renaissance. He was treated as an authority on scientific as well as other topics.

The Nature of Matter

According to Aristotle, physical bodies on the earth are made of the four traditional elements, earth, air, fire, and water. The heavenly bodies are composed of a purer substance, aether. These bodies vary as to their level of actualization; as we saw in chapter 10, such levels may be seen as a hierarchy of entities, with the more highly actualized toward the top and those that are mainly potentiality toward the bottom of the hierarchy. All matter has some form. Prime matter, that is, bare physical matter that has no form, does not exist in the world. Aristotle's concept of matter cannot be reduced to the notion of matter as a stuff from which all things are made. Matter in itself is not knowable. Aristotle was critical of earlier philosophers' attempts to explain

that opposite qualities come out of a single substratum and other interpretations of matter, but he did not deny that there is a substratum; he
viewed matter as potentiality, potential relative to a form, as we saw in
chapter 10.[1]

Matter and Space

Matter has a position; it occupies place or space. Movement occurs in
space. Space has three dimensions; it has size, but it is not infinite.
Space is something, but it is difficult to say what it is. Space is not a
body, and it is not an element in the composition of bodies as is matter.
Space is neither form nor matter. Space, or place, is the body's container, not its material. If space were matter, movement of a body from
one space to another would be hard to explain. Space cannot be a form,
because it has reference to motion. The boundary of a thing is related
to its form, but space is the boundary of what contains a thing at its
surface, where it is in contact with the body contained. Aristotle treated
matter as a cause, but he did not consider space a cause. With this view
of space, Aristotle rejected Plato's view of matter, which Plato called
topos, equating matter with space or place.[2]

Aristotle also rejected the notion of a void, a place devoid of bodies. Such a void is not necessary for motion. There are no bodies that
are not in space.[3]

Time

Time is the measure of motion and of rest. It is not change or movement, but it is not independent of change. It does not exist without
movement. Time is perceived in the before and after of motion; it is
the "number" of motion in respect to the before and after of any event,
or better, it is "the number of precessions and successions in process."
Aristotle made it clear, however, that time, which is "a numberable
aspect" of a process, "is not the sheer number by which we count but is
something counted."[4]

Aristotle described time as continuous. He apparently was trying to
avoid the notion that time could be broken into discrete and separable
moments, which can be easily identified (numerated) by beginnings
and endings, seeing it more as Augustine later described it as a continuum; but the passage that indicates this is difficult.[5]

Aristotle's Astronomy

Aristotle supported a geocentric theory, with the heavenly bodies moving in circular orbits around the earth. The geocentric approach that he accepted was originated by Eudoxus of Cnidus and amplified by Callipus. It was finalized by Ptolemy of Alexandria, and it now bears his name. The theory involves the concept of 55 nested crystalline spheres, each carried in the revolution of its container and also having a rotation of its own oblique to that of its container. The heavenly bodies move in circular orbits because of the superior material of which they are composed, since a circular motion is superior to other motions. It is the only movement that can be continuous, uniform, and infinite.[6]

The Ptolemaic geocentric theory held sway until Copernicus, Kepler, and Galileo established a heliocentric theory during the Renaissance. The geocentric approach endured in spite of growing awareness that astronomical observations do not verify the theory, and that only a theory of component motions, circles within circles, could make the observations fit the theory. The church supported the geocentric theory, but it would probably have been abandoned earlier than it was had it not been for the authority of Aristotle's opinions.

Levels of Entelechies and Living Things

As we saw in chapter 10, Aristotle understood all classes of things to have a fixed level of potentiality and actuality; things were the actualization of certain forms and were potentiality for certain other forms. This gave them a ranking or grade in a sort of hierarchy, with highly actualized species at the top and less actualized (those with more potentiality) at the bottom.

The lowest level of actualization is the four elements, earth, air, fire, and water (plus aether, which is the matter of the heavenly bodies). Inorganic bodies, such as lead, water, and quartz, are higher in grade, since they use the potentiality of the terrestrial elements to actualize forms that the elements do not have. At this level, the use of potentiality is fairly simple. The potentiality of the elements is simply the stuff out of which the inorganic bodies are made.

At the levels of living things the manner in which the lower grade is potential for the higher is not so obvious. The lower grade does not provide the matter in the commonsense physical notion of matter; the matter must be understood here in terms of functions that are realized on a higher level in the higher grades.

Aristotle divided living things according to their functions and called them vegetative soul, sensitive soul, and rational soul. He did not mean "soul" in the sense in which Plato used the term. He also rejected the Atomists' concept of soul and the Pythagorean concept. Aristotle held that soul is not body but is form, the defining form (entelechy) of a body that can have life. He thus defined soul as the entelechy of an organic body, literally a body that has organs. Soul does not exist apart from the body.[7]

Vegetative Soul

The lowest level of living things (and of soul) includes vegetative or nutritive souls. This is, of course, the level of plant life. Of the five powers of soul, the nutritive, appetitive, sensitive, locomotive, and thought, plants have only nutrition and reproduction.[8] Aristotle did not say as much about the vegetative level of soul as he did about the sensitive and rational; he had promised to write a treatise about it later, but if he did this work has been lost. In the De Anima he talked of nutrition as necessary for survival and activity of a living being, and expressed his disagreement with Empedocles' explanation of nutrition in terms of fire; he preferred soul over fire as the principle of nutrition. He thought interpretations of nutrition in terms of like-by-like and opposite-by-opposite were inadequate; he preferred the explanation in terms of potentiality to nourish.[9]

Sensitive Soul and Perception

All animals have at least the sense of touch, the most basic of the senses. Those animals in which the senses are more highly actualized have all five senses. With sensation comes desire or appetite; some sensitive souls possess the power of locomotion. In De Sensu, Aristotle mentioned pain and pleasure in connection with sensation and desire.[10] In keeping with what Werner Jaeger called "the fundamental principle of Aristotle's teleology," that the more highly actualized levels include the lower levels, sensitive souls have the functions of vegetative soul.[11] Nutrition and reproduction are the potentiality for the actualization of the sensitive function. Aristotle was not describing a process of evolution, for species do not evolve into other species; he was only stating that higher level species have the functions of lower level species in a higher form.

Aristotle described sensation as the power of receiving the perceived or sensible form of an object without absorbing its matter. Sensation is not simply passive; Aristotle described it as "a kind of alteration," in that the animal is acted upon, "moved and affected." It is active in that it actualizes potentialities in both the perceived and the perceiver. The perceived object has the potentiality for being perceived, and the perceiver has the potentiality to perceive. Perception is an actualization that uses the potentiality in both. This way of understanding perception overcomes the inadequacy of earlier explanations couched in terms of like perceiving like or perception by opposites. The sense organ is not like the perceived, nor contrary to it, but it must be "neutral" and potentially like the perceived.[12]

The object sensed does not act directly on the sense organ. Sensation acts through a medium; for example, sight requires light and hearing requires air. The object of sense is perceived by the proper organ for its perception. Error does not arise in this aspect of perception; an organ always perceives its proper object. Seeing is not confused with hearing. The perception of sensations proper to each sense is virtually free of error; there is never an error in perceiving whiteness, for example. Error enters with synthetic judgment, as in judging that one is seeing such-and-such a white thing.[13]

Aristotle realized that we perceive "objects" that are not special to any one sense. He mentions movement, rest, number, shape, size, and unity, and says they are common "sensibles." They are sensed by the special senses acting together. This perception is not a special sense in itself, and it has no organ special to it, such as sight has the eyes and hearing the ears. Unlike perception of one of the five senses of an object special to it, which is virtually free of error, the common sense can err.[14]

Aristotle held that sensation is a unity, and the senses function as a unity in perceiving the common sensibles. Another aspect of this unity is our being aware that we are sensing. Explaining our awareness that we are sensing posed some problems. Aristotle saw that it is problematic to say that the individual sense organ "discerns what is doing the discerning." He resisted the supposition that the eye, for example, sees that it is seeing, but to say that something other than the sense organ discerns that it is discerning leads to an infinite regress, to an organ that does know what it is doing.

Separate organs perceiving separate things could not discern that they are separate, in the way we know that color is not taste; we not only perceive but know we are perceiving. The chapter of *De Anima* in which Aristotle tried to explain this matter is not well organized, but we can see that he defended the unity of perception. He did not rely on a merely physiological explanation; he said it "becomes clear that flesh is not the ultimate sense-organ." The potentiality–actuality distinction played a role in his understanding of how a unified power of sensation can do different things. In the *De Sensu et Sensibili,* written after the *De Anima,* Aristotle went into more detail about the several senses.[15]

Aristotle's discussion of sensation in the *De Anima* is followed by a chapter on imagination. By imagination he meant the forming of mental images; he did not mean thinking up fanciful or unreal things. Imagination is closely tied to sensation. Aristotle saw this power of soul as an intermediary between sensation and thought. Imagination cannot occur without perception, and thought requires imagination. Imagination is not sensation, however, for several reasons: Imagination does not share perception's freedom from error. Some animals that have perception do not have imagination. We can have mental images when the eyes are shut, and we can distinguish between perceptions, which we trust, and images, which we question. Also, imagination is not thought, because it does not give the conviction, or serve as the basis of action, that occurs with thought. We correct false imaginations by the use of thought. Perceiving, imagining, and thinking are three different activities.[16]

Aristotle mentions memory in the *Metaphysics,* but he does not treat it in *De Anima.* His full treatment of memory is in *De Memoria et Reminiscentia.* Memory, which some of the lower animals have as well as humans, follows sensation, as the lasting impression of mental images. An experience causes us to remember something that is similar to, contrary to, or contiguous with a present event. We can also make ourselves remember by an effort to recall something.[17]

Rational Soul

Among the faculties of souls, the power of thought is possessed only by humans (and other creatures that may be like or superior to humans). Thought is the highest level of activity that souls can achieve. It is at the top of the hierarchy of souls. Unfortunately, what Aristotle says about rational soul is not always clear or well organized. This has led to a number of different interpretations of what he was claiming about the rational faculties.[18] Aristotle talked of two aspects of rational soul, a potential intellect and an active intellect. Most of our uncertainty is in regard to his view of the active intellect.

It follows from his concept of levels of actualization and the realization in the higher levels of potentialities in the lower levels, that intellect will actualize, as thinking, the sensation and imagination of the sensitive soul. Aristotle seems clearly to hold that thinking is possible based on the foundation of the powers of sensitive soul.

The notion of a potential intellect fits logically with what Aristotle said about sensation and imagination. The intellect, which stands in the same relationship to what can be thought as the powers of perception stand in relation to what can be perceived, enables humans to actualize the materials of sensation and imagination as thought. The images of thinking are analogous to the role of simple impressions in perception. Aristotle does not offer a physiological explanation of this function, and this seems to be a deliberate omission; he wants to separate intellect in some sense from the body. No organ is assigned the work of intellect, and it only exists by thinking. It is nothing except when it thinks. Yet it is clearly dependent upon sense perceptions. There seems to be no basis in Aristotle's description of potential intellect to conclude that it survives in any way the death of the body.[19]

The potential intellect fills the place in Aristotle's hierarchy of entelechies of the soul that actualizes the potentiality of the sensitive soul. This does not explain, however, how we can know certain abstract and theoretical eternal truths, and without this explanation Aristotle's study of the human soul would not be complete.

The active intellect completes the faculty of knowing, but it is not clear exactly what the active intellect is or how it functions. Aristotle's badly organized material on the human soul leaves us with some questions, and scholars have answered them in conflicting ways through the years.

What is the active intellect? Aristotle does not appear to be quite certain about this himself. He said, "The mind seems to be an independent substance implanted in the soul and to be incapable of being destroyed." He also said its operation in a person is affected by old age, intoxication, and disease, but mind itself is not damaged by affections of the body. Again, he said, ". . . it seems to be a widely different kind of soul, differing as what is eternal from what is perishable; it alone is capable of existence in isolation from all other psychic powers."[20] He was surely speaking of the active intellect here, but what is he saying about it? He does not appear to be speaking of soul as the entelechy of an organic body, which may be why he said it "seems" to be another kind of soul. What is clear, however, is that he thought that there is an intellect that is separate from the soul and that does not perish with the soul.

The active intellect, described as a separable substance implanted in the soul, is completely actualized. It is not, like the potential intellect, thinking at one time and not thinking at another. It works in unison with the potential intellect, for thought does not occur without both active and passive intellect. Thus the active intellect enables the thinking of eternal truths, but it is not clear how it does this. Aristotle speaks of it as analogous to light. This suggests that it might enable the soul to recognize that some of its thoughts are of eternal truths, the role that Augustine attributed to the divine illumination (see chapter 19), but this is not stated clearly and might not be what Aristotle had in mind.[21]

The role of the active intellect, which is purely actual, might have been to provide the intellect with the eternal essences by which the nature of things can be understood. This is an attractive suggestion, since a body of essences would certainly be actualized and eternal. This concept of the active intellect is Platonic, and we should not overlook the Platonic element in Aristotle's thinking. Unfortunately, we do not find this way of understanding the active intellect explicitly stated.

Much of the discussion among later philosophers was over the immortality of the active intellect. The De Anima seems clear enough about this; Aristotle said that thinking only takes place with the two intellects acting together. He said that the passive intellect perishes, and the active intellect, which is not affected by anything, has no memory of our individual lives.[22] Philosophers who wanted "the Philosopher," as Aristotle was known in the Middle Ages, to support their belief in immortality were not satisfied with this. The De Anima does not say whether the active intellect is unitary, one intellect for all mankind, or whether each person has an individual active intellect implanted in the soul, ready to work again with the passive intellect, which will return with the resurrection of the body. This gave room for debate about the issue.

The confusing nature of Aristotle's materials gave rise to another issue, the possible connection between active intellect and the unmoved mover. Both are completely actualized, and in the *Metaphysics* Aristotle does not mention an actualized being separate from material things other than the prime mover. This was taken by some scholars to indicate that the active intellect can be no other than the prime mover. There are significant problems with this, however, since it is hard to see the active intellect that is implanted in the human soul and the august prime mover as the same being. Perhaps more important is that the prime mover is described as contemplation contemplating itself, and it is hard to see how this form of intelligence could provide the potential intellect with the means of understanding the nature of things.[23]

Lest we become impatient with Aristotle for careless writing and inattention to detail, we need to remember that all we have are remnants of Aristotle's popular essays and technical writings that do not come directly from his pen. In the *Metaphysics, De Anima, Nicomachean Ethics, Physics,* and other technical writings we have lecture notes or student notes, and materials that were edited several centuries after the death of Aristotle.[24] If Aristotle did not answer all the questions that medieval religionists, and even some modern philosophers, would ask of him, he can hardly be blamed for not anticipating and satisfying their concerns.

In spite of the speculation, passion, and print expended on some of the questions about what Aristotle meant by the active intellect, we should not let these disputes blind us to the primary matters in his thought. The hierarchical relationship of entelechies, in which the lower were necessary for the actualization of the higher, with the higher preserving and bringing to fulfillment the potential of the lower, reaches its highest human level in the two factors involved in intellection. Even though Aristotle clearly considers the active intelligence higher and worthier than the potential, he gave worth and significance to all levels of being, not just to the beings at the apex.

12 ARISTOTLE

KNOWLEDGE AND LOGIC

Aristotle held that the object of knowledge cannot be other than it is; it must necessarily be true. Aristotle shared Plato's belief that knowledge must be of necessary and eternal truths.[1]

Aristotle also thought that knowledge must be about universals, not just about particulars. There can be no knowledge if there is nothing except a large number of concrete individual things. We do not need forms separate from things as Plato posited them, but we do need something more than the individual. We need the species, the universal term that predicates the same properties of many things.[2]

Aristotle's writings on logical subjects illustrate graphically his views on knowledge. Certain features of his thinking about what can be known, how it can be known, and in what terms it can be properly thought about are revealed in his concept of scientific definition, his categories of thought, and his system of logical reasoning.

Definition and Categories

Aristotle said that logical argument, which shows the existence of a thing, is not the same as definition, which shows the nature of a thing. There are, he said, two types of definition. The first type is a statement of the meaning of a name. This does not attempt to show that a thing exists, only what nature is identified by its name. The second type of definition exhibits the cause of a thing. Aristotle calls this a quasi-demonstration of the existence of a thing. The first type of definition is probably Aristotle's major contribution, and it set a pattern that has been followed ever since, in a general way, in scientific definitions.

This kind of definition is a process of division, going from the *infimae species* to the *summum genus,* from the most specific qualities to the broadest class designation. A complete definition gives the qualities, from the most individual to the most general, that make a thing what it is. By taking into account all the classes to which an entity belongs, a definition identifies all the qualities of the species. It shares most of its qualities with members of other classes, but the full range of the properties are present only in the species being defined.

These classes must be listed in correct order. For example, with this sort of definition the human being is rational, two-footed, mammalian, viviparous, animal, living being. Aristotle's idea of the specific classes will seem somewhat odd to us, especially the role given two-footedness.[3] There has been considerable amusement, of the refined philosophical kind, over humans as the featherless biped, but Aristotle's basic approach to classification is sound and a significant contribution to good thinking. This type of definition should remind us of Aristotle's hierarchy of entelechies, but we can use the approach without adopting the value judgments that Aristotle made.

Another aspect of Aristotle's belief about human thought is seen in his categories. Aristotle held that correct thinking must make use of certain categories. They are for correct thought what the parts of speech are for communication. It seems that not as much attention is paid to the categories now as scholars did previously, but they are worth looking at for the light they throw on Aristotle's concept of thinking. These categories come from his books the *Categories,* the *Topics,* and the *Posterior Analytics.* Aristotle held that all correct thought uses the following categories:

1. Substance, for example, horse
2. Quantity, how much
3. Quality, what sort, for example, color
4. Relation, for example, with
5. Location, where
6. Time, when
7. Local position, for example, sits, lies
8. Condition, state, for example, armed
9. Action, for example, running
10. Affected, being acted upon

In the *Posterior Analytics,* some categories are subsumed under the other categories.[4]

It might be difficult to find much agreement about categories to which all correct thinking is limited. Aristotle's approach probably seems restrictive and cut-and-dried to most of us. His categories fit better the mentality of an ancient essentialist than fit our way of thinking about the world.

Knowledge Through Logical Argument

Aristotle's extensive work on logic became the basis of a system of logic that was a primary tool of argument in the Middle Ages and continued to be the standard logical method until it was largely abandoned in Anglo-American philosophy of the twentieth century. Aristotle's logic and the system developed on its foundations were based on categorical statements. The premises of traditional logic declare that such and such is the case. Aristotle believed that knowledge consists of knowing what class, what species, an entity belongs to, and his logic was a method for making discoveries about the properties that accompany class membership. The logical approaches that largely replaced traditional logic in Britain and America treat premises as hypothetical statements. The question becomes, if such-and-such is the case, what follows from that? Anglo-American philosophers were not the first to reject aspects of Aristotle's logical approach. Stoic logic used hypothetical statements and disjunctions (see chapter 16). The choice of a logical system reflects epistemological viewpoints. It is impossible, according to Aristotle, to learn anything from hypothetical statement. Knowledge must be categorical; it is about eternal truths and universal terms.[5]

Premises

According to Aristotle, argument uses previously acquired knowledge, in the form of premises, to acquire additional knowledge. The preexistent knowledge is of two kinds: facts assumed to be true and the meaning of terms.

Premises must be true, primary, better known than the conclusion, and prior to it. Aristotle was aware that "prior" and "better known" are ambiguous terms; they can refer to the order of being or to that of human knowledge. Knowledge through the senses is prior and better known to humans, but those things that are prior and better known without qualification, that are part of the reality of things, are furthest from sense experience. These truths are eternal and necessary truths, which cannot fail to be true under any circumstances. Knowledge requires premises that are "primary and indemonstrable."[6]

Some premises of an argument can be derived from previous arguments, but ultimately knowledge must be based on something more sound than an infinite regress or a circle of arguments.

Intuition and Induction as Sources of Premises

Aristotle held that the intellect has a capacity to intuit certain truths, which are not demonstrable and for which no demonstration is needed. These are not limited to analytic propositions generally recognized as self-evident, such as axioms of mathematics or general logical laws. One kind of intuition includes the simple data of perception, which are error free. These can also be intuited by lower animals, but animals lack the memory to use them as human beings do. Some of the premises of an argument are received by induction, which requires many experiences of the same kind of sense perception. These premises are not known innately nor are they demonstrated; they are results of the capacity for intuition mentioned above. Aristotle compares these intuitions that are acquired with many perceptions to the realization that a rout in a battle is over, as first one, then several, then a large number of soldiers turn and fight.[7]

Demonstration (Deduction)

According to Aristotle, the kind of argument that could produce conclusions that were certain was demonstration. This kind of argumentation came to be known as deduction or syllogistic argument. The form of such an argument is known as a syllogism; it is a formally structured argument in which the conclusion is drawn from premises, which are considered the cause of the conclusion. For it to be an adequate argument, certain very strict principles must be followed. Part of what is involved is the logical relationship of the subject and predicate of a premise.

In explaining how error can occur, Plato pointed out that statements have a subject and a predicate; this enabled him to go beyond the logical impasse created by the Eleatics, who held that it is impossible to think what is not. Another beneficiary of Plato's insight was Aristotle's logic. Aristotle used the subject–predicate form of statements to show how premises can function, or fail to function, in an argument. He showed that the predicate, that is, what is said about the subject, can bear three sorts of relationship to the subject.

Some predicates are accidents, or coincidents, which are connected to the subject coincidentally; for example, "being musical" describes this person but not all people. Statements with these predicates cannot be used in a demonstration because the predicate adds little to our knowledge of the subject. Some predicates are attributes or properties. These are qualities that are coextensive with the species (true of every member) and are expressive of its nature, but they are not ultimate definitions of that nature. Some predicates are essential characteristics of a species. These are qualities that are elements in the essential nature of the thing, defining it (for example, "line" belongs to "triangle").[8]

An essence sets a subject apart from others by constituting its distinctive species. Properties, while not fully defining the species, will always be associated with it. As an example of this, consider the human being: Its essence is being rational, speaking is an attribute coextensive with the species, and speaking Greek is an accident. A logical argument cannot be based on accidents, since they are not true of all members of the species and are not essentially connected with the species. We cannot argue on the basis of a person speaking Greek, as opposed to speaking in general, that something is true of the human species.[9]

The Syllogism

The syllogism is a valid formula for deriving inferences. Its structure, consisting of the arrangement and nature of premises and a conclusion, is very important. Only if it is constructed in the proper form is it a valid syllogism.

Validity

Validity is a crucial aspect of logical reasoning. It has a technical meaning in logic that is stricter than its common street meaning of true, right, okay. In logic, validity is not the same as truth, but it is important in the demonstration of truth. It refers to the formal structure of the argument; if the form is not correct, the argument has not proved its point. If the form is correct, that is, valid, and the premises are true, the conclusion is proved. An example of an argument in which all the statements are true but the form is not valid is as follows:

> No Athenians are Spartans.
> No Englishmen are Athenians.
> Therefore, no Englishmen are Spartans.

This is all true, but nothing has been proved because nothing can be deduced from two negative premises. On the other hand, a valid syllogism might not be true, as in the following:

> No Germans are beer drinkers.
> All artists are Germans.
> Therefore, no artists are beer drinkers.

To be sound, an argument must be valid and have true premises. What is the formal structure for a valid syllogism? There are several rules that must be met. Central to the concept of the syllogism is the middle term. This is the common element in both premises; it is what connects the two premises logically. Technically, the middle term (usually designated "M") connects the minor term, the subject of the conclusion, and the major term, the predicate of the conclusion. It does not appear in the conclusion. The middle terms in the arguments above are Athenians and Germans. The importance of the middle term is obvious; if there is no connection between the two premises, nothing can be proved by putting them together.[10]

There are rules about "distribution" that are a bit more complicated. The middle term must be distributed in one of the premises, and an end term (both the subject and predicate of the conclusion) must be distributed in the premise in which it appears if it is distributed in the conclusion. What, then, is distribution? An argument can only be based on predicates that belong to every member of a class of things. A term is distributed if it applies to every member of the species. Sometimes this is obvious. "All dogs are animals" is about all dogs; "some dogs are brown" is not about all dogs. Some distributions, however, are not obvious and not intuitively recognized. "No bears wear britches" is clearly about all bears; what is not obvious is that it also distributes britches. "Some bears do not like chocolate pudding" is not about all bears, but it distributes chocolate pudding. How can we know these things? Most people simply accept the following principle: universal positive statements (claims that something is true of every member of the species) distribute the term in the subject position; negative statements distribute the term in the predicate position.

For clarity and convenience, universal positive statements are called "A" statements; they distribute the subject term. Universal negative statements are called "E" statements; they distribute subject terms because they are universal and predicate terms because they are negative. Positive particular statements (about part of a class) are called "I" statements, and being neither universal or negative, they do not distribute either subject or predicate. Particular negative statements, "O" statements, distribute the predicate term. A, E, I, and O indicate the quality of the relationship between subject and predicate (whether positive or negative) and the quantity (whether general or particular) of the statement. (See Figure 12.1 for Aristotle's rules regarding distribution.)

The Valid Figures and Moods

Aristotle employed three figures or arrangements of subject and predicate in the premises and the conclusion of a syllogism (see Figure 12.1). In formalizing these arrangements, "S" stands for the subject term, "P" for the predicate term, and "M" for the middle term. A fourth figure was added later by medieval scholars. (See Figure 12.1 for these four figures.)

Several kinds of relationship can exist between subject and predicate in a statement, as we have seen. The predicate may be related to the subject positively or negatively (quality); it may be related to the whole species or to only a part of it (quantity). These are the A, E, I, and O statements of quality and quantity that we saw above. The figures joined with the A, E, I, or O form what is called a mood. The possible combinations would result in a large number of moods, but most of the possible arrangements are not valid; they violate one or more of the rules. Aristotle's rules determining which moods are valid are: (1) The middle term must be distributed at least once (later rules say only once); (2) if an end-term is distributed in the conclusion, it must be distributed in the premise in which it appears; and (3) the number of negative premises must equal the number of negative con-

Figure 12.1. **Aristotelian System of Logic**

Four Figures:	(1) MP	(2) PM	(3) MP	(4) PM
	SM	SM	MS	MS
	SP	SP	SP	SP

S = subject term; P = predicate term; M = middle term.

Valid Moods:

1st Figure	MAP	MEP	MAP	MEP
	SAM	SAM	SIM	SIM
	SAP	SEP	SIP	SOP

2nd Figure	PEM	PAM	PEM	PAM
(all negative)	SAM	SEM	SIM	SOM
	SEP	SEP	SOP	SOP

3rd Figure	MAP	MAP	MEP	MOP	MEP	MIP
(all partial)	MAS	MIS	MAS	MAS	MIS	MAS
	SIP	SIP	SOP	SOP	SOP	SIP

4th Figure	PAM	PAM	PIM	PEM	PEM
	MAS	MES	MAS	MAS	MIS
	SIP	SEP	SIP	SOP	SOP

RELATIONSHIPS between subject and predicate are indicated by:
A = universal positive statement (All S is P)
E = universal negative statement (No S is P)
I = particular positive statement (Some S is P)
O = particular negative statement (Some S is not P)

DISTRIBUTION:
Universal statement - subject term distributed.
Negative statement - predicate term distributed.

Rules for validity (Aristotle's)

1. Middle term must be distributed at least once.

2. If end-term of conclusion is distributed, it must be distributed in one of the premises.

3. Number of negative premises must equal number of negative conclusions.

clusions. Only nineteen moods are valid. (See Figure 12.1 for the valid moods.)

Aristotle considered the first figure the most scientific because it is the only arrangement in which a valid argument can reach a universal positive conclusion. It can do this only in one mood, the syllogism that came to be called "Barbara" (note the a's) because both premises and the conclusion are universal positive statements. In the second figure only negative conclusions can be reached, and in the third no universal conclusions can be reached.[11]

Relation of Logic to Aristotle's Theory of Knowledge

Aristotle's logic underscores his belief that knowledge is of universals and must be certain. The syllogism is based on categorical statements, which declare that a subject is a member of a class of things having a certain essential attribute. Aristotle does not base his logic on hypothetical or disjunctive statements. Knowledge can only be of what is always true, and it can be stated only in categorical terms.

13 ARISTOTLE

ETHICS AND POLITICS

Aristotle's ethical writings are partly in the *Eudemian Ethics,* an early work of doubtful authorship that is considered generally inferior to the work of Aristotle while he was head of the Lyceum, and in the *Nicomachean Ethics.* We will follow the practice of most Aristotle scholars and rely on the work of his maturity as the source of his ethical thought.

Aristotle held that ethics is a science, but not a precise science; the source of its data makes it not precise. He held that it is a mistake to ask too much or too little precision from a particular discipline.[1]

Happiness and Virtue (*Eudaimonía* and *Areté*)

Aristotle's ethics begins with happiness (*eudaimonía*), which is the aim of all human activity. It alone is chosen for itself only and is never the means to another end. Every activity aims at some good, and Aristotle said that everyone agrees that happiness is the good in personal pursuits and in political science. People do not always agree, however, about what constitutes happiness.[2] Some people think that happiness is found in pleasure, others in winning honor, others in making money; but Aristotle did not think that such things are the real goal of life.[3]

That one thing that all people seek for itself alone is not happiness in the sense that usually comes to our mind, that of a joyful or peaceful state or condition. It is an activity of the soul, which is the perfection of the distinctively human function. Translating *eudaimonía* as "happiness" can be misleading, for it is not a state of feeling but the perfection of human existence. Aristotle had no qualms about talking of a human function. Just as a good flute player carries out well the function of playing the flute, and a good eye enables clear vision, the good human fulfills the human function, living a certain kind of life that is an activity of soul. This implies a rational principle and is in accordance with virtue, intellectual virtue most importantly.[4]

Virtue (areté) also did not mean to Aristotle what it means in current English usage. The Greek concept is that of strength and ability. Aristotle spoke of moral virtue as one aspect of fulfilling the human function, but he considered intellectual virtue the most important. (See the discussion of virtue in chapter 5.)

Since eudaimonia is the perfection or fulfillment of the human potential, it requires adulthood and certain of the good things of life: health, length of years, a good family, honor and respect in the city. Aristotle did not consider children the paradigm of happiness or talk about a short happy life.[5]

He held that the highest aspect of human perfection is intellectual, the contemplation of truth. Cognitive reason is the crowning perfection, but practical reason is also necessary. Both are required for the achievement of eudaimonia. Moral virtue is a product of practical reason; it is achieved only with the guidance of reason. Thus, both intellectual and moral virtues that are part of the perfection of the human function.[6]

Pleasure

Pleasure is a product of the perfection of the human function. It cannot be equated with goodness or with happiness. Pleasure is immediate satisfaction; happiness is a more long-range, more complete, satisfaction. Happiness is also an activity, and it is achieved only with the aid of reason and after making many choices. There are good and bad pleasures; some pleasures are proper to human beings, but some pleasures are not. Aristotle did not condemn pleasure. He recognized that pleasure is good, but pleasure is not the good, not the goal of life.[7]

Virtue Ethics

Aristotle's moral philosophy is based on virtue, in contrast to ethics based on duty. Rather than basing ethics on moral obligations to do certain things and abstain from other things, Aristotle bases his ethics on achieving those virtues by which one perfects one's human nature. By engaging in those activities that pertain to the distinctive functions of the human being, one becomes virtuous.

Aristotle believed that moral virtue must be habitual, a state of character. This state of character is the result of training. The way to become virtuous is to practice virtue repeatedly; Aristotle compares acquiring virtue to learning how to be a musician or training to be an athlete. Aristotle believed that people are responsible for their character; by diligence they improve their character; by slackness, they fail to have virtue.[8]

The Golden Mean

Aristotle also defined virtue as avoiding the vices marked by over-indulgence in or over-suppression of an activity. Virtue is the mean between excess and deficiency; courage and a proper confidence, for example, fall between cowardice and rashness. In seeking pleasure, the mean is temperance, while excess is self-indulgence. (Persons who do not seek enough pleasure are so rare that we do not have a name for their behavior.) In the use of money, liberality is the mean between meanness and prodigality. Proper seeking of honor lies between undue humility and vanity.[9]

This idea of a mean or a middle way, called Aristotle's "golden mean," has had great popular appeal, but what many people have seen in it, a simple and clear way to tell right from wrong, is not what Aristotle had in mind. The author once read of an English clergyman who mused, "As a follower of Aristotle's ethics, I must have three wives, for one is a deficiency and five would be excessive." If he was serious he did not understand Aristotle; perhaps he was making fun of the penchant many people have for accepting an unexamined slogan, such as "take the middle of the road," as a serious moral guidepost.

Aristotle did hold that virtue is intermediate between the extremes of excess and deficiency, but he said clearly that it is not an arithmetical mean. It is a mean relative to us, and it is not the same for all people, for what is excessive for one might not be enough for another. For example, an athlete needs more food than a sedentary person. Aristotle realized that judgment of conduct must not be too general; we must consider the facts of individual cases.[10]

The "golden mean" is not the way to determine what is right and wrong; it is an interpretation of what virtue is. Knowing that virtue is a mean does not tell us which behaviors constitute the mean. The mean cannot be reduced to a mechanical "middle of the road." We have seen one reason why this is so; the mean must take account of individual situations. Another reason is that for some activities one extreme is further from the mean than the other. Aristotle thought that cowardice differs from courage more than does rashness.[11]

Aristotle held that some activities and feelings admit of no mean. There is no right way to be spiteful, shameless, or envious. Adultery, theft, and murder are bad in themselves, not only in an excess. To be unjust, cowardly, or voluptuous is wrong in any degree.[12]

In describing virtue as a mean, Aristotle was not trying to lay down a simple rule. Doing what is right is not a simple matter. He said that the right action involves proper motives and feelings and the right method. Anyone can spend money or get angry, "but to do this to the right person, to the right extent, at the right time, with the right motive, and in the right way, that is not for everyone, nor is it easy; wherefore goodness is both rare and laudable and noble." Determining the virtuous thing to do in a situation requires the use of practical reason. Aristotle said, ". . . it is no easy task to be good." The golden mean does not make careful thought and judgment unnecessary. Aristotle knew that ". . . it is no easy task to find the middle. . . ."[13]

Moral Responsibility

Aristotle was concerned with the issue of when people are morally responsible for what they do. He held that people are responsible when they act knowingly and without being under compulsion. People are acting under compulsion when the "moving principle" is outside them, and they are contributing nothing to the passion or action. Aristotle compared people then to objects blown about by the wind. Actions done because of great fear or threat of danger are not clearly voluntary or involuntary. They are "mixed"; but they are nearer to voluntary. We cannot be said, however, to choose if it is not in our power. A person is only properly blamed or praised for actions under that person's power, which are done knowingly.[14]

Aristotle made an important distinction between acts that are done *from* ignorance and acts done *in* ignorance. Acts done from ignorance are involuntary. They are not intended by the agent, and afterward the agent is pained by them and repents of them. The one doing the action is ignorant of some particular fact of the situation. Aristotle had in mind such things as thinking mistakenly one's son is one of the enemy or not knowing that the button has come off a spear. He also mentioned accidental things, such as the unintentional release of a catapult. Another example is giving a draught meant to heal a sick person, but as a result the patient dies. In these cases the causes are outside the person acting. When a person acts in ignorance, however, the person acting, who might be drunk or in a rage, does not know what he is doing, but the cause of the action is the rage or the drunkenness. Such actions are not completely involuntary.[15] This distinction remains an important one in Roman Catholic moral teaching.

Incontinence

Aristotle did not agree with the view of Plato, which Plato attributes to Socrates, that moral evil is always the result of ignorance about the nature and consequences of an action. He held that such a view contradicts the observed facts. He believed that there are people in whom desire overrules reason. This he called incontinence.[16] The person who is a victim of vice wants to commit an evil. Aristotle explores the question of incontinence throughout the seventh book of the *Nichomachean Ethics,* examining a number of opinions about incontinence, the kind of knowledge or lack of it held by the incontinent person, the difference between incontinence and self-indulgence, and the possibility of the incontinent person's being cured.

Justice

Justice is both an important ethical concern and a political matter. Aristotle spoke of justice in one sense as "virtue entire," while injustice is "vice entire." He did not equate justice with virtue generally; the essence of justice and the essence of virtue differ, for justice involves a relationship to other people. Unlike Plato, who looked upon justice as a state of the individual soul, Aristotle thought of justice in a broadly political sense, involving human relationships. He also saw justice as a state of character that makes people "act justly and wish for what is just."[17]

Humans are social beings; social relationships are necessary for the development of human functions and the virtues. Aristotle said that without friends no one would chose to live. Friendship is needed by all people at all ages, whether they are strong or weak, rich or poor. Friendship seems to hold states together, and fractious elements are expelled as threats to the state.[18]

Aristotle said that people associate for three reasons, and all of these are called friendship, even though only one deserves the name. Some relationships involve using people for pleasure. Other relationships are for the sake of utility or for benefit to be derived from the other. The truest friendships are those between good people, who wish their friends well for their own sake. These are the lasting relationships that also bring the most good and pleasure because of the fine qualities of the people involved; these friendships bring mutual enrichment.[19]

Between friends there is no need for justice, but good friendships are infrequent; the people who can be real friends are rare, and building such a friendship takes time.[20] The friendships of those who seek pleasure or profit from their associates are unstable and short lived; they are not based on a love of enduring good.[21] They do not replace the need for justice.

Aristotle defined justice as the lawful and the fair. Justice as fairness is a familiar idea, but calling the lawful "just" raises questions. Did Aristotle accept as just the demands of each and every law? He said that laws enacted by the legislature are in a sense just, but he qualifies this claim when he says that we consider just the laws that produce happiness and social benefit. He makes a distinction between "rightly framed" and "hastily conceived" legislative acts. He says the law bids us be brave, temperate, and good-natured, and to live by the other virtues. In light of Aristotle's objection to tyranny, it seems clear that he did not mean to accept all laws as just laws.[22]

Aristotle's point about justice and lawfulness is that justice does not exist apart from law. He said, "Justice exists only between men whose mutual relations are governed by law. . . ." [23] This is a widely supported principle, which was strongly affirmed by founders of modern political philosophy such as Thomas Hobbes and David Hume, and is recognized by many philosophers as one of Aristotle's major contributions to political theory.[24]

In explaining justice as fairness, Aristotle described two different applications of the principle of justice: distributive justice, which con-

cerns the distribution of benefits such as honor or money, and rectificatory justice, which seeks to correct harm that a person has suffered at
the hands of another. These apply to different situations and employ
different principles.[25]

In the distribution of benefits, justice requires that the division be
intermediate, equal, and relative to the respective merits of the people
involved. "Being intermediate" between too much and too little refers
to the mean we have already seen. "Being equal" and "relative to
personal merit" seem contradictory, but Aristotle did not mean equal in
the absolute sense of the same shares. The equality he had in mind was
the ratio between reward and merit. Those who are equal in merit
should receive equal shares, but the unequal should not receive the
same rewards. If one person is twice as meritorious as another, their
rewards should reflect the same ratio: the person of greater merit
should receive twice as much as the other, and so on for other ratios.[26]

Rectificatory justice makes right a situation that has been made
wrong by someone who harmed another, either deliberately or inadver-
tently. It can be understood as compensatory, corrective, or remedial
justice. Unlike distributive justice, merit plays no role in determining
rectificatory justice. This aspect of justice is not punitive; it seeks to
restore a balance between the original situation and the changed situation. It does not matter whether a good person or a bad person has
caused the harm. The determination is mathematical. The offender
must pay to restore a balance that is intermediate between gains and
losses. The term "gain" is used, even though the harm to another might
be of no actual benefit to the perpetrator. It is simply a way to reckon
what the offender must pay to the one who suffered the loss.[27]

In most cases money is used to make amends. If one person has
done physical damage to another, doing the same damage to the offender would not be appropriate. A monetary value must be established and payment made to rectify the situation. The same applies to
damage to property.[28]

Justice in the Family and in the State

Aristotle did not think the justice required of a master or a father is the
same as the justice required of a citizen. Slaves and minor children are
a man's chattels; they are parts of himself. A man cannot be unjust to
them, since a person cannot be unjust to himself. As a citizen, how-

ever, one acts in relationship to others who have an equal part in governing. More justice can be practiced toward a wife than toward slaves and minor children, for the relationship with a wife involves "household justice."[29] Even though household justice is not the same as the justice of a citizen, and the governance of a statesman is not the same as that of the manager of a household, Aristotle views household justice in political terms. The most elemental form of association is the family. The household involves the three relationships of master and slave, husband and wife, and parent and child.[30]

The most elemental aspect of governing a household is the relationship of master and slave. The slave is property, an instrument to serve the household. Aristotle knew that some thinkers considered slavery contrary to nature and held that there is no natural difference between slave and master. They saw the institution of slavery as a convention based on force and not having a just basis.[31] Nevertheless, he held that some slaves are slaves by nature.[32] He was critical, however, of the practice of taking slaves in war. He was familiar with arguments by jurists and philosophers against the practice and was critical of the arguments used to justify it. These slaves were often not "slaves by nature" but people forced into slavery.[33] Aristotle did not condemn slavery when the slaves were slaves by nature. The head of the household, in the role of a monarch, rightly rules over slaves and free persons over whom he has authority.[34]

The head of the household continues his monarchical reign over his wife and children. Aristotle believed that the male is naturally superior to the female, and it is natural that the male should rule the female. The male head of the house possesses three different kinds of rule, that of the freeman over the slave, that of the male over the female, and that of the mature man over the minor child. The male has the faculty of deliberation that makes these forms of rule possible. The slave has no power of deliberation. The female has it, but it is without authority. In the child the power of reason is not developed. Not only is the power of reason different in these elements of the household, but their virtues are different. The master must possess moral goodness in its full form. Less is required of the slave, the wife, and the child. Justice, courage, and temperance are not the same for a man and a woman. Aristotle thought that women exercise their virtue in being quiet and acquiescent.[35]

Political Theory

Aristotle considered the city, the polis, to be the "final and perfect" form of association. The polis exists by nature, and as a self-sufficient political association it is definitive of the political art, the "final cause" politically.[36] The forms of governance that Aristotle considered legitimate in the polis are not patterned after the monarchical role of the head of a household. In the polis the associations are between peers, and the statesman is not like the master of a house, as we have seen.

The purpose of the state is to promote the highest good, which can be reached only by a person living in a polis. The human is a political animal, and the person who of his own nature lives apart from a polis, not needing the city, is the worst sort of animal or a super-human, either "a beast or a god." Aristotle held that nature "makes nothing in vain," and the power of speech, the fact that humans are not individually self-sufficient, and the concept of justice and injustice, which humans alone have, show that humans are political by nature.[37]

Kinds of Constitutions

Aristotle was little interested in the concept of an ideal state; Books VII and VIII of the *Politics* are thought to be from an early period, when Aristotle was under Plato's influence. He held that there are three types of lawful government, with constitutions, and three perverted forms of government. He defined the types of constitutions according to the number of rulers, but the number of rulers does not of itself make the rule a bad or good one. Rule by one person can be kingship, if lawful, or tyranny, if not lawful. Rule by a few can be a lawful type, aristocracy, or it can be oligarchy, which is a perverted form. For practical purposes Aristotle favored a polity, the rule of a middle-class majority; the perverted form of government by many is a democracy. In lawful governments the rulers rule for the common good; in perverted forms of government they rule for their own benefit.[38]

The Polity

There is no traditional name for the form of government that Aristotle recommends for those cities that have a large middle class. Plato does not mention this form of government. Aristotle gave it the generic name for constitutional government, a polity. A polity is not simply a government by the majority. Economic class is involved. In a polity the middle class governs; in a democracy the poor govern. Theoretically the majority in a city could be rich, but in actuality there are a few people who are rich and many who are poor.[39]

Aristotle did not support the polity because of its inherent superiority. He did not think of it as an ideal form of government for all cities, but he considered it a constitution that most cities could employ. It does not require a standard of excellence that ordinary people cannot reach. Aristotle thought that a city is fortunate to have a large middle class. People in this economic group will listen to reason, while the very rich are too arrogant to reason with and are prone to serious offenses. The poor find it hard to live by reason, and they fall into petty crimes. The middle class will accept responsibility, while they neither seek nor try to avoid public office. Aristotle thought that seeking and avoiding office are both dangerous to the city. The middle class will be obedient to the law, while those nurtured in luxury have not learned obedience, and those reared in poverty are too ignorant, mean, and poor-spirited to be good citizens. The secure people of the middle class do not desire the possessions of others or plot against others. Under the leadership of the middle class there is less dissension and there are fewer factions than in other forms of governance.[40]

Kingship

Aristotle did not advocate a polity for every city. Some cities do not have the large middle class on which a polity is based. He believed the form of government should be suited to the particular city. In chapters 1 through 10 of Book IV of the *Politics* he describes various forms of government.[41] One of the main forms of lawful government is a monarchy. Aristotle mentioned five types of kingships, including one that gave the king charge of military matters but little power over internal governance; a form of elective kingship; the hereditary absolute power he thought most common among barbarians; kingship in the Heroic Age; and absolute monarchy. He wrote most about the absolute monarchy, a constitution he considered appropriate for some cities.[42]

Absolute monarchy is not a perfect form of government; it has some serious problems. Part of the appeal of kingship in the early days when cities were small was that people who had the ability to rule were uncommon, but Aristotle thought that in his day there were more people of ability. People with the ability to rule can still deteriorate in character and enrich themselves at the expense of the public, however; this leads to a degeneration from kingship to oligarchy. Aristotle does not look with favor upon rule by inheritance. The children of a good king often are not suited for kingship, and the king will seldom refuse to let his children take the crown. Aristotle also held that the king should not have enough power to control the whole people. He must be able to defend the law, but only with enough power to control individuals and factional groups.[43]

One of the claims of supporters of monarchy is that it is best to have one person interpret and govern the application of the laws; as we saw, Plato supported this view. Aristotle understood the difficulty of making laws that fit all cases, and he thought that enforcing a law in cases where it does not fit is bad, but he was not convinced of the idea that one person can apply the law best. One person, he notes, can be corrupted by anger or another emotion. Aristotle thought that using a jury of capable people was better than leaving all decisions to one person.[44] We do not have much written by Aristotle about aristocracy; scattered passages indicate that he felt it has advantages and difficulties similar to those of kingship, and his main concern seems to be that it not degenerate into oligarchy. The one general principle of politics from which Aristotle never wavered is that constitutional government is better than any form of non-constitutional government. Aristotle did not trust government by experts; he did not treat governing as an exact science, and he indicated that the quality of the people determines the quality of their government.

14 HELLENISTIC CULTURAL BACKGROUND

After the death of Aristotle philosophy began to change in several ways. The motivation for philosophy was no longer the wonder and desire to know for the sake of knowing that Aristotle believed to be the reason for philosophizing. Philosophical method also changed. It was not the death of Aristotle that brought these changes about. Philosophy changed because social and political conditions changed, and this fact changed people's needs and interests. The cause had more to do with Alexander the Great than with Aristotle.

The Hellenistic Period

The period following the death of Alexander is called the Hellenistic era in contrast to the Hellenic era, during which Greece was independent. It is called Hellenistic because Greek culture continued to dominate the fine arts and matters intellectual. The cultural influence of Greece is part of the legacy of Alexander. He wanted to create one Greek world, not by destroying everything that was not Greek but by adding Greek culture to the life of barbarian peoples. He built Greek cities in the areas he conquered, he settled his veterans in foreign territories, and he encouraged intermarriage, so that Greek culture would come to be dominant in these once barbarian lands.

By the time of his death in 323 B.C., Alexander had conquered the then-known world. The successor kingdoms, led by the people Alexander had left in charge of the main regions, Antigonus in Macedonia, Ptolemy in Egypt, and Seleucus in Syria, carried on the process of Hellenization. The wealthy people in the conquered cities adopted Greek styles of architecture and dress; it became fashionable to play Greek games, attend the Greek drama, and follow other Greek customs. The spread of Greek culture went fairly smoothly, except in Palestine, where it provoked the Maccabean revolt.

The successors to Alexander were not able to bring political unity to the world until Rome finally created one political world. The Romans also adopted Hellenistic culture, and the world became a "melting pot" of various ethnic and cultural groups.

Historians date the beginning of the Hellenistic era from the death of Alexander in 323 B.C., but the end of the period is not as definite. Some historians consider the era to have closed with the end of the Roman Republic; the battle of Actium in 31 B.C. is a convenient marker. Others use the term Hellenistic for a longer and less definite period of Roman political power and Greek cultural influence. It seems to make little difference for the history of philosophy. The Epicurean philosophers of note, Zeno and Lucretius, lived in the period before 31 B.C. The Greek shapers of Stoicism fall within the same period. The Skeptics range from Pyrrho in the third century B.C. to Sextus in the second century A.D. The Roman thinkers who were influenced by Stoicism promoted a moderated version of the original philosophy as part of some broadly eclectic intellectual systems. We can do well enough in speaking of Greek and Roman philosophers and leaving to others the debate about the closing date of the Hellenistic era. The cultural and social changes that came about in the Hellenistic era are very important in understanding what happened to philosophy after the death of Aristotle, however; we need to look at this era in some detail.

Hellenistic Culture

The Hellenistic era was a time of significant advances in learning, commerce, and the fine arts. For the first time in history there was one major language, a simplified version of Greek known as *koiné* or common Greek; it served as the language of diplomacy and trade. This enabled not only the growth of commerce but the dissemination of thought and other aspects of culture. Learning was fostered by large new universities at Alexandria and Antioch in Syria. The great library at Alexandria had half a million classified entries and was an important center of study. Athens also remained an important center of learning until the emperor Justinian closed the Academy in 529 A.D. There were advances in mathematics; this was the time of Euclid and Archimedes. Eratosthenes, Pythias of Marseille, and Aristarchus of Samos contributed to the study of geography and astronomy. Polybius and Heironymus of Cardia were two noted historians.

The growth of trade throughout the world was stimulated by cooperation between trade centers, the growth of commercial credit, and improved navigation and map making.

This was a period of city planning and the erection of fine public buildings. The world was said to be a prettier place than it had ever been. Many people were exposed to the fine arts. Some of the art works that many people today know as Greek art, especially works of sculpture such as the Venus de Milo, the Victory of Samothrace, and the Dying Gaul, are Hellenistic.

The Hellenistic era is called the Silver Age, in contrast to the Golden Age of Athenian greatness. The implication is that the fine arts of the Hellenistic age are inferior to those of the earlier period. The references to silver and gold can also indicate that the fine arts were available to more people than ever before. The talk of a Silver Age might reveal some prejudice or snobbery, but there is more to it than that. Without denying that some people feel that what many people enjoy cannot be very good, we should understand that the lesser valuation of Hellenistic art rests on some basic beliefs about great art. The art of the later period is naturalistic. It pictures people who would never be the subjects of the classical art, and people were pictured realistically, without the formal balance with which gods and goddesses, and a few heroic figures, were portrayed in the Golden Age. Most people like Hellenistic sculptures because they are interesting and humanistic. They appeal because they lack the formality that some art historians consider one artistic merit of earlier works.

If we put aside the aesthetic controversy about art in the two periods, we can see something important to philosophical history. The Hellenistic art works reflect the interests and concerns of the people of the period. Often these works picture the anxiety, the soul-searching, and the desperate hope of the people. These works, whether "gold" or "silver" (and neither, by the way, is a base metal), can be one window onto the nature of the people, the lives they led, and the needs that philosophy was trying to meet.

Social Conditions in the Hellenistic Era

In spite of the growth of learning, commerce, and fine art, the Hellenistic world did not gladden every heart. The lot of the common people was hard; poverty and slavery contributed to unhappiness and dissatisfaction with life for many. Many small farmers were ruined and had to join the urban poor. The power of masters over slaves was virtually unlimited for much of this period. Aristotle would surely have had a difficult time providing a justification for slavery as it was practiced under the Romans. Many of the slaves were military prizes; other slaves were exposed children, abandoned children, or children of the very poor, and some slaves were more cultured and better educated than their masters. The suffering of the slaves and poverty of the masses of people did not tend to give them determination and the strength to struggle for a better life. From time to time there were outbreaks of armed resistance to Roman power, but these were usually on the fringes of the Empire in areas not completely subjugated.

What had happened to the people? One aspect of their demoralization was that military conquests had broken down old political structures and thrust people out of their previous sources of support. Old sources of individual identity, security, standards of value, and control over conduct were lost. Home, if it still existed at all, was for many people far away and could no longer be reached. This was for many people a time of desperate need, in which they did not know where to turn or what to believe.

Old religions faced foreign faiths and new systems of belief. Religious certainty and ethnic solidarity were lost, as people experienced contrasting customs and beliefs. In this uncomfortable situation the individual person was forced to fall back upon his or her own resources; a sense of community gave way to an individualism for which few people were prepared. Too, comfortable localism and provincialism gave way to a cosmopolitanism for which most people were not ready; the world was too large and diverse to be comprehended as "home."

The world citizenship concept that had challenged some of the sophisticated Sophists was beyond the comprehension of most people, but their previous citizenship had been destroyed. This led to a quest for inner peace and security, and it is not surprising that there was an increased interest in an afterlife. There was no shortage of religions in this period; new religions developed and old ones evolved to meet the new concerns.

Philosophy could not escape being changed by the new cultural conditions. Gilbert Murray says that the philosophical schools of the fourth century B.C., Epicureanism and Stoicism, belong to the history of religions.[1] Even though Epicureanism and Stoicism do not clearly look like religions, and Epicureanism arose as a defense against religion, both were trying to meet urgent personal needs. After Aristotle the philosophies of Greece offered a kind of secular salvation but led to the later period that Gilbert Murray refers to as "the failure of nerve" and describes as a "rise of asceticism, of mysticism, in a sense, of pessimism; a loss of self-confidence, of hope in this life and of faith in normal human effort; a despair of patient inquiry, a cry for infallible revelation; an indifference to the welfare of the state, a conversion of the soul to God."[2]

The Effect on Philosophy

Philosophy as a quest for knowledge for its own sake could no longer meet the needs of people adrift in a world too large and too strange, and philosophies became quests for salvation. This quest was not as obvious in some of the earlier Hellenistic philosophies, such as Stoicism and Epicureanism, as it was in others, such as Neo-Pythagoreanism and Middle Platonism, that were religious philosophies. Stoicism and Epicureanism were not, however, simply satisfying curiosity; they were answering personal needs. They were, in a sense, functioning as secular substitutes for religions. Skepticism also, in a way, was providing some relief from the anxiety that people were facing. Even when philosophers were treating the same questions that had been discussed in earlier centuries, the purpose behind the explorations was not the same as it had been.

Later in the Roman period, the pagan philosophy that had the most influence upon philosophy in the following centuries, Neo-Platonism, was an intellectualistic religion, and Augustine was a theologian first, a philosopher second.

Another aspect of philosophy at the time was eclecticism, the practice of taking material from various philosophies and mixing it together in a scheme that might hang together quite loosely. This is not the same as being influenced by previous thinkers, as most philosophers have been. Plato, for example, took the various influences on his thinking and digested them to create his own cohesive system of thought. Eclectic philosophy, however, sometimes takes from older systems of thought large or small elements that are used just because they support in some way the claims of the philosopher who uses them. These materials, often drastically out of their original context, are "shoehorned" into a philosophy that is not really derived from them.

Epicureanism and Greek Stoicism borrowed heavily from the metaphysics of Democritus and Heraclitus, respectively. The Epicureans did not just take parts of Democritus's thought and put it into a melange that was alien in spirit to the system of Democritus; they were honest, studious, and creative disciples. They were also critical and discriminating, as can be seen in Epicurus's opposition to the implications of Democritus's determinism for human freedom. The Stoics created a monumental philosophy that incorporated the metaphysics of Heraclitus, which they treated with great respect. They did not simply take pieces of Heraclitean thought to support a point here and there. Epicureanism and Stoicism, however, were the great philosophical schools of the Hellenistic era. This greatness, however, limited their appeal for many people, and lesser and much more eclectic philosophies arose in response to the needs of the people. The philosophers of these schools took ideas and concepts without always showing due regard for consistency or the integrity of the systems recycled.

The Academy continued to be an important philosophical institution. At first it emphasized mathematical interpretation of reality, along with expanded interest in the religious interests of Plato. In the third century B.C. the Academy took a remarkable turn and became skeptical; after it had housed Middle-Platonism, it accommodated the middle period of Skepticism. After this the Academy became eclectic, generally treating Plato and Aristotle as one system, although some Middle-Platonists resisted the influence of Aristotelianism.

After the death of Aristotle, the Lyceum was led by two capable thinkers, first Theophrastus, then Strato, who continued Aristotle's approach and improved his logic. The Lyceum also became more naturalistic, dropping the emphasis on teleology and the unmoved mover. After Strato, however, the Academy was important only for its Aristotelian moral teaching; later it was virtually absorbed by Neo-Platonic thought.

15 EPICUREANISM

Epicureanism, Stoicism, and Skepticism can be seen as philosophies that responded to the need that people in the Hellenistic period felt for some kind of salvation. These philosophies did not give way entirely to the failure of nerve that created philosophical religions of most of the Hellenistic and Roman philosophies; however, they did not offer immortality, with the hope that a better life would come after this hard life was over. They did offer ways of coping with the troubles of this life through philosophy and an attitude toward life.

The Epicureans

Epicurus was born in 341 B.C. to an Athenian family living on the island of Samos, where he was reared. Diogenes Laertius reported that he began his study of philosophy at age fourteen. He went to Athens at age eighteen, when Aristotle had moved to Chalcis and Xenocrates was head of the Academy. He lived in Colophon for a while and traveled as a schoolmaster. Apparently he turned from the study of literature to serious study of philosophy because of dissatisfaction with literature and discovery of the works of Democritus. He returned to Athens and founded his school in a garden in Athens; his philosophy is sometimes referred to as the Garden. He remained in Athens the rest of his life and died in 270 B.C.

Epicurus was a prolific writer, but most of his work has been lost. Diogenes Laertius cited a number of titles and preserved Epicurus's work *Principle Doctrines* and letters to three of his disciples, Herodotus, Pythocles, and Menoeceus. There is a Vatican collection of fragments, some thought to be from specific books, some not identified with a specific book, and some from correspondence.

Diogenes Laertius reported that Epicurus was attacked by some of the Stoics and other writers who accused him of excessive indulgence and pleasure seeking, hypocrisy, ignorance, and other character flaws. Diogenes said the creators of these charges were mad and dismissed their claims as false.[1] Some of the accusations probably grew out of a misunderstanding of Epicurus's philosophy; other attacks were probably provoked by sharp disagreement with his hedonism, his ideas about the gods, and his denial of immortality.

Diogenes named a number of disciples, most of whom are little known. The only noted follower was Lucretius, a Roman poet who lived from about 99 to 55 B.C. and of whose life little is known; he is thought to have been a reclusive invalid. His poem, *De Rerum Natura* (On the Nature of Things), a defense of Epicurean philosophy, is considered a masterpiece of Latin literature.

The Epicurean Way of Life: Salvation Through Philosophy

Porphyry quotes Epicurus as saying that the words of a philosopher are empty if they do not relieve human suffering. Philosophy is like medicine that does not heal if it does not get rid of the suffering of the soul.[2] Epicureanism used philosophy as a way to personal salvation, which sought to meet the needs being felt in the Hellenistic period, but its approach was for very sophisticated thinkers. It required an intellectual acuity and openness of mind that is uncommon in any era. The goal of Epicurean philosophy was securing happiness through erasing fear of death and of the actions of divine beings. It did not promise a life after death but sought to show that death is nothing to fear. Its treatment of the gods was subtle, so much so that it is still uncertain whether Epicurus and Lucretius believed that the gods actually existed as substantial beings rather than idealizations in people's minds.

The Gods and Death

The Epicureans held that belief in the gods arose from people's dreams about blessed beings who are free of all trouble and concern and never perish.[3] It is not clear whether this explanation of belief in the gods as idealized humans was meant to deny that the gods exist in reality. Did the Epicureans think that the gods were more than images? We cannot

answer this with certainty. Epicurus and Lucretius claimed to be be-
lievers; Epicurus wrote to Menoeceus that the gods exist and knowledge of them is self-evident. He told Menoeceus, however, that the
gods "are not such as the many believe them to be." The common
beliefs, he believed, are harmful. "The impious man is not he who
denies the gods of the many, but he who attaches to gods the beliefs of
the many about them."[4]

The purpose of Epicurus and Lucretius may not have been to deny
that the gods exist but to explain that there is no need to fear them.
They are blessed and imperishable beings, who do not become angry at
humans. They have no needs or concerns, so they do not expect anything of people; they are distant and untouchable. Consequently, they
do not touch human life, except for their appearances in dreams. Fear
of the gods and concern lest one offend them is the result of mistaken
beliefs about the gods.[5]

The Epicureans held that death was not to be feared because death is
nothing to us; it does not bring punishment in an afterlife, and the
fearful mythological creatures and places associated with death, such
as Cerberus, the Furies, and Tartarus, do not exist anywhere.[6] Epicurus
wrote to Menoeceus, "all good and evil lie in sensation, whereas death
is the absence of sensation." He told Menoeceus that a correct understanding of mortality rids us of a desire for immortality. Natural philosophy enables us to overcome fears based on mythological notions.[7]

Hedonistic Ethics

The ethics of the Epicurean way of life was hedonistic; Epicurus considered pleasure the yardstick for judging whether something is good.
He was not endorsing an unrestrained pursuit of pleasure, however; he
advocated a simple life, with simple food. No pleasure is bad in itself,
but some pleasures cause stress greater than the pleasure they give.
Dissipation and excess are counterproductive. Not all desires are bad;
some are necessary for happiness, some for freedom from stress, and
some for life itself. The Epicurean goal in life is freedom from physical pain and mental disturbance, a kind of serenity called *ataraxia*.[8]

The Epicureans held a negative concept of pleasure, as absence of
pain. Diogenes Laertius reported that they recognized kinetic and static
pleasures, unlike the Cyrenaics, who held that all pleasures are motions, therefore kinetic. Joy and delight were seen as kinetic pleasures;

the examples given of these are relief from thirst and restful refresh-ment, which can be taken as relief from pain. Freedom from pain and disturbance are static pleasures. The greatest pain is mental, such as fear; pleasure is made possible by rationalizing the causes of fear.[9]

Epicurus advised against the pursuit of wealth, position, or power; he recommended avoidance of politics. He placed great value on friend-ship.[10] Epicureanism resulted in a quiet, ethical, almost ascetic life. Epicurus expressed no enthusiasm for family life. Diogenes reported Epicurus's opinion that the wise man will marry and have children, but he will not fall in love. He said that the pleasures of sex were never beneficial, and one is fortunate if they are not harmful.[11] This is quite unlike the modern connotation of the term "epicurean." In ancient times Epicurus's hedonism was subject to being misunderstood,[12] and his name has been associated with such misunderstanding ever since.

The Metaphysical Basis of Epicureanism

Epicurus held that religion, which promotes fear of the gods and of death, is the greatest enemy of serenity (*ataraxia*). He argued that gods do not concern themselves with human affairs, and he interpreted death as an absence of sensation; thus there is nothing to fear after death. He did not simply declare that there is nothing to fear from death or the gods; he used the atomic theory of Democritus to explain the basis for his beliefs.

According to Democritus's metaphysics, all that exists is bodies and the void in which movement occurs. Bodies are aggregates of the primary substances, which are atoms. The void is not the absolute lack of being denied by Eleatic logic, but is a space not occupied by a body, a space that a body can enter or pass through. It was called "intangible substance" by Sextus Empiricus. The atoms and the void have always existed; nothing comes into being from nothing, and the atoms never disappear into nothingness.[13]

The observable properties of things, such as shape, color, and weight, are not themselves substances or incorporeal things; they are accidents of bodies. The only real things are the atoms and the space in which they move. Time is not something in itself but is an attribute of the observable bodies. Sextus said time was considered an accident of accidents.[14]

Atoms have no qualities beyond shape, weight, and size; the observ-able qualities of things, their shapes and colors, odors and tastes, come from the way the atoms are arranged. Atoms can have "unimaginably many" different shapes, but the kinds of shapes are not infinite. Atoms have different sizes, but the size of atoms also has upper and lower limits. As atoms, they are of course "uncut" (*a-tomē*); even in theory, they are not infinitely divisible. The number of atoms in a body is vast, but it is not infinite.[15] Reality itself, however, is infinite. The Epicureans held that reality could have no extremity, no boundary. There would need to be, of course, an infinite number of atoms in an infinity of reality.[16]

Epicurus's claim that atoms have weight has been seen as a conceptual problem. Does the notion of weight have any meaning as an attribute of the atoms themselves? As we will see, the notion of atoms falling because of their weight was used by Epicurus in his defense of human freedom from fate. Is the notion merely a fault in his thinking, brought on by his ethical interests? This is arguable. Epicurus was aware that the notion of an up and a down has meaning "in relation to some point," and that up is used "to project a line above our heads to infinity."[17] Perhaps he was thinking about atoms having weight relative to what is up and down to us. Remember, he thought that atoms and the void have always existed, and he might have thought that there was never a time in which there were no bodies composed of atoms, bodies that would have been a reference point for an up and a down. Within the context of the presence of bodies and the relativity of motion, the concept of atoms having weight can have a clear meaning.

The Epicureans held that atoms have always been and must ever be in motion, vibrating, knocking together, and recoiling "continuously for ever." In a void, where they do not collide with others, atoms would all move at the same speed, regardless of size, and they move faster than the speed of sunlight.[18]

Lucretius described two different kinds of motion. One is the result of collisions between atoms that can send atoms caroming in any direction. Let us call this induced motion. Another form of motion is that of atoms moving of their own nature, without any induced motion. According to the Epicureans this motion is always downward, it is never oblique. Lucretius said that atoms have no intrinsic power to move obliquely, which implies that their intrinsic power is to move downward. Let us call this inherent motion. As we have seen, in the context of certain reasonable assumptions, this concept of inherent motion is a meaningful notion.

The Epicureans did not stop with the description of downward atomic inherent motion that occurs in the absence of induced motion. They held that atoms swerve slightly, no more than a small distance, which is their width. This swerve puts them in the paths of other atoms and results in collisions. This notion of a swerve was criticized because no cause for it was given, but this need not be a serious problem. It could simply be the nature of atoms, which come in many shapes and weights, to be unstable as they fall, perhaps spinning or vibrating of their own nature. Lucretius did give what he took to be evidence for the swerve; collisions could not have occurred if all atoms fell straight down, since they all fall at the same speed, which rules out rear-end collisions.[19]

There is a problem with Lucretius's explanation. If the atoms "continuously and forever" have been colliding and careering off into spaces to the side, above, and below, Lucretius's evidence of the swerve is undercut. He may have been thinking of an original state of affairs before the induced motions began, in which there was only intrinsic motion, but this would return us to a state in which the notion of atoms having weight would be highly questionable. In such a highly speculative physical theory a little inconsistency could easily creep in; the more serious problem with the swerve, however, is that the Epicureans tried to use it to account for freedom of the will. For this argument they are rightfully criticized.

Freedom of the Will

The Epicurean philosophy is based on Democritus's deterministic metaphysics, but Epicurus resisted the implication that since all events are determined no one is responsible for his or her behavior. He objected strongly to the belief that the human being is "a slave to 'fate'," a belief he attributed to the natural philosophers. He held that some things occur to a person that are necessitated and for which the person is not morally responsible, and some events in a person's life are due to good or bad fortune. Some behaviors, however, "depend on us."[20]

Epicurus held that people are responsible for their behavior, but they blame their behavior on the atoms, even when "the nature of their atoms has contributed nothing to some of their behavior, and degrees of behavior and character, but it is their developments which themselves possess all or most of the responsibility for certain things."[21]

The wording of Epicurus's claim was awkward, but what he seems to be saying would now be considered unexceptional; that is, even though our atoms, that is, causality in the physical world, cause some behavior and dispose us to some other activities, we develop our character over a long period of time, so what we have become makes us responsible for much of what we do.

Our beliefs determine our responses to those environmental influences from which we never escape. We experience our freedom, Epicurus held, when "we rebuke, oppose, and reform each other as if the responsibility lay also in ourselves." Epicurus refused to let theory override experience, and he said that infinitely claiming that each action is necessitated by physical causation is self-refuting and is not reasoning empirically.[22] This is an approach with which many of us are sympathetic, but the Epicureans were not simply satisfied with this defense of freedom and based their defense on a theory of indeterminacy in physical nature. The concept of the swerve, questionable in itself, was put to an even more questionable use. The Epicureans appealed to the postulated swerve of atoms in their downward movement for explanation of how "the mind should not itself possess an internal necessity in all its behavior, and be overcome and, as it were, be forced to suffer and be acted upon. . . ." The claim was that "a tiny swerve of atoms" brought about freedom of the will.[23]

This defense of free will was attacked even in classical times. Cicero, for example, held that the Epicureans were mistaken in looking for an external cause of freedom, rather than seeking it in a cause internal to the mind itself.[24] The Epicureans reasoned that the swerve, which was not caused, broke a rigid chain of determined causes, and thereby enabled the mind to act apart from the physical causation that governs the rest of nature. The mistake in this is not hard to see; if our minds were to act without being caused to act, this would not give us freedom and moral responsibility. It would make us victims of accidents; it would be as though we were tossed about by uncertain winds, even if the shifting gales are in our own minds.

Denial of Teleology

Lucretius held that there is nothing to prevent there being an infinite number of worlds. If there are other worlds, they are not the result of design or purpose but are simply the result of "individual entanglements," that is, the locking together of atoms upon colliding with each other. These worlds would not be eternal but for various causes would disintegrate; our own world is not an exception to the non-purposive formation of worlds.[25]

The denial of teleology played an important role in the Epicurean philosophy; freedom from fear of the gods required that the gods not create or govern the world. Lucretius held that the world is not de-signed and that there is no divine providence looking after it. This struck some people as a denial of something that gave them comfort, but the subtle basis of comfort offered by the Epicureans was based on an atomistic philosophy, according to which mechanical laws govern what comes into being. According to this philosophy, the various things in the world are not products of design. He wrote, ". . . nothing has been engendered in our body in order that we may be able to use it. It is the fact of its being engendered that creates its use." The eyes, for example, were not created so that we might see. The world is not a product of the gods, nor is anything in the world.[26]

Epicurean Psychology and Epistemology

The metaphysics of Democritus served well the salvation philosophy of the Epicureans, and the psychology of Democritus served equally well. Following the doctrine that only bodies and void exist and that the bodies are composites of atoms, Lucretius held that the soul (the mind) is a "fine-structured body, diffused through the whole aggregate," that is, the human body. The soul has the major responsibility for sensation, feelings, and thought as well as voluntary motion. The mind or soul develops as the person develops, and it ages with the person. It is affected by disease and degeneration. When the body disintegrates, the soul disintegrates and is dispersed. As we have seen, this is nothing to dread. Rather than being terrifying, death, which is the end of all sensation, saves us from any terrible experiences in an afterlife.[27]

The Senses

The Epicureans explained sense experience as Democritus had done. It is caused by effluences or emanations from bodies in the form of small atomic copies of the bodies perceived. The emanations have the same configuration as the body. The process of these emanations acting upon our sense organs is almost instantaneous; it happens as fast as thought. The Epicureans believed these small images sometimes become distorted by collision with other atoms, as Democritus had said. Democritus held, however, that even finer images escape this distortion and give us correct information about the world. He did not justify his claim or give a clear account of how this works. It is not even clear that he was talking about perception and not reason.

Epictetus gave a clearer explanation of perception. The images that reach us intact are not a special kind of emanation; they are simply those that escape being damaged in collisions. There are many successful transmissions of images, and even though there are failures, the frequent transmissions preserve the unity and continuity of the impressions. Our sense impressions, therefore, can be accepted as true. Error and falsehood "are always located in the opinion which we add."[28] Lucretius said that we should not be puzzled at perceiving objects even though we do not perceive the individual images that enable us to see the objects. He compares this to feeling the wind beat upon us but not feeling every particle of wind. When we touch a stone we do not feel the colored surface of the stone but the hardness "deep down within the stone."[29]

More imaginatively, Lucretius held that many images that are "more delicate-textured than the ones that fill the eyes and stimulate vision" are all about us. They "wander variously in every direction." These images are the cause of our seeing imaginary things. This happens especially when the memory is not awake, which is why it happens frequently in dreams. The ready availability of images also helps explain why the mind can think a thing it wants to remember.[30]

The Epicurean epistemology is based on trust of the senses. Nothing has greater reliability than the senses; ". . . whatever impression the senses get at any time is true." Life depends on trusting the senses. Lucretius did not accept optical illusions as indications that the senses are misleading us. He said the senses work separately and cannot refute each other. He took the approach that Augustine took later, which is that the senses perceive what they ought to perceive. If a square tower appears round when viewed from a distance, the sharpness of the corners is blunted because the image has had to travel a long way. The image is not as sharp as the image of a round tower seen near by. The eye has not been deceived by the far tower. If a person judges that the distant tower is round, it is a failure of the mind to reason properly. The eye should not be expected to do the work of the mind, but the reason depends on the senses, and if the senses cannot be trusted reason is false.[31]

Epicurus said, "If you fight against all sensations, you will not have a standard against which to judge even those of them you say are mistaken." Perhaps he realized that we have no way to judge any sense experience except on the basis of other sense experiences.[32]

The Epicurean stress on sense experience should not be made trivial or taken to be less sophisticated than it is. The discussion of sense experience has come a long way from the notion attributed to Protagoras. Epicurus and Lucretius were not saying that every sense impression reveals to us the nature of the world. Lucretius said, "The eyes cannot discover the nature of things." Epicurus held that it is necessary to put opinions to the test, and some criteria are needed to test for truth. The criteria of truth for the Epicureans were sensations, preconceptions, and feelings. Sensations need to be tested against the mental images of memory and the general ideas we have of things, the preconceptions. Then, opinions face another test of experience, which is related to the direction of conduct. This test involves the feelings, especially pleasure and pain. These feelings are practical tests of whether one is correct or mistaken. Feelings of pleasure indicate what people should do, while feelings of pain indicated behaviors to avoid.[33]

Truth

Sextus Empiricus explained the Epicurean tests of truth in a clear way, saying that true opinions are those that are attested and are not contested by clear evidence. "Attestation is perception through a self-evident impression of the fact that the object of opinion is such as it was believed to be." He used the example of believing that Plato was approaching at a distance; this is still a "conjectural opinion." When Plato draws nearer, there is further testimony that this is Plato approaching. Finally it is attested that this is Plato. "Non-contestation" relates to belief in something that is not self-evidential, such as belief in the space that makes motion possible. The belief is non-contested if nothing that is evident conflicts with the belief; in this case motion does exist. Attestation and non-contestation indicate true beliefs; their opposites indicate false beliefs.[34]

Social Theory

The Epicureans believed that society was based on a compact among persons to mutually refrain from harm. Epicurus said that justice is nothing more than a contract not to harm or be harmed. The motive for keeping the contract is fear of punishment, and no one who breaks the contract can be confident of escaping detection. Epicurus said, "Let nothing be done in your life which will bring you fear if it should be known to your neighbor."[35]

Justice is useful in social relations, but justice is not the same for everyone. Justice changes, and it varies "in the light of what is peculiar to a region." Laws should be judged on the basis of their social utility.[36]

Lucretius anticipates the concept in modern social theory of a state of nature and a social contract. He said that people turned to laws, constitutions, and magistrates to escape from bloodshed and disorder.[37] The social utility of society fits well the goal of the Epicurean life. Epicurus said that the just life "is most free from disturbance, but the unjust life is full of the greatest disturbance." The social dimension of *ataraxía* was clearly recognized.[38]

16 STOICISM

Stoicism, as did Epicureanism, sought to meet human needs with a way of life that was supported by a philosophy. It was in some respects more complicated than Epicureanism, and it underwent more changes as the original Greek Stoicism became popular in Rome, becoming part of the eclectic thinking of Cicero, Seneca, Marcus Aurelius, and others.

The writings of the Greek Stoics have mostly been lost except for fragments and references in the writings of non-Stoic thinkers, some of whom were hostile to Stoicism. For English-speaking students, Volume I of *The Hellenistic Philosophers* by A.A. Long and D.N. Sedley will be the most valuable source of fragments.

The Old Stoa

The Greek originators of Stoicism flourished in the fourth and third centuries B.C. The founder was Zeno of Citium, who lived from about 340 to 265 B.C. He moved to Athens about 315 B.C., where he studied first with Crates of Thebes, a Cynic. Diogenes Laertius wrote that he attended the lectures of Xenocrates, head of the Academy from 339 to 314 B.C., and studied under Polemo, his successor. He had conflicts with Arcesilaus, a skeptical leader of the Academy, who saw him as a rival and attacked him.[1] Zeno also studied under Diodorus Cronus, leader of the dialectical school, who is known for his interest in logical problems and fallacies. Diodorus's use of dialectic was called eristic, that is, very competitive, often employing logic merely to win arguments. This mode of argumentation is thought to have influenced Stoicism. Diogenes Laertius reported Zeno's study with Diodorus and quoted many examples of Zeno's repartee. Some of these show a rather sharp, even caustic, tongue.[2]

Zeno lectured at the colonnade known as the Painted Porch (*poikilē stoâ*). His school was named the Stoa, hence the name Stoicism. His group of followers was also referred to as the Porch.[3]

Zeno was respected for his moral earnestness. He was highly honored in both Athens and Citium. When he was eighty years old, he was invited by King Antigonus of Macedonia to visit and instruct him in philosophy; he declined because of his old age and infirmity but sent two of his disciples, which seems to have been a satisfactory arrangement. Diogenes Laertius preserved the correspondence between Zeno and the king.[4]

Zeno lived frugally; he was noted for his simple diet. He lived to a very old age, by some reports ninety-eight years. He fell and broke a bone, which he may have interpreted as a message from the gods that it was time for him to die. Reports of the exact manner of his death vary from his dying on the spot to his fasting to death. Diogenes Laertius gives a list of nearly twenty writings by Zeno, all of which have been lost. Diogenes also listed a number of disciples.[5]

On Zeno's death leadership of the school fell first to Cleanthes of Assos, who lived from about 331 to 232 B.C. Diogenes Laertius reported that Cleanthes was a boxer, who arrived in Athens with only pocket change. He was noted for his size and strength and he worked for his living as a gardener. He was not noted for great intellect, but he was respected for his good humor and his ability to live in poverty with dignity. Diogenes cited fifty titles of works by Cleanthes, which he described as "very fine writings." Cleanthes fasted to cure a disease of the gums; but when told to resume his usual diet, he continued to fast until he died.[6]

Cleanthes gave Stoicism a religious expression, but the religious approach of Stoicism was naturalistic. Cleanthes is noted for his *Hymn to Zeus,* the only surviving work of Stoic authorship. R.D. Hicks calls this work "the truth of natural religion in poetic form." He says it is "a curious personal form of pantheism."[7] The Stoics referred to the gods, but treated them as symbols of aspects of nature.

Chrysippus of Soli, who lived from about 282 to 206 B.C., succeeded Cleanthes. Diogenes Laertius said he achieved eminence as a philosopher, especially in the practice of dialectic. Stories are told of his use of catch-question arguments. He is reported to have had an exalted opinion of himself. Chrysippus was a diligent writer; according to Diogenes he had a good reputation as a writer and left over 700

works, which Diogenes cited arranged according to topics. Some crit-
ics held that his writing were weak in content, often treating the same
topic repeatedly; he was accused of using indecent and coarse language. He was also accused of approving of cannibalism and incest. It
is impossible to know whether there is any truth in the stories that put
him in a bad light. The opponents of the Stoics and Chrysippus's
jealous rivals might have exaggerated tales of his appearance, deport-
ment, and limitations. There are a number of conflicting reports of his
death. He may have committed suicide, as did his two predecessors.[8]

Chrysippus was probably not an original thinker, but he was a copi-
ous writer and an able systematizer and defender of Stoic doctrine. He
seems to have had greater ability in dialectic than either Zeno or
Cleanthes.

The Middle and Late Stoa

Stoicism was brought to Rome by some prominent scholars and diplo-
mats who tended to moderate some of the harsher features of the Old
Stoa. The leading figures of the Middle Stoa, as this period of Stoicism
is called, were influenced by other schools of thought, and the Romans
who were attracted to Stoicism did not find all of the doctrines of the
Old Stoa appealing.

Three Stoics of the middle period are well known. Diogenes of
Seleucia, called the Babylonian, who lived in the second century B.C.,
was a pupil of Chrysippus and succeeded him as head of the Stoa. He
was recognized especially for his work in the study of language and
logic. He visited Rome in 155 B.C.[9] Panaetius of Rhodes, born about
185 B.C., was a student of Diogenes. He visited Rome and was influential among the aristocrats. Panaetius moderated Stoic doctrines and
humanized its ethics, dropping some of the harshness of the Cynic
influence and placing more value on the amenities of life. He held that
the end of the virtues is happiness. Living according to nature is the
fulfillment of natural human tendencies, and people live in accordance
with nature in different ways.[10] Posidonius of Rhodes, born about 135
B.C., a pupil of Panaetius, was a gifted and influential writer. He is
reported to have built an armillary sphere, an astronomical device
showing the relationship of the heavenly bodies to the earth. He admired Plato's philosophy and adopted his concept of the tripartite soul.
He resisted the tendency to soften Stoic doctrines and stressed the

religious aspects of Stoic thought, holding that god is the substance of the world. He was critical of Chrysippus and others for their ethical doctrines, which he thought led to considering pleasure or freedom from pain the end of life. He held that we must not be influenced by the irrational parts of the soul.[11]

The Late Stoa consisted of the eclectic Roman thinkers who were influenced by Stoic thought, such as Horace, Virgil, Cicero, Scipio Africanus, and Hadrian. The most important of these as sources of information on Stoicism are Seneca, Epictetus, and Marcus Aurelius. Seneca, who flourished in the first century A.D., was an eclectic and independent thinker, who was influenced by moderate Stoicism. Epictetus, who was born about 50 A.D., was a highly educated slave. He wrote the *Discourses* and the *Manual*. He was concerned primarily with the ethical and religious aspects of Stoicism and stressed the virtues of independence and self-control and indifference to worldly fortune, along with love for all humanity. Marcus Aurelius, born of an influential Spanish family in 121 A.D., was adopted, at the wish of the Emperor Hadrian, by Antoninus Pius, heir designate of Hadrian. Marcus was well educated and was influenced by Epictetus and other Stoics. He became emperor in 161 A.D. and died in 180. Marcus practiced a modified Stoicism; he believed in a rational world order directed by a divine reason. He did not believe in personal immortality, but thought that at the dissolution of the body its reason was reunited with the world reason. Even though he was a broadly eclectic thinker, Marcus Aurelius is one of the best-known Stoics because of his *Meditations,* which has been a popular classic for many centuries.[12]

The Stoic Way of Life

Stoicism stressed self-control and independence (*autárchia*), virtues advocated by all of the Greek moral philosophers. They aimed to achieve self-control through *apátheia,* which is indifference to that which is not in a person's control. Their goal was serenity in the face of good or bad worldly fortune. We should resist the temptation to translate *apátheia* as "apathy." It does not have the negative connotations of apathy; it is not indifference to things about which a good person should be concerned. Diogenes Laertius indicated that the Stoics were aware of and disapproved of the sense of apathy typical of callous bad people.[13] The attitude the Stoics advocated was avoidance of useless agitation over what one cannot prevent and useless longing for what one cannot count on.

Stoics held that what happens to a person is neither good nor bad, but indifferent; what counts is the person's attitude toward it. The wise person, the sage, knows that what is good is virtue, meaning justice, prudence, courage, and temperance, for example. What is bad is vice, meaning injustice and foolishness. Health, pleasure, beauty, strength, wealth, and the like can bring harm as well as benefits. Death, disease, pain, poverty, and the like are not to be seen as bad things that always do harm. Motivation alone is of moral significance.[14]

The Stoic attitude of *apátheia* was not as extreme as it might at first appear. Some of the Stoics said that certain morally indifferent things can be preferred. If circumstances allow, one prefers health to illness. If something is in accordance with nature, even the Stoic prefers it, by a kind of natural impulse. Aristo of Chios denied that some indifferent things should be preferred, however; that the wise person will be utterly indifferent to everything except vice and virtue. He seems, though, to have been exceptionally rigorous in taking this approach.[15]

The proper functions for a wise person are in accordance with nature and dictated by reason. Such actions as honoring parents and siblings, acting patriotically, treating friends well, and taking care of one's health are reasonable and in keeping with nature. The exact way of carrying them out will depend on the circumstances.[16]

Virtue and the Good Life

The Stoics did not consider the pursuit of virtue a burden. The Stoic way of living was in keeping with considering happiness to be the goal of life. Zeno said, "Happiness is a good flow of life." This good flow consists of living virtuously, which is also described as living according to reason and living in accordance with nature or in agreement with nature. Chrysippus described happiness as "living in accordance with experience of what happens in nature," but this can also be seen as self-fulfillment, because our natures are parts of the whole of nature. For Chrysippus the nature in accord with which we must live is the nature common to all things and that particular to humans. Cleanthes, however, thought of nature only as the common nature of all things.[17]

The eclectic Roman Stoics maintained the basic principles of the Stoic way of life. They held that the end of life is tranquility through a life of reason in accordance with nature.[18]

In acknowledging that happiness is the goal of life and that happiness consists in virtue, the Stoics had no intention of making virtue merely a means to an end. They held that virtue is praiseworthy and is to be chosen for its own sake. They held a strong belief in the unity of the virtues. Whoever acts in accordance with one virtue acts in accordance with all. The virtues apply to different aspects of life, which gives them different perspectives, but they are inseparable. Diogenes Laertius reported at length Stoic opinions on the virtues and the good. More severe Stoics, such as Aristo and Menedmus of Eretria, held that there are no degrees of virtuousness and no differentiations between virtues.[19] Belief in the unity of the virtues was not a new idea; Plato had made it an important aspect of his moral theory. The Stoics were divided on the question of degrees of virtuousness.

The Old Stoa believed that there can be no stages of progress toward becoming a Stoic sage; it happens suddenly, and some Stoics said finally. Cleanthes thought that one cannot lose the state of being a Stoic. Chrysippus, however, held that a sage could "back-slide." The Stoics of the middle period tended to be less severe about levels of moral achievement; they did not all hold that virtue came by a sudden conversion to complete wisdom. Panaetius is reported to have answered a youth, who asked whether a sage could fall in love, that we would have to wait and see what the sage will do, since we are a great distance from being sages. We should ensure, he told the youth, that we do not fall into a disturbed state of affairs that is worthless to us. Cicero reports that a Stoic, probably Panaetius, said that since life is passed in the company of people who are not perfectly wise but do well to show some likeness to virtue, we should not neglect one in whom some mark of virtue is found.[20]

The Roman Stoic Epictetus said that it is not possible to remain faultless. We can, he said, "be continually intent on not doing wrong. We must be content if we avoid at least a few faults by never relaxing this attention."[21]

The Emotions

The popular picture of a Stoic as a person without emotions is largely a misunderstanding. The Stoics thought that many of the emotions are detrimental to *apátheia,* but some emotions are rational and appropriate. The passions are impulses that are contrary to nature; the primary irrational passions are appetite, fear, distress, and pleasure. Appetite includes such emotions as anger, intense sexual desire, craving, and love of riches and honor. Pleasure includes rejoicing in the misfortune of another and trickery. Fear includes shame, superstition, and dread. Distress includes malice, envy, jealousy, pity, grief, sorrow, and worry. The passionless state of the Stoic sage is a godlike freedom from harmful and useless emotions.[22]

There are, however, good emotions: joy, watchfulness, and wishing. Joy is the opposite of pleasure, watchfulness is the opposite of fear, and wishing is the opposite of appetite. The good emotions include kindness, generosity, warmth, affection, respect, cleanliness, delight, sociability, and cheerfulness.[23] This does not support the picture of a glum and frowning misanthrope, which is the commonplace notion of the Stoic.

Problems of personality, such as proneness to illness, irascibility, malevolence, and a quick temper, are the effects of wrong beliefs about what is important, what should and should not be sought. They are related to faulty judgment. Epictetus said that it is not things themselves that disturb people, but their judgments about things.[24]

Seneca held that certain bodily effects, things that "rouse the mind fortuitously," should not be considered passions. Bodily drives such as sexual arousal, pallor, or the coming of tears are not passions. Passions arise not in the passing impressions, but in surrendering oneself to them. Anger becomes an impulse to act when the mind assents to it. Gellius said that a terrifying sound can cause the Stoic sage to be moved and frightened, which is a rapid and involuntary movement. Soon, however, the sage withdraws mental assent from such impressions and finds in them nothing to fear.[25]

The Stoics on Suicide

The Stoic attitude toward suicide throws some light on Stoic beliefs and disagreements over the relationship between a virtuous life and those things held to be morally indifferent but preferred goods. Is the loss of preferred good things important enough to justify suicide? Some Stoics held that suicide is sometimes a right action for the wise person, and some considered it a duty in circumstances that prevented living a virtuous life, as in situations in which the bulk of one's circumstances are not in accord with nature. There was some approval of suicide on behalf of one's country or friends, or if one falls victim to unduly severe pain, mutilation, or incurable illness. While Seneca considered suicide justified by the infirmity of old age, incurable disease, or loss of mental powers, Epictetus denied that these are unnatural and grounds for taking one's life. It might be a mistake to assume that there was widespread approval of suicide among Stoics. R.D. Hicks thinks that the tradition that Zeno, Cleanthes, and Chrysippus committed suicide might account for the impression that the Stoics were generally supportive of suicide.[26]

Stoic Metaphysics

The popular notion of the Stoic as a person of such courage and self-determination that nothing could disturb the hearty soul is a parody. The Stoics did not achieve a godlike calm nor claim to be living rationally and according to nature by the sheer force of stubborn determination. Their thought was undergirded with a philosophy that made their way of life rational, even in accordance with nature. Diogenes Laertius credited Zeno and Chrysippus with a threefold division of philosophy into the ethical, which we have examined as the Stoic way of life; the physical, which we will study as the metaphysical basis of Stoic life; and the logical, which we will examine later.[27]

The Stoic metaphysics was based closely on the philosophy of Heraclitus. Diogenes Laertius wrote that the Stoics defined nature "as a force moving of itself, and producing and preserving in being its offspring in accordance with seminal principles."[28] This definition refers to the seminal reasons (*spermatikoi lógoi*), which played a significant role in Neo-Platonic and medieval metaphysics. These seminal principles are seed ideas that give rise to the things of the world and a rational order of the universe. They originate in the rational mind (*lógos*) that gives rise to the world and is the substance of the world. This is the divine fire we first saw in the philosophy of Heraclitus. God is the substance of the world as well as the divine providence that makes all things work out for the good. The Stoics employed arguments such as the familiar ontological, cosmological, and teleological arguments to argue for the necessity of an ever-lasting and self-moving force.[29]

This philosophy is religious, but it is naturalistic without a transcendent concept of deity. God is considered a body, for only bodies are capable of acting or being acted upon.[30] This is, however, a very sophisticated form of pantheism. The basic reason (*lógos*) is un-generated and indestructible. A substratum that is the prime matter of all bodies is subject to continuous change but is never destroyed; but the elements of earth, air, fire and water return to the original fire, the divine fire that designs and creates the world in periodic conflagrations. The element of earthly fire, which exists through the use of fuel, is not the same as the creative fire, which is the reason of the universe.[31]

The doctrine of world conflagrations, occurring at fated times, when the primary fire that contains the seminal reasons of all things returns all to fire and then reconstitutes the world, was borrowed from Heraclitus. The members of the Old Stoa held that the world will recur infinite times following the conflagrations. Each time it will be restored to what it was before, or a form only slightly different. Belief in periodic conflagrations was largely abandoned by the Stoics of the Middle and Roman periods.[32]

If the belief is held that nature is the divine reason that created and maintains the world, so that by divine providence all events work together for the good, failing to accept whatever happens would be to rebel against nature. This would be irrational since all things happen according to divine reason and are good.

In regard to soul and body, some of the Stoics spoke of soul in two senses, that which sustains the living being, and the commanding faculty or reason. In speaking of soul and body the latter definition is referred to. The soul was held to be engendered by the body. Its activity is seen in breath, in perception, and in impulse to act. It is seated in the heart but acts throughout the body. The soul was thought to be an offshoot of the world reason. The Stoics did not agree about the immortality of the soul. The soul is subject to generation and destruction, but some Stoics held that the souls of the virtuous survive until the periodic conflagrations.[33]

Stoic Physics

While it is true that the Stoics used the metaphysics of Heraclitus to undergird their ethical approach, it would not be accurate to portray them as nothing more than devotees of a philosophical religion. Their interest in physics was not limited to ideas that supported the Stoic way of life. They dealt seriously with physical issues such as the nature of bodies and space and the nature of time. They held that space, or the void, being unoccupied by a body, was infinite. They distinguished "place," occupied by a body, from "room," occupied by a large body. They held that the world, which is a whole, is finite, whereas the "all," which includes the surrounding void, is infinite.[34]

Zeno held that time is the dimension of all motion, but Chrysippus said it is the dimension of the world's motion. The Stoics held that time is infinitely divisible. Past and future subsist, and present time alone "belongs," but no time is wholly present and is only "broadly" said to exist. This view of time is close to Aristotle's view, but all of the Stoics may not have held exactly the same view, and Stoic expressions seem to lack the reference to measurement that was part of Aristotle's definition. They seem to have held that present time is partly past and partly future, part of a continuum, but the least perceptible time between past and future.[35]

The Stoic teaching on the origin of the world, like the rest of prescientific theory, is metaphysical speculation. Stoic astronomy, on the other hand, made some interesting advances over earlier views. The Stoics held that the earth is spherical and that the sun is fire and is larger than the earth. They also understood the cause of eclipses.[36]

Fate and Freedom

As we saw, the Stoics held that only a body can act or be acted upon. The causes of all events are corporal, and there is a necessity between the presence of a cause and the occurrence of an event. All things, they held, are fated.[37] Fate is a sequence of causes, "an inescapable ordering and interconnection."[38] Chrysippus used a variety of expressions for fate. He called it "the rationale of the world," "providence's act of government in the world," "truth," "nature," "necessity," and other similar terms. Note two things in Chrysippus's words: the affirmation of a determined system of order, and belief that this order is directed providentially by the reason that governs the world.[39]

Their belief in determinism and fate, the belief in the uniformity and inevitability of cause and effect, justified divination for some Stoics, but Panaetius denied the truth of divination.[40]

In spite of a strong belief in fate, the Stoics also believed in freedom and moral responsibility. Chrysippus held that some causes are complete and primary; these causes effect events whether or not a person assents to them. Other causes, however, are auxiliary and proximate.

Fate is an auxiliary cause. A person's own nature and actions affect the results of external causation. What happens according to fate is co-fated. The fated event does not happen regardless of what a person does. Marcus Aurelias believed that people are compelled to act as they do, but their own beliefs are part of the causation.[41]

Language and Logic

The Stoics held that dialectic is a necessary part of philosophy; the sage will always be a dialectician. Dialectic gives the wise person freedom from being precipitate in giving the mind's assent to sense impressions. Dialectic gives the wariness that enables the Stoic to question what at the moment seems probable. It gives the sage use of right reason and enables the development of strong arguments.[42]

Dialectic falls under two headings: language and discourse. The Stoics studied the elements of language: types of statements, the parts of speech, errors in syntax, verbal ambiguities, and aspects of diction. The other aspect of dialectic covered the study of impressions, that is, the immediately given data of consciousness and experience, along with propositions that consist of a subject and predicate, the nature of genera and species, and arguments.[43]

The Stoics called the subsistent constituents of language "sayables" (*lekta*). R.D. Hicks defined a *lekton* as "the content of notions, judgments, and syllogisms." A sayable can be complete or incomplete; a noun by itself has meaning, but it does not really say anything significant. The incomplete *lekton* "Prince" does not make a claim, but *lekta* such as "Prince was the best dog I ever had" or "Prince always watched over my children when we went camping" are complete sayables. The Stoics saw that sayables could be propositions, but they could also be questions, commands, oaths, or other forms of utterance. Some sayables can be true or false. They seem to be very much like what is meant by "speech acts" in twentieth-century ordinary language analysis.[44]

Chrysippus defined a simple proposition as "that which is true or false, or a complete state of affairs which, so far as itself is concerned, can be asserted."[45] To be true or false, a proposition must be a complete sayable. The Stoics used the notion of contradictories and realized that not every denial of a proposition is a contradictory. A contradictory is the negation of a proposition. "It is day" and "it is not day" ("P" and "not P") are contradictories. The negation of a true proposition is false. "It is day" and "it is not light" are not contradictories.[46] The Stoics thought that a true proposition is one that corresponds to reality. As Diogenes Laertius put their view, "it is day" is true "if it really is day," otherwise the proposition is false. The Stoics also applied the concept of true or false to sense perceptions and to arguments. A true argument is valid and has true premises.[47]

The Stoics made a number of distinctions among propositions. They can be true or false, and they can be definite ("this person is sitting"), indefinite ("someone is sitting"), or intermediate ("a man is sitting"). If a definite proposition is true, the indefinite will also be true, and if the definite is false, so will be the indefinite be false.[48] A significant contribution of the Stoics to logic was their treatment of types of propositions not dealt with in Aristotle's syllogistic. They described several kinds of non-simple propositions. Conditionals, such as "if it is day, it is light" were analyzed in terms of antecedent and subsequent propositions. Subconditionals are similar, but the antecedent and subsequent are connected with "since." Conjunctions join simple propositions with the connective "both–and," and disjunctions with "either–or." A sound conditional does not have a true antecedent and a false conclusion. Conjunctions are false if one conjunct is false. Disjunctive propositions are false unless one of the simple propositions is false and one true.[49]

Stoic logic, unlike that of Aristotle, was not based on categorical statements and did not consider universal affirmations the most import aspect of knowledge. The Stoics dealt with the logic of hypothetical statements or conditionals, that is, implication, in the logical forms we now know as *modus ponens* and *modus tollens.* They also recognized valid arguments based on disjunctions and conjunctions, and realized the logical modalities, "necessarily true," "possible," and "impossible."[50]

Sextus Empiricus listed four types of invalid argument recognized by the Stoics. *Disconnection* occurs when there is no connection between the premises and the conclusion. In *redundancy,* something superfluous is added to a premise. When the extraneous matter is removed, the form is valid. An argument can be posed in an *invalid form,* such as, for example, what we now know as denying the antecedent. In *deficiency,* something needed is missing from the premises. The example given of this is treating two statements in a disjunction as contradictories and denying one of them to reach the conclusion that the part not denied has been demonstrated: "either wealth is good or wealth is bad" ignores the possibility that wealth is indifferent.[51] The Stoics dealt with many sophisms and logical puzzles that seem to have been commonplace at the time and paid attention to problems of ambiguity and other logical difficulties. A number of treatises dealing with ambiguity and problematic arguments are attributed to Chrysippus.[52]

The logical theory of the Stoics receives scanty treatment from some historians of philosophy. Eduard Zeller held that the Stoics lost sight of the important aspects of logic in attending in great detail to trivial matters. He claims that their theories on semantics were no more than dressing the logic of the peripatetics in new terminology. He says, "No very high estimate can therefore be formed of the formal logic of the Stoics."[53] It is hard to see how Zeller can dismiss Stoic logic, however, unless he also rejects the importance of all logic that is not based on categorical statements. Benson Mates defends Stoic logic against Zeller's claims. He holds that Zeller's objections are not supported by evidence, and says that Zeller is wanting in his understanding of Stoic logic and failed to understand several technical terms used by the Stoics.[54]

Stoic Epistemology

The difference between Stoic logic and Aristotle's logic reflects their differences in epistemological theory. A critical difference is that the Stoics were not essentialists; they did not consider universals to be the essences of things in the world. They treated general terms as concepts produced by the mind. A concept is not a something. Only particular things exist.[55] Aristotle did grant that particular things exist, but sensory perception of particulars did not account for knowledge, as it did in Stoic epistemology.

Sense Impressions

The Stoics saw sensory impressions, which they called presentations, as of primary importance. They held that the mind is like a blank sheet of paper at birth, and on this blank surface we inscribe conceptions. This process starts with sense impressions, and with increasing memory of similar impressions we have experience and form conceptions. The conceptions are formed naturally, and with attention to them we form preconceptions, or general notions.[56] There are differences between a cognitive impression coming from a real object and a semblance, such as occurs in dreams. An impression was understood in a literal sense, as being like the impress of a seal in wax. An impression comes from a real object and agrees with that object. Some impressions are not sensory data that are conveyed by a sense organ. They are appearances received by the mind; they purport to come from real objects, but the Stoics held that we can know the difference, since they are not as clear and distinct as cognitive impressions coming from real objects, and we need not give mental assent to these appearances.[57]

We become aware of the qualities of things through sense impressions, and knowledge is developed by the mind as it builds up mental perceptions. From sense impressions we develop concepts by analogy.[58]

Knowledge

The standard of truth by which we apprehend impressions that come from real objects was described in various ways. Chrysippus said the standard is sensation and preconception, or general notions. These general notions are conceptions of universals and general concepts, but his emphasis seems to have been upon perceptions that have a peculiar power to convince the mind, which accepts them voluntarily. The general notions are necessary for knowledge and the making of correct decisions.[59]

Later Stoics made weaker claims for the criterion of cognitive impressions than did the Old Stoa. They held that it applied only when it had no impediment. A strong cognitive impression might be unbelievable in circumstances that belied it. The cognitive impression was not accepted unconditionally as the criterion of truth.[60]

The Stoics did not claim that cognition by itself is knowledge. Cicero reported that Zeno used hand gestures in explaining scientific knowledge (*epistēmē*). Spreading the fingers of one hand represented an impression. Closing the fingers a little represented assent to an impression. Closing the hand into a fist represented cognition. Gripping the fist with the other hand, he said, is the scientific knowledge of the wise person.[61]

Sextus Empiricus said that the Stoics thought that cognition lay between knowledge and opinion (*doxa*). A cognitive impression cannot be false. Scientific knowledge is cognition that is firm and cannot be changed by reason. Opinion is false assent to a noncognitive impression. Only the wise person has knowledge, while only the inferior person has opinions. Both the wise and the inferior have cognitions, though, and cognition is the criterion for separating knowledge and opinion. If Sextus reports correctly, that the Stoics held that wise and inferior persons both have cognition, it is hard to see how cognition serves as a criterion of truth, as the Skeptics pointed out.[62]

The criterion of truth is built around cognitive impressions, but it seems to involve a critical attitude toward impressions and a willingness to suspend judgment in some cases rather than resort to holding opinions. To avoid acceptance of non-cognitive impressions, assent should not be given hastily. Opinions are weak and changeable assents to an impression, and the sage does not give such assent. The inferior person is precipitate, but the virtuous wise person is not hasty. The Stoics considered the giving of assent carelessly to be a moral failure.[63]

Perhaps we can understand the Stoic criterion better if we do not see it as focused on individual and isolated cognitions. Stobaeus says that the Stoics thought of knowledge systematically. Knowledge is a system developed by a person with a disposition for accepting only cognitive impressions.[64] This describes a criterion that is not subject to much of the easy criticism of the criterion of truth as it is usually presented, which may be an incomplete and overly simple notion of the criterion.

17 SKEPTICISM

The salvation offered by Skepticism would have little appeal for the person who had been captured in battle and sold into slavery. It would promise nothing to the person whose village had been destroyed and who was now part of the desperate urban poor. It was a sort of salvation, however, for some intellectuals, who were through it relieved of needing to make sense of the world. The benefit of being a Skeptic is described as not being perturbed, which seems much like the *ataraxía* of the Epicureans and the *apátheia* of the Stoics. Pyrrho of Elis was admired for his lack of concern, and freedom from the adopting and defense of opinions and theorizing about unresolved issues. His pupil, Timon of Phlius, called Pyrrho god-like, and compared him to the sun in its journeys around the earth.[1]

Skepticism began as a philosophical movement with Pyrrho, who lived from 360 to 270 B.C., and for whom Skepticism is still sometimes called Pyrrhonism. Pyrrho had the ability to discourse at length and engage in questioning. He was respected and honored both in Athens and in his native city, Elis, and he was admired by Epicurus. Pyrrho studied under the Skeptical philosopher Anaxarchos, who compared experience of existing things to the experience of insane people and dreamers. Pyrrho advocated agnosticism and suspension of judgment about the nature of the world. His Skepticism also applied to matters of ethics; he held that nothing is just or honorable by its nature. Human actions, he held, are governed by custom and convention.[2]

Pyrrho considered human pursuits vain folly, and he advocated fortitude in the face of pain and trouble. Even though he was admired for his composure and described by Timon as like a god, he was aware of his own human weakness and admitted that he could become frightened or angry.[3]

Pyrrho's leading pupil, Timon, who lived from about 325 to 235 B.C., was known as a satirical polemicist. He wrote lampoons of many earlier philosophers, such as Parmenides and Zeno of Elea, Xenophanes, some of the Sophists, Epicurus, Zeno of Citium, and Aristotle. His sarcastic comments were not very informative or perhaps even fair, but he was known as a good writer and composer of verses. He held that Skepticism gives freedom from disturbance.[4]

When Arcesilaus from Pitane (in Aeolia) succeeded his teacher Crates as head of the Academy in Athens in about 273 B.C., a new period of Skepticism began, the "New Academy," which some writers called the Middle Academy. Arcesilaus was noted for his ability in argumentation; he liked to distinguish the meaning of terms, and he was outspoken and satirical. Diogenes Laertius reported some of his sharp witticisms. At the same time, however, Arcesilaus was generous and charitable.[5]

Arcesilaus advocated suspension of judgment (*epochê*) and living reasonably and prudentially; he said a person doing so will act in a morally right way. Accusing Arcesilaus of denying the knowledge that would support ethics but acting ethically anyway, Cleanthes said that he argued one way and acted another.[6]

Arcesilaus's arguments were directed mainly against Zeno the Stoic, who was his main intellectual rival. He argued against the Stoic criterion of truth, denying that cognition could be the criterion between knowledge and opinion.[7]

Arcesilaus was succeeded by Carneades of Cyrene, who was born about 213 B.C. and died about 129 B.C. and who had studied under the Stoics but turned against Stoic doctrine and argued against several aspects of it. He rejected not only the Stoic criterion of truth, but any criteria whatever; impressions and reason can both be misleading. The false impression cannot be distinguished from the true, and reason is dependent on the impression. Carneades attacked Stoic belief in a divine mind governing the world, rejecting also belief in divination and in fate.[8]

Carneades advocated acting upon probability and held that different impressions had different probabilities of being true. While remaining skeptical, he recognized that some impressions are convincing enough for judgment and action. The lowest level of probability was that of impressions based on little observation, with only an even likelihood of being true. A higher level is reached by undiverted impression, that is, impression based on more frequent observations with no contradicting impressions. The highest level of probability possible is that for impressions based on thorough observation. Sextus Empiricus seems to report Carneades' recognition of probability with his approval. Carneades was known as a "formidable controversialist," but he wrote little and his views are preserved by his pupils, especially Cleitomachus.[9]

Carneades was succeeded by Cleitomachus, who was head of the New Academy from about 128 to about 110 B.C. Diogenes Laertius wrote that Cleitomachus was a diligent scholar, who composed four hundred treatises. He held that convincingness of sense impressions does not show that they are cognitive, and the wise person will not give assent to them. The sage does not ignore sense experience, however, and some experiences impel us to act.[10] He was succeeded by Philo of Larissa, head of the New Academy from about 110 to about 79 B.C. Philo is considered a revisionist, who allowed qualified assent to opinions that are known to be opinions and not knowledge. Rifts and defections troubled the Academy during Philo's tenure. Philo's pupil, Antiochus of Ascalon, rejected Skepticism and founded what he called the Old Academy. He considered himself a disciple of Plato, whom he interpreted in Stoic terms. He was accused of teaching Stoicism in the Academy.[11]

Opposition to Philo's approach to opinions, which was considered too lenient, and the Stoic influence of Antiochus, led to the Alexandrian period of Skepticism. Anesidemus of Crete, who taught in Alexandria and whose dates are uncertain but who probably lived in the first century A.D., separated himself from the Academy and supported what he considered the original Pyrrhonism. He wrote *Pyrrhonean Discourses,* in which he attacked Stoicism. He advocated suspension of judgment and held that all we can know is what appears, that is, phenomena. There is no basis for deciding between conflicting perceptions and conceptions; tastes and moral beliefs are matters of convention. He explained ten modes, or tropes, that are kinds of agreement and disagreement in perceptions and ideas that justify the adoption of Skepticism. Little is known of his successor, Agrippa. Diogenes Laertius mentioned him as adding to the grounds for Skepticism. Sextus Empiricus reported that he reduced the ten tropes to five.[12]

The best known figure of Alexandrian Skepticism is Sextus Empiricus, a Greek who taught about 200 A.D. He is our best ancient authority on the history and doctrines of Skepticism, and he contributed much to our knowledge of other Hellenistic philosophies. Sextus advocated suspension of judgment as a way to achieve "unperturbedness."[13] Being unperturbed enabled some scholars to cope with the tribulations of life in the Hellenistic and Roman periods. Judgment is suspended without denying all value to sense perception. Appearances are separated from judgment. Without declaring as a fact that things are such and such, the Skeptic reports how things appear at the moment and may question whether objects actually are as they appear.[14]

Sextus held that the Skeptic's position, which he described as "nondogmatic," differs from that of the New Academy. He objected to the Academic's practice of saying that all judgments are probable. In respect to judgments of good and evil, for example, he said, "When we describe a thing as good or evil we do not add it as our opinion that what we assert is probable, but simply conform to life nondogmatically that we may not be precluded from activity."[15] This nondogmatic approach does not lead to the kind of skepticism that asserts that nothing will ever be known. Sextus said that the Skeptic will "keep on searching."[16] This sort of Skepticism does not lead to inability to act and respond intelligently to events as they appear to be. It is a pragmatic approach rather than a doctrinal approach.

Sextus did not abandon Skepticism, however. He was critical of the Stoics' attempt to establish a criterion of truth, which he held leads to an infinite regress. He explained the tropes or modes that are grounds for refuting dogmatic philosophies.[17] His refusal to deny all value to appearances must be seen in relation to his statements about the problems of sense perception. He held that sense experience varies greatly from one perceiver to another and one experience to another. Differences in perspective, the organs of perception, states of health, the effect of previous perception such as exposure to sunlight, and other conditions keep perception from being dependable.[18]

Sextus denied the reliability of syllogistic reasoning and rejected the concept of logical proof. He called syllogistic argument redundant, inconclusive, and circular. He consider inductive reasoning "insecure," since particulars that are not treated in an argument might contradict the generalization reached by induction.[19]

Sextus's skeptical approach did not preclude his reaching some philosophical conclusions. He held that there are problems in the claim that God exists. He pointed to the lack of evidence to support the claim. He noted difficulties with the notion of divine foreknowledge, the denial of which would be impious, but the affirmation of which leads to logical problems. He wrote of the problem of evil in a world created by a good and omnipotent deity. He held that the concept of a divine providence is refuted by the observation that "the good fare ill and the bad fare well."[20]

18 NEO-PLATONISM

Epicureanism, Stoicism, and Skepticism were salvation philosophies, in the sense that they helped intellectuals cope with life in the Hellenistic and Roman eras. They made concessions to the need for meaning and inner peace that did not seriously compromise their philosophical integrity. Other philosophies of the Hellenistic and Roman period are better understood as religious philosophies or as philosophical religions. They tended to be very eclectic, adopting philosophical traditions that could be used to give intellectual foundation to their religious goals. Their main purpose was to meet religious needs. This is the phenomenon that Gilbert Murray referred to as a failure of nerve.[1]

The ultimate development of a pagan philosophical religion in the Roman era was Neo-Platonism, but it was preceded by Middle Platonism and Neo-Pythagoreanism, which provided some of the concepts that were employed by Neo-Platonism.

Middle Platonism

Middle Platonic thought emphasized divine transcendence and intermediary beings between God and humanity, along with other mystical elements. Both ideas, the transcendence of the highest deity and the intermediaries, seem to be responses to religious desires that have been seen in other eras. In a time when life is very hard and evil appears common, the religious mind seems to want to put God above and beyond all that is wrong in the world. At the same time, a completely transcendent God is too distant to be approachable or available to succor and assist his devotees. What happened in the Roman era appears to be psychologically the same as what occurred in Byzantine Christianity, which can be seen in the church art of the time; Jesus

Christ became an austere figure, usually pictured as the stern judge of the last judgment, and Mary became the approachable representative of heaven. With the Middle Platonists, the concept of God had reached a state of development that justifies use of the capital "G."

There are two well-known representatives of Middle Platonism, Plutarch and Philo of Alexandria. Plutarch was a prolific writer, best known for his *Lives* of famous Greeks and Romans and *Moralia,* a collection of essays on moral subjects, as well as other works on philosophical and religious subjects. Born in the middle of the first century B.C., Plutarch studied in Athens, visited Rome, and learned Latin literature.

Plutarch was an eclectic thinker, influenced especially by ideas of the Platonists and Aristotelians, but opposed to the Skepticism of the New Academy and generally against the Stoics, possibly because, as R.H. Barrow holds, he did not understand the Stoicism current in his time. There was much in Stoic teaching that should have appealed to him. He was not so much a critical and creative thinker as a moral teacher, and it is surprising that he did not appreciate the moral earnestness of the Stoics. Barrow thinks that he was put off by some of the thought of the Old Stoa and was not aware of the practical and moral approach of Roman Stoicism, as can be seen in his essay *On the Self-contradictions of the Stoics.*[2]

Plutarch sought a reasonable and universal approach to religion, along with common sense and good morals.[3] He stressed the transcendence of God, whose nature cannot be known in this life, a common view among the Middle Platonists and Neo-Pythagoreans. Plutarch was opposed to atheism but was more strongly opposed to religious superstition. He saw superstition not as belief in divinities but as dread of them as the cause of pain and injury, an approach that "utterly humbles and crushes a man."[4] Plutarch referred to the classical gods and goddesses, treating them as aspects of the universal deity. He did not totally reject the Egyptian use of animal symbols for God. He was critical of most religious festivals and sacrifices and the worship of idols as deities, not symbols of the one deity. He accepted oracles and revelations in dreams, but he saw a danger in superstitious attitudes toward them.[5]

Plutarch's theology included belief in demons and lesser gods and goddesses as intermediaries between God and humanity. He attributed evil and the imperfection of the world to an evil principle and to demons. In this dualistic approach, God is not responsible for any wrong or imperfection. In his essay *Isis and Osiris,* evil is personified as Typhon, the enemy of Isis. Frederick Copleston says that the evil principle seems for Plutarch to have become the world soul that created the earth but that remains in opposition to the divine goodness.[6] The human soul shares the good and evil aspects of the world, having a good part associated with reason and an evil part associated with bodily desires and personified as Typhon, which is "impressionable, impulsive, irrational, and truculent."[7]

Plutarch's concept of salvation was the Platonic notion of eventual release of the soul from rebirths, but he does not present a clear picture of the afterlife. He seems to have held that good souls are reincarnated in human form, but bad souls might become plants or nonhuman animals. Souls of the very virtuous are said in his *Life of Romulus* to become heroes, then demigods, and finally gods.[8]

Philo Judaeus, who was born about 25 B.C. in Alexandria and died about 40 A.D., was a product of diaspora Judaism, that is, Judaism in Roman cities, away from Jerusalem. In his time more Jews lived outside Judea than in it, and many of them spoke Greek and had little or no knowledge of Hebrew. Their holy scripture was the Septuagint, a Greek version of the Hebrew bible, and they were exposed to Greek ideas. Interestingly, Philo wrote about Essene and Therapeutae, Jewish cults that reflected Greek ideas in their theology and religious life.[9] The religious communities that produced the Dead Sea scrolls seem to be similar to the religious communities described by Philo.

Philo wrote in *koiné* Greek, a simplified version of Greek used throughout the Roman territories. He cited passages from the Greek translations of the Hebrew scriptures. He also shows familiarity with a wide range of Greek literature.

Philo attempted a reconciliation of Jewish scripture and Greek philosophy, especially Plato, as interpreted by Middle Platonism, and some Stoic ideas. Samuel Sandmel says that Philo's basic religious ideas were Jewish, but he explained them in terms of Greek philosophy, largely Platonic and Stoic.[10]

The reconciliation of Hebrew scripture and Greek philosophy was an exercise in the use of allegory, by which the scriptures were interpreted on two levels, the literal level and a higher nonliteral level. Philo seems to have believed that scripture is true on both levels, but his interest was obviously in the nonliteral philosophical level. On the higher level, characters in Hebrew history were interpreted as people who represent virtues or traits. Some of Philo's allegories were based on the Hebrew roots of the people's names, but when these were not suitable to him he made up meanings. The allegories frequently seem forced upon the biblical text, and some of them are quite strained.[11]

An example of Philo's allegorical interpretation is his using Abraham's journeys as an allegory for spiritual development. The story in Genesis 14 of Abraham's war with four kings allied with the king of Sodom and four kings from Eastern nations represented for Philo the warfare between the mind and the five senses and four passions, a struggle to which any Platonist could relate.

Philo was a very prolific writer. His writings were not only numerous but diverse. Sandmel describes the kinds of works Philo wrote, and a listing of his titles is in volume X of the Loeb Classical Library edition of his works.[12]

Philo adopted the Platonic distinction between the sensible and the intelligible and related it to spiritual development. His interest in numbers, which he credited to the Pythagoreans, was not in using them intellectually like Plato but the product of an interest in numerology.[13]

Philo called God "To On" (*to ón*), which is a definite article and a participial form of the verb to be. It means, literally, "the Being." Later on Plotinus held that God is too transcendent to be described as existing, but Philo had no difficulty with his description. In other respects, however, Philo described a God who was as transcendent and unknowable as the deity described by the Neo-Platonists.

To the transcendence of God Philo also joined the concept of intermediary beings. This partly anticipates the role of such beings in Neo-Platonism. Philo wrote of a Logos, a Divine Reason possessing the ideas that are the intelligible realm. He described the Logos as the first-born son of God, which was one of the aspects of Philo's work that appealed to the Christians who preserved his writings. As the possessor of archetypal ideas, the Logos would have an important role in the creation of the world. The Logos does not leave the intelligible world.[14]

In addition to the Logos, Philo also wrote of Powers, which are described as activities of God in creation and governance of the world; they are subordinate to the Logos, and unlike the Logos they act in the sensible world. Their relation to the Logos is similar to that between Plotinus's Divine Intellect and World Soul (see below).[15]

Lesser known Middle Platonists treated the transcendent God and the intermediary beings as trinities. Eudorus of Alexandria in the first century B.C. described a trinity consisting of the supreme God, from whom proceeds "the one," and indeterminate duality; in Pythagorean thought, the one represents order and duality disorder. Albinus, in the second century A.D., fused Platonic and Aristotelian elements to create a trinity of the first God, mind, and soul (*psyche*). He held that the first God is the unmoved mover, mind possesses the Platonic ideas, and psyche is a world soul, as in Plato's *Timaeus*. Maximus of Tyre, in the second century A.D., held that there are lesser gods and demons, a view we saw in Plutarch; and Apuleius, also in the second century, included the Olympian deities and the Platonic forms in a hierarchy of lesser gods.[16]

Neo-Pythagoreanism

After a long period of obscurity, Pythagoreanism emerged as an influential religious sect, and in the second century A.D., highly eclectic thinkers such as Nicomachus of Gerasa and Numenius of Apamea combined elements from Plato, Aristotle, and the Stoics with Pythagorean mathematical concepts, a strong soul/body dualism, and mystical elements such as revelation and direct intuition of the deity. They also developed trinities that used Platonic and Aristotelian concepts as divine principles.[17]

Neo-Platonism

The founder of Neo-Platonism, Ammonius Saccas, was a highly respected teacher in Alexandria in the first half of the third century A.D. Little is known of his life; he left no writings, but his lectures were considered brilliant. Many talented pupils attested to his greatness. One of his best-known pupils was Plotinus, whose book *The Enneads* is the primary source of knowledge about Neo-Platonic thought.

The parents of Plotinus were Roman citizens living in Egypt. He was born about 204 A.D. He had little interest in talking about his early life and placed little value on living in a body. We know the little we do about his life from a biography written by his pupil Porphyry. At age twenty-eight Plotinus was a pupil in Alexandria of Ammonius Saccas, with whom he studied for eleven years. Upon the death of Ammonius, he went with the Emperor Gordian on a military expedition in order to study the wisdom of the East. When Gordian was assassinated, Plotinus went to Rome, where he was well received and gained considerable prominence. He died in retirement in 270 A.D. after a long illness.[18]

Philosophical Religion

Plotinus was a religious thinker who used philosophy, primarily that of Plato, to explain and support his religious views. In his writing he talked about mystical experience, and Porphyry reported that four times he became one with God, which sounds like the *via negativa* (negative way) mysticism of some Jewish and Christian mystics.[19]

Plotinus did not write until he was fifty years old, by which time he was losing his eyesight. He wrote with little regard for style or penmanship. Porphyry edited these writings to some extent and published them in six groups of nine chapters. The book is known as *The Enneads,* that is, "The Nines." Plotinus's writings are often repetitious and obscure, but in the main points they are the profoundest and most philosophical development of pagan religion in the Roman period.

Plotinus based his doctrines primarily on the philosophy of Plato, but they should not be treated as an explication of Plato's thought. Unlike Plato, Plotinus was not interested in governmental matters, nor was philosophical exploration and discussion an important concern for him. He used elements from Platonic thought dogmatically in support of philosophical paganism. His use of Plato was selective, but he employed some of the basic ideas of Platonism. He based his thought on the mythological notions of the fall of the soul when it entered material human life, and the reincarnation of the soul and its final salvation when it escaped from the flesh. We cannot tell whether Plato believed literally in these ideas, which seem to have originated in Orphism and to have been adopted by the Pythagoreans, but Plotinus treats them with a greater seriousness than did Plato. In addition he adopted the Platonic concept of the difference between sensible things and an unchanging intelligible reality. What Plato saw as the philosophical need to overcome the allure of the world of the senses and to attend to intelligible truth, Plotinus saw as the way of religious salvation. Correct thought was a central aspect of his religious program. Through dialectic one is able to rise above the sensible and grasp the intelligible. Dialectic, he held, is one part of philosophy, the most important part.[20]

The Deity

Plotinus described God as a trinity of the One, the Divine Intellect, and the World Soul. The highest nature of God, the One, is too transcendent to be described as soul, mind, active reason, or anything in the sensible or intelligible realms, or even to be said to exist. In this central aspect, God is utterly inscrutable, even transcending the realm of ideas. There can be no adequate name for the One. Plotinus thought of God as absolute unity, but held that God is not a substance that has unity as an attribute. The unity of God is not that of a numerical unit or a geometrical point. The One is indivisible, not in respect to magnitude, for the One does not occupy space, but in respect to power and self-sufficiency. Other terms for God are even more problematical. The One can be called good but is superior to goodness and may be called good by analogy, as it is good for the things that participate in the deity. The One cannot be described as being or beauty or intellect, although the One is the source of these things.[21]

The One can be known only in mystical ecstasy, a state in which all distinctions, such as those between subject and object, thinking and what is thought, are transcended. It is impossible to describe the One, who has no determinate form.[22] Union with the One cannot be described as one would describe an earthly encounter. Certain aspects of this union will be discussed below.

Emanation

It is the nature of the One to expend divine reality by a process of emanation until all levels of reality are realized. Emanation is a sort of effusion or outflowing of divine reality, by which the One produces the Divine Intellect and, through the Intellect, the World Soul. The World Soul produces the world. Plotinus compared emanation to the sun's giving of heat and light. The One is not diminished by these emanations, just as Plotinus thought the sun was not diminished. Plotinus considered the emanation of the two lesser parts of the trinity and finally the world to be necessary. The One is the source of all things. If the One were alone, there would be nothing in existence. The One begets all things but is not one of them, not even Being or Intelligence. The One does not think.[23]

The first emanation is the Divine Intellect, which is pure contemplation, perceiving at a glance the whole of reality. It does not think discursively, that is, moving from one topic to another. In the Divine Intellect are ideas of particulars as well as of generalities. These ideas are the *protoi lógoi* of Stoic thought, the *lógoi spermatikoi* or "seed ideas," that are reflected in the World Soul and are known in medieval thought as seminal reasons. The Divine Intellect possesses ideas of everything that is real, but all things in the Intellect are good; there is no evil and no thing that decays. Plotinus speaks of these ideas in the Intellect as existing and spoke of intelligence and being as one nature. The Divine Intellect contemplates the One and is aware of its separation from the One.[24]

The second emanation is the World Soul, which possesses the ideas of the Divine Intellect but engages in discursive and synthetic reasoning. Time emerges with the World Soul, which thinks in time, one thing after another, and addresses itself to things in the changing world. The World Soul contemplates the Divine Intellect and knows its separation from the Intellect. It is important that the separation of the three aspects of the divine trinity not be thought of in spatial terms. The members of the trinity are not material entities but are omnipresent in all reality.[25]

Plotinus attributed to Plato the view that there are levels of being and identified the World Soul with Plato's world soul.[26]

Human Souls

Individual souls are parts of the World Soul, but have a distinct identity. Their existence does not diminish the World Soul. The soul is not extended, not a body or a harmony of parts of the body. It is an intelligible being and part of the divine. Souls are tripartite, with reason, desire, and spiritedness. They are also described as having a lower part that is turned toward the body and a higher part turned toward the mind. Plotinus qualified this by saying that the body has faculties, not parts; reason, desire, and perception are faculties of the soul.[27]

Plotinus spoke of the soul's entering the body as a descent, which was necessary to make the universe complete, and he described the soul as being imprisoned in the body; but the soul does not enter the body completely, and it can turn toward the intellect. Souls forget their origin in the divine, however, and love and seek earthly things. The salvation of the soul lies in an ascent above bodily matters and the senses. This ascent is in contemplation of the World Soul and the Divine Intellect, and in ceasing to love sensible things but loving the intelligible.[28]

The ascent of the soul in contemplation is a mystical experience that is difficult to explain because it transcends the particularities, distinctions, and separations of ordinary experience. After the mystical experience, God, the One, still cannot be described because of the nature of the experience and the nature of the One.[29]

Contemplation of the deity is accomplished through intelligence, but this union with and knowledge of the One does not come through science or pure thought, as we know other things. Science involves discursive reasoning and multiplicity and when so engaged the soul does not act in its unity; but in contemplation, through the intellect, the soul acts as a unity. To enter into contemplation, the soul must be in a purified state; it must be turned away from the sensible, from external things; it must forget all things. It must lose its sense of personal identity.[30]

Plotinus described the mystical experience of union with the deity as a divine dance in which the soul sees the source of life, intelligence, and being; it sees the cause of good and the source of the soul. He said it is happiness and bliss, comparable to the bliss of sexual union but directed toward a reality that does not perish. The soul is part of the eternal divinity, at one with the One.[31]

Mystical experiences are not permanent. The soul cannot stay in the world above; it is not yet completely detached from earthly things. The ultimate salvation of the soul lies ahead in an eventual reunion with the One, in which the soul is no longer aware of its history in the body. Scholars do not agree on how Plotinus viewed the role of reincarnation in the future of the soul. He said that souls are reincarnated in bodies, the nature of which is determined by the dominant part of the soul in the past life; those dominated by appetite become plants, and those too spirited become wild animals, but there is some doubt regarding his literal belief in the rebirth as vegetable or beast.[32]

The Sensible World

Emanation of the sensible world is not the same as that of the divine trinity and human souls. In the emanation of the Divine Intellect, the World Soul, and human souls there is no diminution of being, while in the emanation of the world there is a mixture of being and matter. In

the emanation beyond soul there is a diminution of being, an unform-
ing. In this metaphysical doctrine, matter is nothing; it is an absence of
being. Matter, which is nothing in itself, becomes the principle of evil
as negation or privation. In his descriptions of matter, Plotinus mixed
Platonic and Aristotelian concepts. Matter was described both as a
substratum with the potentiality to embody form and as a nothingness,
comparable to a shadow or an illusion.[33] Plotinus attacked the
Gnostics' claim that the world is evil, however. It is a faithful copy of
the intelligible world from which its reality comes. The emanation of
the divine in order to realize all levels of reality makes the existence of
the world necessary. The world cannot be as perfect as its archetypes,
but no world can be better. Plotinus blamed wicked behavior on individual souls, but these souls were necessary to make the universe
complete. Souls are free in the sense of being self-determined; they can
turn away from the sensible to the reality of the intelligible. The individual soul is free when acting rationally.[34]

The Arts and Reality

Plotinus's aesthetic theory is closer to Aristotle's than to Plato's. He
saw art as revealing the form in an object or event, enabling the reality
to be observed more clearly than it can be seen in the object itself.[35] It
was this aesthetic approach that was followed by subsequent Platonists, including the influential Platonic Academy in Florence during
the Renaissance.

Successors and Influence of Plotinus

Porphyry, in the third century A.D., was the pupil, biographer, and
editor of Plotinus. His most important work, in addition to editing the
Enneads was a commentary on Aristotle's *Categories,* an important
book for medieval philosophers. Porphyry stressed the religious aspect
of Neo-Platonism and was an important opponent of Christianity.

Porphyry's pupil, Iamblichus, a fourth century Syrian, was less philosophical than his teacher; he increased the number of elements in the
divine hierarchy and added occult elements such as miracles, divination, angels, and demons. Pupils of Iamblichus added polytheism.

Proclus, a fifth century Athenian, wrote commentaries on various
works of Plato. He was well acquainted with philosophers of the Neo-

Platonic tradition as well as with Plato and Aristotle, but he was not a very systematic thinker, and he included many additions and subdivisions in the basic Neo-Platonic scheme of emanations.

Alexandrian Neo-Platonists were more interested in science and logic; they were more philosophical and placed less emphasis on religion. They tended generally to avoid superstitious elements and complicated speculations.

The influence of Neo-Platonism would be hard to exaggerate. Until the works of Plato were made available to Western scholars by Marsilio Ficino during the Renaissance, only the *Timaeus* was available. Plato was known through the writings of Neo-Platonists. The influence of Plato on philosophy during this long period was the influence of Neo-Platonism.

19 AUGUSTINE

Augustine was born in 354 A.D. in North Africa of a Christian mother and a pagan father, who was later converted to Christianity. He studied and taught in Carthage, then in Rome and Milan, and was greatly influenced by Ambrose, Bishop of Milan. He devoted nine years to the study of Manichaeism, a dualistic religious movement that he eventually decided could not answer his questions; he studied the writings of Plotinus and was a student of Christianity. After a religious experience he converted to Christianity. He became a zealous leader in the church and was made Bishop of Hippo.

Augustine's best known writings are the *Confessions* and *De civitate dei* (The City of God), but he wrote *De trinitate* (On the Trinity), *De doctrina christiana* (On Christian Doctrine), *De libero arbitrio* (The Problem of Free Choice) and numerous other theological works and attacks on heretical groups. Much of his extensive writing is of little philosophical interest; it is devotional literature and works on liturgical and other church matters. Most of his theological treatises expounded Christian beliefs on the basis of tradition and authority, but within his works are argued positions, what is called philosophical theology, and these passages are of philosophical interest.

Augustine was the church's main defender against certain heresies of his time. He was well-suited to play this role because of his firm belief in doctrines such as original sin, which the heresies called into question. It is possible that his role as opponent of these heresies might have strengthened his commitment to the doctrines. As he looked back on his life, he saw himself as exceedingly wicked, even though he was an obedient child, a good student, and certainly not wild or debauched. He had a relationship with a woman who bore him a child, but his mother made him send the woman back to North Africa, which may have been the most wrongful aspect of his whole early life.[1]

Attitude Toward Philosophy

Augustine was first and foremost a theologian, but he had an unusual appreciation of philosophy, especially Platonic thought. Unlike Tertullian and some other Christian leaders, he did not scorn everything of pagan origin. He did not oppose use of music or the pagan classics. He held that wherever truth is found, it belongs to God.[2] He was selective in his use of philosophy, however, being favorable toward Platonic thought but rejecting much of Aristotle and the Stoics. He considered religious faith primary; even though he evinced curiosity about philosophical questions, he gave believing primacy over knowing. As should be expected, the various aspects of Augustine's thought are presented in the context of his theology.

Theology

Augustine's concept of the deity is that of orthodox theism. In his *Confessions* he recalls his growth in thought about God as he moved toward his understanding that God is one, eternal, unchanging, impassible, omnipotent, all-knowing, and omni-present. Neo-Platonists would accept many of these qualities of God, but Augustine's theology built also on ideas from Hebrew culture, such as the emphasis on the goodness of God and God's concern for individual persons. He held that God is the creator and sustainer of the world, not out of necessity as the Platonists held, but out of his divine love. He held that God is too transcendent to be completely comprehended by reason, but such concepts as "good," "wise," and "omnipotent" approximate his nature.[3]

Augustine described the Son, the second person of the divine trinity, in terms that are compatible with Neo-Platonic ideas about the Divine Intellect and World Soul, such as the possession of the Platonic forms. He said that all things are in the Son.[4]

Frederick Copleston holds that even though Augustine employed several arguments to prove the existence of God, such as the necessity of a first cause, the rational nature of the universe, and universal belief in the existence of God, the most important argument was built on understanding God as the ground of eternal and necessary truths.[5]

Some of Augustine's writings show his belief that knowledge of the truth points to the existence of God. In *De libero arbitrio,* for example, he wrote of unchanging truth and called it the supreme good next to God himself. He wrote, "if there is anything more excellent (than truth), it is this which is God, but if there is nothing more excellent, then truth itself is God. Which ever is the fact, you cannot deny that God exists. . ."[6]

Paul Tillich interpreted Augustine as more mystical, less rationalistic, in his approach to God's existence. Augustine, he said, understood the relationship to God not as meeting a stranger but as being reconciled with a friend from whom one has become estranged. According to Tillich, *"God is the presupposition of the question of God.* This is the ontological solution of the problem of the philosophy of religion. God can never be reached if He is the *object* of a question and not its *basis."* Tillich held that Augustine's view is the approach taken by the medieval Franciscans; he contrasts it to the approach of Thomas Aquinas and the Benedictines.[7]

Support for Tillich's interpretation of Augustine can be found in Augustine's writings. In the *Confessions* he wrote that God has created us for himself and our hearts are restless until they find their rest in him. Strong support for seeing the soul's relationship to God as reconciliation is found especially in the *Third Discourse on Psalm 32,* in which he wrote, "In your soul is the image of God; the human mind contains that image. It received it and by stooping to sin defiled it. He comes to refashion it who first of all fashioned it."[8]

Creation of the World

Augustine's view of creation of the world, the orthodox view of Judaism and Christianity, is that the world was created by God out of nothing (*ex nihilo*). This view of creation stands in opposition to Aristotle's view that the world is eternal, Plato's view of a creation out of previously existing material that is ordered according to the forms, and Plotinus's concept of creation by emanation from divine reality, interpretations of the origin of the world that Augustine saw as contrary to the Christian position.[9]

Had the world been eternal or made of preexisting matter, the world or some aspect of it would be coeternal with God, which is contrary to theistic belief. Belief in creation of the world by emanation tends toward pantheism, or identification of the material world with God; this tendency remained a problem for theologians for centuries. Giordano Bruno was burned at the stake in the sixteenth century on the suspicion that he held such beliefs.

Augustine's doctrine of creation was not simple. He held that matter was created *ex nihilo* before time as a formless something (prime matter). In itself, matter is a "nothing," but it can receive form. Matter is infused with seminal reasons (which we saw originally as the Stoic *lógoi spermatikoi*), which are created by God. The appearance of entities in the material world is the actualization of forms that are already present in matter as seminal reasons. This enables the whole of creation to occur at once, before time, thus solving the theological problem of an unchanging God acting in time.[10]

The Problem of Evil

Augustine faced the theological problem of reconciling evil in the world with the goodness, power, and knowledge of its creator. He employed several arguments to account for evil. One argument builds on the Neo-Platonic concept of evil as an unavoidable aspect of a material world. Augustine argued, against the Gnostics, that the world is good and beautiful. Matter itself is not evil, but it suffers an absence of being; it is good in that it has form, but in itself it is deficient. The world's limited goodness is necessary and not the fault of God.[11]

This account of evil worked better with Neo-Platonism, in which the formation of the world was a necessary and un-willed result of divine reality, than it does with a theistic concept of creation as an act of loving will. Augustine did not accept the Neo-Platonic concept of emanation. Trying to combine the notions of a willed creation and evil as a necessary absence of being is something of a *tour de force*.

Augustine also argued that apparent evils are good in the total providence of God. This aesthetic argument holds that what seems to be evil is good in the total order of things. Augustine used the example of sounds in music that, unpleasant in themselves, contribute to the beauty of the whole work.[12] This is like the Stoic claim that everything works for the good, and like it, must appeal to faith that the whole of reality is better than the parts we are experiencing.

In explaining moral evil, Augustine blamed it on the individual person; he employed the concept of an evil will, the perverted will. An evil will makes itself evil by desiring lower things; the evil will is not totally corrupt, but it is deficient in goodness.[13] The followers of the Pelagian heresy denied original sin; they held that new souls are sinless and have free will, which enables them to choose whether they will sin. Augustine led the church's fight against the Pelagian heresy; in arguing against Pelagius, Augustine stressed the importance of original sin. The doctrine of original sin held that humans are corrupted by the disobedience of the first man and woman. They are unable to use their full powers to be morally good without special help from God.[14]

The Human Soul

Augustine held that the soul is not material, but a spiritual entity or substance. Each soul is created by God. Augustine did not believe that the soul is preexistent or that it emanates from God. Augustine also leaned toward traducianism, the belief that the soul is inherited from the parents, to explain the transmission of original sin; this is not consistent, however, with his other beliefs about the soul. Augustine's approach to the relationship between soul and body was dualistic; he held that a person is a union of soul and body, and he spoke of the soul using a body.[15]

The existence of the soul is not in doubt; Augustine held that the soul knows that it is, that it lives, and that it has understanding. He gave a proof of the existence of the soul which anticipates Descartes' famous proof, "I think, therefore I am." Augustine said that even if he doubted his existence he must exist (*dubito ergo sum*), and even if he only dreamed that he existed or his thoughts were mistaken (*si fallor, sum*), his existence is still demonstrated.[16]

Augustine used several arguments for the immortality of the soul, including the Platonic argument that the soul is the principle of life and death is its contrary. He also argued from the soul's apprehension of eternal truths and the soul's desire for beatitude. The latter argument considers belief in immortality to be a response to the soul's relationship with God. It follows that nonhuman animal souls, lacking apprehension of eternal truth and the desire for beatitude, are not immortal.[17]

Free Will and Divine Foreknowledge

In combating the heresies of his time Augustine stressed divine foreknowledge, but he wanted to show that there is no contradiction between this doctrine and freedom of the will. In arguing that God does not know events "before" they happen, he appealed to the eternity of God, his being entirely outside of time, and presented a picture of the divine intellect similar to that of Plotinus's Divine Intellect. It knows all things at once, without discursive thought. Augustine held that all time is present to God, and events are "before" and "after" only to human consciousness. Even though this line of thought has an impressive history, it does not of itself show that the human will is free. Augustine coupled the idea with the claim that God works through the human will; the will is part of God's orderly providence. Augustine may be seen as combining Neo-Platonic and Stoic notions. He wanted to show that even though God has what we interpret as foreknowledge, it is the human person who chooses.[18]

Time

An example of Augustine's interest in philosophical issues because of his theological concerns is his approach to the question of time. Augustine held that God is eternal, which means that God is not in time or affected by time. God, Augustine held, created time. Augustine understood time in relation to motion; time exists in the motion of a body, in its passing, but it is not the motion itself. The first moving bodies created by God were the angels, and their movement marked the first moment of time.[19]

While the relationship between time and motion had been explained similarly by Aristotle, Augustine did not stop here. He examined the experience of time, holding that all time is present as the present of things past, the present of things present, or the present of things future. He was explaining time as an experienced continuum.[20]

Augustine's interest in time was not primarily a matter of phenomenological curiosity, however; it was related for him to theology and the philosophy of history. A central premise of theism is that time is not cyclical, as the pagans believed, but is linear, moving from a beginning in the creation to a fulfillment in God's victory over evil at the end of time. A cyclical interpretation of time, with history meaning a recurrence of the seasons or the epochs that have occurred before, views such as we have seen often explicitly stated in the philosophies we have studied, is contrary to the divine revelation on which Judaism, Christianity, and Islam are based. A marked difference between the theistic religions and paganism is in their concept of history. Theistic religions are called historical religions, which does not mean that they are old, but that they place great importance on history as the story of salvation. It begins with creation and concludes with God's triumph, which is somewhat differently described by the three theistic religions.[21]

Augustine explains unfolding history as warfare between the City of God, which consists of those in all ages who are faithful to God, and the Earthly City, composed of those who are not devoted to God. He sees Cain as the first member of the Earthly City and Abel as the first member of the City of God. Sarah was of the City of God, Hagar of the Earthly City.[22] He continues through several chapters of *De Civitate Dei* to trace the warfare of good against evil in biblical times and more recently. Finally, the City of God will triumph and its members enjoy a heavenly reward; the wicked will suffer eternally in hell, which Augustine saw as an actual place of physical punishment in material fire. Augustine did not consider the church the City of God; as closely related as the two are, he saw that the membership of the two is not identical.[23]

Knowledge

Augustine's treatment of epistemological questions was also in the context of his theological concerns, which were knowing and loving God. Even though God is too transcendent for reason to grasp his nature fully, Augustine had no doubt that the faithful could know God; he rejected Skepticism and wrote against the Skeptics of the New Academy. He was not interested in arguments about whether knowledge in possible; his question was how knowledge comes about. His writing on knowledge is scattered throughout numerous works.[24]

Augustine did not deny the usefulness or reliability of sense experience; he considered it a gift from God. He recognized the superficiality of skepticism based on the supposed failures of sense perception. The senses do not lie—they give the impressions they should in every circumstance; for example, in water an oar should look bent. Sense impressions are relative to the physical condition of the person sensing.

Augustine did not want to exalt sense experience above higher aspects of intellect, however. He wanted it understood that in sense experience the body does not act upon the soul; the soul uses the body in perception as it perceives changes made in the body by external stimuli. Although sense experience is reliable, it cannot give knowledge of eternal truths. Things of the world are not the most worthy objects of intellect; there can be no real knowledge of such things because they are mutable and deficient. We do learn something from our sense experience and the experience of other people, however, even though sense-knowledge is the lowest and least certain part of our knowledge. This kind of knowledge is practical, directed toward action in pursuit of the necessities of life. It is a lower use of the intellect than is wisdom, which is exercised in contemplation.[25]

Memory plays an important role in knowledge. Augustine equates memory and mind: "Memory itself is mind."[26] He defines the contents of memory broadly. In addition to images of past experiences, it contains emotions and learning, including knowledge that does not come directly from sense experience, in the sense of something remembered with the aid of mental images. This knowledge is produced by the mind, which organizes scattered bits of experience. Also attributed to memory are more abstract types of knowledge, including analytic truths.[27]

Augustine held that some things can be known with certainty. Some of these are analytic truths, logical and mathematical. Others rest on self-awareness, which Augustine treats as knowledge. The fact of doubting, the fact that we receive sense impressions, and the fact of one's own existence as a living, understanding, and willing being are known with certainty.[28]

Augustine held that only a few people can attain knowledge of eternal truths. Sense experience alone cannot give this level of knowledge, which is accomplished by divine illumination. The philosophical inspiration for the concept of divine illumination seems to have been Plato's parable of the sun and the Form of the Good, in which things are made visible or intelligible. As Frederick Copleston interprets Augustine, the divine illumination does not impart eternal ideas to the mind but enables the mind to recognize, by its illumination, that they are eternal truths. Augustine is not clear about how the mind forms these ideas, and he claims that only a few minds form them. Perhaps the ideas are formed by a process of abstraction from sense experience.[29]

Ethics and Social Theory

Augustine followed Plato in relating virtue to wisdom. He looked upon moral goodness as both an end in itself, a life enlightened by knowledge of God, and the means to happiness, by which he meant beatitude, a state of peace with God. Happiness in not found apart from God, for the human being is a mutable creature and not self-sufficient. As a rational creature, the human seeks God.[30]

Augustine's moral approach is an ethic of love. He accepted Plato's view that all love is erotic (see the chapter on Plato's philosophy of love). He held that all love is *amor,* the Latin equivalent of *eros.*[31] Morality, however, aims at making all love and desire a striving for God, the true good. Virtue is the right ordering of love, directing it to God, the only right object of love. This does not forbid love of one's spouse or child or love of neighbor, but one must love God through these loves.

That our good actions are done in love of God is critically important to Augustine. Virtuous acts done without reference to God or inflated with pride are actually vice. The ethic of love is obviously not an easy or sentimental matter. Augustine held that a person needs God's help to live morally; he needs not only the divine illumination to show the moral truth, but the help that comes through Christianity. Augustine held that the demands of moral law should drive a person to seek the help of Christ.[32]

Compared to some other church leaders Augustine was not a radical ascetic, but his ethics might seem very demanding. He saw seeking to please the senses as sinful, even in such matters as enjoying food. He advocated taking food as we would medicine, because we need it, but not enjoying it. He believed that sex for procreation was not morally wrong, but he expressed the wish that conception could take place without the pleasure of intercourse.[33]

Augustine's political theory was concerned with the role of the church in society. He did not hold, as we saw above, that the church is the same as the City of God, but the church is superior to the secular state and should influence it. He did not advocate church control over the state, but he believed that only a Christian state can be truly just and moral. He held that the state is established by God for the purpose of punishing the wicked; the members of the City of God should obey the state as an instrument of God. Even bad rulers are sent by God to punish and are given their power by God. Augustine's social and political ideas are most clearly expressed in his concept of the two cities, the City of God and the Earthly City. His interest was primarily theological, though, and his view of the state was secondary to his vision of the eventual triumph of God over all evil.

Augustine died in 430 A.D. as barbarian invaders were breaching the walls of Hippo: His death can be seen as a symbol of the end of an era. He can also be seen as one of the architects of medieval philosophy. His life ended as the so-called Dark Ages, a time that changed the cultural and intellectual life of the West, began, but his writings provided one of the main foundations on which the intellectual life of the Middle Ages was built. He was the premier theologian of Christianity in his day and remained so even when Thomas Aquinas became an important rival, never replacing him. Augustine, then, provided a bridge between the Roman era and the Middle Ages.

NOTES

Chapter One. Greek Cultural Background

1. John Burnet, *Early Greek Philosophy,* 80.
2. W.K.C. Guthrie, *The Greeks and Their Gods,* 132; see also B.A.G. Fuller, *A History of Philosophy,* 17–19.
3. The *Odyssey* XI, 487–491; Fuller *History of Philosophy,* 20.
4. Gilbert Murray, *Five Stages of Greek Religion,* Chapter II, Guthrie, *The Greeks and Their Gods,* 132.
5. Ibid., 130.
6. Fuller, *A History of Philosophy,* 31; Burnet held that "hylozoism" is a misleading term, in that it implies a more developed concept of matter than was available to Ionian thinkers (*Early Greek Philosophy,* 12 *n.3*).
7. For scholarly description of the mystery cults see Harold Willoughby, *Pagan Regeneration: A Study of Mystery Initiations in the Graeco-Roman World,* Chapter II.
8. Ibid., Chapter III.
9. Ibid., 95–97.

Chapter Two. The Primary Stuff and Structure of the World: The Milesians and Pythagoreans

1. Diogenes Laertius, *Lives of Eminent Philosophers* I, 22; Herodotus, *Histories,* Book I (Clio), 74, 75, and 170; Aetius, *Opinions,* I 3, 1, IV 1, 1; Proclus, *In Euclidem,* and others. See Kirk and Raven, *The Presocratic Philosophers,* 74–86, for English translations.
2. Aristotle, *Politics* I, 11, 1259a9.
3. Plato, *Theaetetus* 174a.
4. Simplicius, *Physics;* Diogenes Laertius, *Lives* I, 23.
5. Aristotle, *Metaphysics* Alpha 3, 983b20.
6. Aristotle, *De Caelo* II, 13, 294a28.
7. Aristotle, *De Anima* I, 5, 411a7; Plato, *Laws* 10, 899b; Diogenes Laertius, *Lives* I, 24; Aetius, *Opinions* I, 7, II.

8. Diogenes Laertius, *Lives* II, 1–2; Herodotus, *Histories,* Book II (Euterpé), 109.

9. Themistius, *Orations* 26; Diogenes Laertius, *Lives* II, 1–2.

10. Strabo, *Geography* I.

11. Parts of Theophrastus's account of the *ápeiron* have been preserved in Simplicius, *Physics* 24, 13; Hippolytus, *Refutatio* (Refution of All Heresies) I 6, 1–2; and Pseudo-Plutarch, *Stromateis* 2. See Kirk and Raven, 104–107, for translations. For commentary on Aristotle's treatment of the *ápeiron,* see Kirk and Raven, 110–115.

12. See Kirk and Raven, 109; see also F.M. Cornford, "Mystery Religions and Presocratic Philosophy," in *The Cambridge Ancient History,* vol. 4, 542.

13. Aristotle, *Physics* Alpha 4, 187a20.

14. Pseudo-Plutarch, *Stromateis* 2; Hippolytus, *Refutatio* I, 6, 3–5; Aristotle, *De Caelo* II, 13, 295b10–15.

15. Aetius, *Opinions* V, 19, 4.

16. Pseudo-Plutarch, *Stromateis* 2; Hippolytus, *Refutatio* I, 6, 6; Plutarch, *Symposiakon* VIII, 730E.

17. Diogenes Laertius, *Lives* II, 3.

18. Aristotle, *Metaphysics* Alpha 3, 984a5, *De Caelo* II, 13, 294b13–15, and *Meteorologica* Beta I, 354a28; Simplicius, *Physics* 24, 26; Hippolytus, *Refutatio* I, 7, 1 and 4–6; Plutarch, *De primo frigido* 947F; Pseudo-Plutarch, *Stromateis* 3; Aetius *Opinions* II, 14, 3–4.

19. Appolonius, *Historia miraculorum* 6; Diogenes Laertius, *Lives* VII, 6 and IX, 1.

20. Porphyry, *Vita Pythagorae* 9; Diogenes Laertius, *Lives* VIII, 3; Iamblichus, *Vita Pythagorae* 249; Herodotus, *Histories,* Book IV (Melpomene) 95.

21. Porphyry, *Vita Pythagorae* 19.

22. Diogenes Laertius, *Lives* VIII, 36; Porphyrius, *Vita Pythagorae* 19.

23. Iamblichus, *Protrepticus* 21; Porphyry, *Vita Pythagorae* 7; Diogenes Laertius, *Lives* VIII, 19.

24. Porphyry, *Vita Pythagorae* 37; Aristotle, *Metaphysics* Alpha 5, 985b23; Proclus, *Euclidem.*

25. Aristotle, *Metaphysics* Alpha 5, 985b32.

26. Theophrastus, *De sensu* 25–26.

27. Aetius, *Opinions* V, 30, 1; Aristotle, *Metaphysics* Alpha 5, 985b23–986a8, *Nichomachean Ethics* II, 6, 1106b29; and *De Caelo* II, 9, 290b12.

28. Aristotle, *Metaphysics* Alpha 5, 986a15, Mu 6, 1080b16–20, and Mu 8, 1083b8.

29. Aristotle, *Physics* III, 4, 203a10–15.

30. Aetius, *Opinions* I, 3, 8; Aristotle, *Metaphysics* Alpha 5, 986b8.

31. Aristotle, *Nichomachean Ethics* Beta 5, 1106b29 and *Physics* III 4, 203a10; Simplicius, *Physics* 455, 20.

32. Aristotle, *Metaphysics* Alpha 5, 986a15 and 987a13–19, Alpha 8, 990a18f, Mu 6, 1080b16–20 and 1083b6, and Nu 3, 1090a20; Aetius I, 3, 19.

33. Aristotle, *Metaphysics* Alpha 5, 985b26 and Mu 4, 1078b21.

34. Aristotle, *De Caelo* II, 9, 293a20–25; Simplicius, *De caelo* 511, 26.

35. Diogenes Laertius, *Lives* VIII, 8.

Chapter Three. Change, Stability, and Permanence: Heraclitus and the Eleatics

1. Diogenes Laertius, *Lives* IX, 1 and 6.
2. *Ibid.* IX, 1; Clement, *Stromateis* V, 104, 1 and 3; Plutarch, *De E apud delphos* 8, 388 D; Sextus Empiricus, *Adversus mathematicos* (Against the Professors) VII, 129; Aristocritus, *Theosophia* 68; Clement, *Protrepticus* 22 and 34.
3. Diogenes Laertius, *Lives* IX, 1 and 5. See Kirk and Raven, *The Presocratic Philosophers,* 183.
4. Aristotle, *Physics* Theta 3, 253b9; Eusebius, *Praeparatio Evangelica* (Preparation for the Gospel) XV, 20; Plutarch, *De E* 18, 392B; Plato, *Cratylus* 402A; Hippolytus, *Refutatio* IX, 9, 1 and IX, 10, 4.
5. Sextus Empiricus, *Adversus mathematicos* VII, 132 and 133; Pseudo-Plutarch, *Consolation to Apollonius* 10, 106E; Pseudo-Aristotle, *De mundo* 5, 396b20; Hippolytus, *Refutatio* IX, 10, 8.
6. See Kirk and Raven, *The Presocratic Philosophers,* 161, 200.
7. Clement, *Stromateis* V, 104, 1 and 3; Plutarch, *De E* 8, 388 D.
8. Origen, *Contra Celsus* VI, 42; Hippolytus, *Refutatio* IX, 9, 4; Aristotle, *Eudemean Ethics* Eta I, 1235a25.
9. Diogenes Laertius, *Lives* IX, 9–10; Aristotle, *Meteorologica* Beta 2, 355a13; Plutarch, *De exilio* II, 604A.
10. Aristotle, *Physics* Theta 3, 253b9; Sextus Empiricus *Adversus mathematicos* VII, 132; Themistius, *Orations* 5; Hippolytus, *Refutatio* IX, 9, 5; Diogenes Laertius, *Lives* IX, 1.
11. Clement, *Stromateis* VI, 17, 2; Stobaeus, *Anthologium* III, 5, 7 and 8.
12. Clement, *Stromateis* I, 64, 2; Diogenes Laertius, *Lives* IX, 21–23; The *Suda,* "Zenon."
13. Diogenes Laertius, *Lives* IX, 18; Plato, *Sophist* 242D; Aristotle, *Metaphysics* Alpha 5, 986b18; Simplicius, *Physics* 22, 26.
14. Sextus Empiricus, *Adversus mathematicos* IX, 193; Diogenes Laertius, *Lives* VIII, 36 and IX,18; Clement, *Stromateis* V, 109, 2 and 3; VII, 22, 1.
15. Clement, *Stromateis* V, 109, 1; Aeschylus, *Supplices* 96–103; Simplicius, *Physics* 23, 11 and 20; Sextus Empiricus, *Adversus mathematicos* IX, 144.
16. Sextus Empiricus, *Adversus mathematicos* VII, 49 and 110; Plutarch, *Symposiakon* IX, 7, 746B; Stobaeus *Anthologium* I, 8, 2.
17. Simplicius, *Physics* 189, 1; Sextus Empiricus, *Adversus mathematicos* X, 34; Hippolytus, *Refutatio* I, 14, 5.
18. Plato, *Parmenides* 127A; Diogenes Laertius, *Lives* IX, 21–23; Strabo 6, p. 252; Plutarch, *Adversus Coloten* 32, 1126A.
19. See Kathleen Freeman, *Ancilla to the Pre-Socratic Philosophers,* 41–46 for translations of fragments of the poem.
20. Aristotle, *De Anima* Alpha 2, 404a16; Proclus, *In Timaeum* I, 345, (Diels 18, frag. 2 and 3); Simplicius, *Physics* 117, 4 and 147, 7; Plato, *Sophist* 237 A; Sextus Empiricus, *Adversus mathematicos* VII, 114.
21. Simplicius, *Physics* 145, 1, 23, and 28; 146, 15.
22. *Ibid.,* 30, 14 and 180, 9; Theophrastus, *Epitome of Physical Opinions* frag.

6 and *De sensu* 1–3; Aristotle, *Metaphysics* Alpha 5, 986b31; Simplicius, *Physics* 31, 13 and 39, 14.

23. Kirk and Raven, 286; Strabo 6; *The Suda,* "Zenon."

24. Plato, *Parmenides* 128c. 29; Simplicius, *Physics* 139, 8, 140, 29, and 141, 1.

25. Aristotle, *Physics* Zeta 9, 239b9, 11, and 14; Aristotle, *Topics* Theta 8, 160b7.

26. Aristotle, *Physics* Zeta 9, 239b30 and 33; Kirk and Raven, 296.

27. Diogenes Laertius, *Lives* IX, 24; Plutarch, *Pericles* 26; Simplicius, *Physics* 29, 22 and 109, 20, 31 and 34; Simplicius, *De caelo* 558, 21; Hippolytus, *Refutatio* 1, 11, 2.

Chapter Four. Reconciliation of Eleaticism and Experience: The Pluralists and Atomists

1. Diogenes Laertius, *Lives* VIII, 51, 62, and 74; Aristotle, *Metaphysics* Alpha 3, 984a11; Simplicius, *Physics* 25, 19; Clement, *Stromateis* VI, 30.

2. Hippolytus, *Refutatio* VII, 29; Plutarch, *De exilio* 17, 607c; Clement, *Stromateis* III; 14, 2, V, 81, 2, and VI, 30; Diogenes Laertius, *Lives* VIII, 62; Ammonius, *De interpretatione* 249, 6.

3. Porphyry, *De abstinentia* II, 21 and 31; Sextus Empiricus, *Adversus mathematicos* IX, 129. Cf. Hesiod, *Works and Days* 109.

4. Diogenes Laertius, *Lives* VIII, 77; *The Suda,* "Empedocles." See John Burnet, *Early Greek Philosophy,* 203f and G.S. Kirk and J.E. Raven, *The Presocratic Philosophers,* 413.

5. Plutarch, *Adversus Coloten* 12, 1113c; Aetius I, 3, 20 and I, 18, 2; Diels, fragments 11–14.

6. Simplicius, *Physics* 25, 21; 33, 21; 158, 1, 8, and 13; and 159, 21. See John Burnet, *Early Greek Philosophy,* 232, and Eduard Zeller, *Outlines of the History of Greek Philosophy,* 77.

7. Hippolytus, *Refutatio* VII, 27; Diels, fragments 27–29; Simplicius, *Physics* 32, 13 and 158, 1; Aristotle, *Metaphysics* Alpha 4, 985a23; Aristotle, *Generation and Corruption* Beta 6, 334a1; Aristotle, *Physics* Beta 4, 196a20 and Beta 8, 198b29; Aristotle, *De Caelo* Gamma 2, 300b25 and 30; Aristotle, *De Anima* Gamma 6, 430a28; Simplicius, *De Caelo* 529, 1 and 587, 1 and 20; Plutarch, *Adversus Coloten* 28, 1123b; Aelian, *On the Characteristics of Animals* XVI, 29.

8. Aristotle, *Generation and Corruption* Beta 7, 334a5 and *De Caelo* Gamma 2, 301a14; Simplicius, *De caelo* 587, 24.

9. Simplicius, *De Caelo* 529, 1 and *Physics* 32, 13; Stobaeus, *Anthologium* I, 10, 11.

10. Kirk and Raven, 347–348.

11. Fragments 65 and 67 (Diels); Aetius, *Opinions* V, 19, 5; Simplicius, *Physics* 32, 6 and 300, 21. See Kirk and Raven, 340.

12. Aristotle, *De Respiratione* 7, 473b9.

13. Aristotle, *Metaphysics* Beta 4, 1000b6; Theophrastus, *De sensu* 7; Plutarch, *Questiones naturales* 19, 916d.

14. Fragments 42, 45, and 48 (Diels); See Kathleen Freeman, *Ancilla to the Pre-Socratic Philosophers,* 57–58, for translations of the fragments.

15. Plato, *Phaedrus* 270a. In the golden age of Athens, its ruler Pericles brought together a circle of such people as Phidias the sculptor, Callicrates the architect, Thucydides, Sophocles, Euripides, and others, including his consort, Aspasia. Aspasia was a cultivated, well-educated woman, which was remarkable in a time when women generally were not educated and played no role in public life. When Pericles died, the Athenians banished Aspasia. Conventional, provincial Athens did not seem to be able to tolerate a capable and educated woman.

16. Diogenes Laertius, *Lives* I, 16 and II, 7; Plato, *Phaedrus* 270a and *Apology* 26d; Strabo 14.

17. Herodotus, *Histories* II (Euterpé), 22.

18. Simplicius, *Physics* 34, 29 and 164, 26; Aristotle, *Physics* Alpha 4, 187a23; Aetius *Opinions* I, 3, 5; Diels, fragment 10 (see Freeman, *Ancilla,* 84, for translation).

19. See Kirk and Raven, 367–368, and 386, and John Burnet, *Early Greek Philosophy,* 264–265.

20. Simplicius, *Physics* 153, 13 and 164, 24 (Diels, fragment 12), Kathleen Freeman translation.

21. John Burnet, *Early Greek Philosophy,* 268; Eduard Zeller, *Outlines,* 77.

22. Simplicius, *Physics* 34, 21, 155, 22 and 163, 20 (Diels, fragments 1, 4, and 17).

23. Ibid., 35, 14, 300, 31, 156, 13 and 164, 24.

24. Plato, *Phaedo* 98b7; Aristotle, *Metaphysics* Alpha 4, 985a18.

25. Kirk and Raven, 384, note 1. The limited and virtually mechanical role of mind weakens the claim (mentioned by Zeller, *Outlines,* 80) that Anaxagoras was a dualist with two basic principles, mind and infinite substance, as indicated in Theophrastus, *Epitome of Physical Opinions.* This is nothing like the two-substance dualism of Orphism and its followers, since mind was probably considered corporeal (see also Kirk and Raven, 375).

26. Simplicius, *Physics* 155, 31 and 179, 3 and 8.

27. Ibid., 27, 11; Diogenes Laertius, *Lives* II, 8.

28. Hippolytus, *Refutatio* I, 8, 3–10.

29. Simplicius, *Physics* 35, 3 and 157, 9.

30. Theophrastus, *De sensu* 27ff; Sextus Empiricus, *Adversus mathematicos* VII, 90 and 140.

31. Hippolytus, *Refutatio* I, 8, 12; Theophrastus, *Inquiry into Plants* III, 1, 4.

32. Aristotle, *Physics* Delta 6, 213a22.

33. Simplicius, *Physics* 28, 4; Diogenes Laertius, *Lives* X, 13.

34. Diogenes Laertius, *Lives* IX, 45; Aetius I, 25. See Kirk and Raven, 403, for an account of Leucippus's writings.

35. Diogenes Laertius, *Lives* IX, 35 and 45.

36. Simplicius, *Physics* 28, 4.

37. Cicero, *Academica* II, 37, 118; Aristotle, *Generation and Corruption* Alpha 8, 325a2, *Metaphysics* Alpha 4, 985b4, *De Anima* Alpha 2, 405a11 and *De Caelo* Gamma 4, 303a12

38. Diogenes Laertius, *Lives* IX, 31; Aetius, *Opinions* II, 7, 2; Sextus Empiricus, *Adversus mathematicos* VII, 117.

39. Aetius, *Opinions* I, 26, 2; also Diogenes Laertius, *Lives* IX, 45 and Aetius, *Opinions* I, 25, 4.

40. Aristotle, *Physics* Beta 4, 196a24.

41. Diogenes Laertius, *Lives* IX, 31; Hippolytus, *Refutatio* I, 13, 2.

42. Simplicius, *De caelo* 242, 21.

43. Aristotle, *De Caelo* Gamma 2, 300b8; Kirk and Raven, 417.

44. Aetius, *Opinions* I, 23, 3; Kirk and Raven, 418.

45. Aristotle, *Generation and Corruption* Alpha 8, 326a9; Theophrastus, *De sensu* 61; Aetius, *Opinions* I, 3, 18.

46. Fragments 9 and 11 (Diels); Aetius, *Opinions* IV, 8, 10 and 4, 19, 3; Theophrastus, *De sensu* 50; Alexander, *De sensu* 56, 12; Sextus Empiricus, *Adversus mathematicos* VII, 135, 139.

47. Fragments 7, 8, 9, 11, 117, and 125 (Diels); Sextus Empiricus, *Adversus mathematicos* VII, 135 and 139; fragment 125; fragment 117 (Diels). See Kirk and Raven, 423–424. For translations of the fragments see Kathleen Freeman, *Ancilla,* 93 and 104.

48. Fragment 41 (Diels).

49. Fragment 34 (Diels).

Chapter Five. The Sophists

1. Aristides, *Orationis* 46. See W.K.C. Guthrie, *The Sophists,* 27–34.

2. Plato, *Sophist* 231d. All translations of Plato's dialogues are from *The Collected Dialogues of Plato,* edited by Edith Hamilton and Huntington Cairns.

3. Aristotle, *Sophistical Refutations* I, 165a21.

4. Xenophon, *Memorabilia* I, 1, 11 and *On Hunting* 13, 18.

5. W.K.C. Guthrie, *The Sophists,* 41–48.

6. Untersteiner, *The Sophists,* 42–49, 54, 86f; Guthrie, *The Sophists,* 8, 47.

7. Guthrie, *The Sophists,* 48 (n. 1), 55–116.

8. Ibid., 60–84.

9. Plato, *Protagoras* 322a–d.

10. Aristotle, *Politics* III 9, 1280b11.

11. Guthrie, *The Sophists,* 152–153.

12. Ibid., 312; Untersteiner, *The Sophists,* 341.

13. Aristotle, *Rhetoric* III 3, 1406b11; Untersteiner, *The Sophists,* 341.

14. Plato, *Republic* 338c–339a.

15. Plato, *Gorgias* 483b–d, 491d–492c.

16. Untersteiner, *The Sophists,* 63 and *passim;* Guthrie, *The Sophists,* 117–131.

17. The best ancient sources for Protagoras's life are Diogenes Laertius, *Lives* IX, 50 and Philostratus, *Lives of the Sophists* I.10.494–95. For modern treatments of his life and teaching, see Untersteiner, *The Sophists,* especially 1–92, and Guthrie, *The Sophists,* passim, especially 21, 45, 63–64, 183–84, 220–21, 230–31, 234–35, 262–69. For translations of fragments of the Sophist's work, see *The Older Sophists,* edited by Rosamond Kent Sprague.

18. Plutarch, *Pericles* 36; Isocrates, *Panathenaicus* 169.

19. Aristotle, *Rhetoric* III 5, 1407b6 and *Sophistical Refutations* XIV 173b17.

20. Diogenes Laertius, *Lives* IX, 50.

21. Plato, *Protagoras* 319a, 326b, 329b, 339a, and 349a.

22. Eusebius, *Chronicle;* Sextus Empiricus, *Adversus mathematicos* IX 55, 56; Plato, *Theaetetus* 91d and 162d.

23. Diogenes Laertius, *Lives* IX 50; Plato, *Theaetetus* 252a and *Cratylus* 385e; Sextus Empiricus, *Outlines of Pyrrhonism* I 217 and *Adversus mathematicos* VII 389.

24. Untersteiner, *The Sophists,* 41–2, 86–7.

25. Diogenes Laertius, *Lives* IX 50–51; Sextus Empiricus, *Adversus mathematicos* IX 55, 56; Hesychius, *Onomatologies;* Eusebius, *Praeparatio Evangelica* XIV 3, 7.

26. Clement, *Miscellanies* VI65; Seneca, *Letters* 88, 43; Plato, *Theaetetus* 166d-167d; Aristotle, *Rhetoric* II 24, 1402a23.

27. Plato, *Protagoras* 322a-d.

28. Xenophon, *Memorabilia* II 1, 21; Plato, *Symposium* 177b and *Protagoras* 340c-d; Philostratus, *Lives* I.12.496. See Untersteiner, *The Sophists,* 336, on pessimistic aspects of the philosophy of Critias and others, including Prodicus.

29. Plato, *Protagoras* 315e and 341a, *Symposium* 177b, *Theaetetus* 151b, *Cratylus* 384b, and *Hippias Major* 282c.

30. Galen, *On the Elements* I 9 and *On the Physical Faculties* II 9; Sextus Empiricus, *Adversus mathematicos* IX 18; Philodemus, *On Piety* 9, 7; Themistius, *Orations* 30. See Untersteiner, *The Sophists,* 212–213 and Guthrie, *The Sophists,* 279.

31. Plato, *Protagoras* 337a–c, 340a–b, *Laches* 197d, *Charmides* 163d, and *Euthydemus* 277e; Aristotle, *Topics* II 6, 112b22.

32. Guthrie, *The Sophists,* 269–274; Diogenes Laertius, *Lives* VIII, 58–59; Philostratus, *Lives* I, 9, 1.

33. Sextus Empiricus, *Adversus mathematicos* VII, 65; Aristotle, *Rhetoric* III 14, 1414b29 and 1416a1; Philostratus, *Lives* I.9.492–494. See Sprague, *The Older Sophists,* 42, 50–63, for translations of *On Nature,* "Helen," and "Palamedes." See Untersteiner, *The Sophists,* 101–138, especially 117.

34. Guthrie, *The Sophists,* 193–196; Untersteiner, *The Sophists* 163–164. See Sprague, *The Older Sophists,* 46, for Sextus's paraphrase of the argument of *On Nature,* translated by George Kennedy. Guthrie, 196–200, and Untersteiner, 140–162, give detailed summaries of the argument.

35. Plato, *Philebus* 58a-b. See "Helen" 13 in Sprague, *The Older Sophists,* 53.

36. Untersteiner, *The Sophists,* 185–193, relates Gorgias's aesthetics to his epistemology.

37. Philostratus, *Lives* I, 9, 1; Plato, *Protagoras* 337c; Guthrie, *The Sophists,* 44, 150, 162.

38. Plato, *Protagoras* 315c and 317c, *Hippias Major* 281a-b, 282a, d–e, and 285c-e, *Hippias Minor* 362c-d, 368b, and *Protagoras* 315c; Xenophon, *Symposium* 4, 62; Philostratus, *Lives* I.11.495–496; Guthrie, *The Sophists* 280–282; Untersteiner, *The Sophists* 272–274.

39. Plato, *Hippias Major* 286a-b; Xenophon, *Memorabilia* 4, 4, 12–14; Guthrie, *The Sophists,* 283–285; Untersteiner, *The Sophists,* 284.

40. Plato, *Protagoras* 337c–d; Xenophon, *Memorabilia* 4, 4, 14–16; Untersteiner, *The Sophists,* 280–282, 289; Guthrie, *The Sophists* 70, 119 *n.2,* 143, 145, 162–163, 284–285.

41. Plato, *Protagoras* 337d, *Hippias Minor* 366c–d, 367d, *Protagoras* 318e; *Dissoi Lógoi* VIII; Untersteiner *The Sophists* 279–180.
42. Guthrie, *The Sophists,* 33.
43. Ibid., 11; George Grote, *A History of Greece from the Earliest Period to the Close of the Generation Contemporary with Alexander the Great.*

Chapter Six. Socrates

1. Plato, *Apology* 32b–e and *Epistle* VII 324e–325a; Diogenes Laertius, *Lives of Eminent Philosophers* II.22–24. See *The Philosophy of Socrates,* edited by Gregory Vlastos, and *Essays on the Philosophy of Socrates,* edited by Hugh H. Benson, for articles on various aspects of Socrates.
2. *Apology* 23b.
3. *Apology* 30e.
4. *Apology* 20e–23b.
5. Plato, *Theaetetus* 149–150d.
6. Plato, *Meno* 81c–d, 82–85c and *Phaedrus* 247c–e.
7. Plato, *Crito* 49b–54e.
8. See, for example, Plato, *Laches* 190e–192b and *Euthyphro* 6d–e.
9. *Laches* 190e, 191e.
10. *Euthyphro* 6d.
11. Xenophon, *Memorabilia* I, 2, 1 and I, 3, 5; See A.R. Lacey, "Our Knowledge of Socrates," in *The Philosophy of Socrates,* edited by Gregory Vlastos, 22–49, for detailed treatment of sources on the life and teachings of Socrates.
12. *Memorabilia* I, 1, 10.
13. Ibid., I, 2, 64.
14. Ibid., III, 8, 2 and 3. Quotations of the *Memorabilia* are from the Loeb Classical Library version, translated by E.C. Merchant.
15. Ibid., III, 8, 4.
16. Ibid., III, 9, 14; IV, 2, 33.
17. Ibid., IV, 5, 12.
18. Ibid., I, 2, 64; Diogenes Laertius, *Lives* II.40.
19. Plato, *Apology* 23b and 30e.9.
20. Diogenes Laertius, *Lives* II.42.
21. Xenophon, *Memorabilia* IV, 5, 12.
22. *Apology* 23c-24a.
23. Diogenes Laertius, *Lives* II.106–112.
24. Ibid., VI.1–19.
25. Ibid., VI.20–81.
26. Ibid., VI.3.
27. Ibid., II.65.
28. Ibid., II.87 and 89.
29. Ibid., II.84–85, 92–103.

Chapter Seven. Plato: Metaphysics and Theology

(Unless otherwise stated, works cited are by Plato.)
1. The main ancient source of information on Plato's life is Diogenes Laertius,

Lives of Famous Philosophers 3, 4. There is some information in Plato's *Epistles* and other writings and in Aristotle. There are excellent lives of Plato and surveys of his writings in A.E. Taylor, *Plato: The Man and His Work* (Cleveland and New York: World Publishing Co., 1956), 1–22 and in other histories of philosophy.

2. Aristotle, *Metaphysics* Alpha 6, 987a32.
3. *Apology* 34a1 and 38b6–9 and *Phaedo* 59b10.
4. *Epistle* VII, 324b8–326b4.
5. *Epistle* VII 324a, 338c, 339a. 350a, *Epistles* IX and *Epistle* XII.
6. For example, *Symposium* 201c–d and *Phaedo* 114d.
7. *Timaeus* 29c–d.
8. *Phaedrus* 247c–e.
9. *Republic* VI 507b and X 596a.
10. *Parmenides* 130c–d.
11. *Phaedo* 65d and *Hippias major* 287 c–d.
12. *Republic* VI.508–509.
13. *Parmenides* 131–132 and 134b–135a.
14. *Philebus* 23c–27 and *Timaeus* 53–56.
15. Aristotle, *Metaphysics* I 9, 991b–992b.
16. *Timaeus* 48e–49a, 52b.
17. *Symposium* 201c, 210b–211e; *Republic* 452e; *Gorgias* 474d; *Lysis* 216d; *Hippias Major* 297b–c.
18. *Republic* 587e; *Hippias Major* 287c–d, 289d; *Phaedo* 100c–d.
19. *Hippias Major* 287e–289b, 289e, 290b–e, 291d, 293e–294e.
20. Ibid., 291d–e, 293a–b.
21. Ibid., 295c–296d, 296e–297c. See also *Lysis* 216d and *Symposium* 201c.
22. *Hippias Major* 297e–303d.
23. Ibid., 294b.
24. See Paul Oskar Kristeller, "The Modern System of the Arts," in *Journal of the History of Ideas* vol. 12 (1951), 465–527, and vol. 12 (1952), 17–46.
25. *Republic* 597e, 598b–c.
26. *Sophist* 235a–c, 235d–236c; *Republic* 377d.
27. *Republic* III 395c–d, 396b, 399a–400e, X 595b.
28. Ibid., II 377a–383c, III 386a–400c, 401b, 402c, X 595, 607a; *Laws* VII 801c-d, 817d, VIII 829d.
29. *Gorgias* 503d–504a.
30. *Ion* 533c–534e; *Phaedrus* 245a, 265b; *Laws* III 682a, IV 719c.
31. *Ion* 533d–e, 535a–536d, 542a–b.
32. *Republic* II 379b–383c.
33. *Laws* X 896a–899e; *Philebus* 30a–c; *Timaeus* 30b, 34b.
34. *Laws* X 896e–897d, 898–899.
35. *Timaeus* 27d–28c, 29a–b, 29 d–e, 30a–b, 34a, 37c–e.
36. Ibid., 28c, 29d, 71d.
37. *Laws* 907d–910d.
38. *Phaedo* 70c–72d.
39. Ibid., 761–77c.
40. Ibid., 78b–84d.
41. Ibid., 85e–86d, 871–88b.
42. Ibid., 104e–105e.

43. *Phaedo* 245c-3; *Laws* X 894d–896d.
44. *Timaeus* 27c–92c.
45. Ibid., 29d, 71d.

Chapter Eight. Plato: Theory of Knowledge

(All works cited are by Plato.)
1. *Republic* V, 509d, VII, 514–517.
2. Ibid., VI, 509d–11e.
3. *Parmenides* 134b–135a.
4. *Phaedrus* 247c–e; *Meno* 81c–d, 82–85e.
5. *Phaedo* 114d.
6. *Theaetetus* 146e, 151e–186e, 187b–201c, 201c–210d.
7. Ibid., 191c-c, 195d–196c.
8. Ibid., 197c–198b, 200a–c.
9. *Sophist* 236e–237e, 240c–e, 241d.
10. Ibid., 249c–d, 250, 254d.
11. Ibid., 253a and d, 261, 262.
12. *Phaedo* 95–99e.
13. *Timaeus* 29d.
14. Ibid., 35b–37c, 39e, 41.

Chapter Nine. Plato: Ethics and Politics

(Unless otherwise stated, all works cited are by Plato.)
1. *Republic* I 343b–344c and 348c–349a; 358b–367e.
2. *Gorgias* 472e, 473d, 475c–d, and 480c–d.
3. *Republic* II 361e.
4. *Gorgias* 483b–d, 491d–492c.
5. Ibid., 496–499e.
6. Ibid., 507c–d.
7. Ibid., 523–526d; A.E. Taylor, *Plato: The Man and His Work,* 27–28, 65–66,
145.
8. *Republic* II 359–360.
9. Ibid., 329c–330b, 330e–331e, 332a–b, 333b–c, 349d, 349e–351a.
10. Ibid., 329–334, 357b–358d; *Meno* 87e, 88a–d.
11. *Protagoras* 329–334, 357b–358d; *Meno* 81d–85c, 82b–85b.
12. *Gorgias* 494c–495a, 497d–e; *Protagoras* 358a; *Laws* II 663a, 667b–e, IX
863b; *Philebus* 11b, 60d, 67a; *Republic* III 402e, VI 505a–c.
13. *Gorgias* 494c–e, 495b; *Republic* IX 582e–583b, 586d; *Protagoras* 357b–e.
14. *Republic* VI 485d–e; *Phaedo* 64d–65a; *Philebus* 21c, 22.
15. *Philebus* 31d–32a, 44a–d, 66c.
16. *Symposium* 176a–188e.
17. Ibid., 189a–197e.
18. Ibid., 200a–207a.
19. Ibid., 207c–209e, 210a–212b.

20. Ibid., 247a–253c, 255c–256b.

21. *Phaedrus* 238d–241d; *Republic* III 403a–b; *Symposium* 217–219e; *Laws* VIII 835a–841e.

22. *Republic* II 368c–369a.

23. Ibid., II 369–371, 373.

24. Ibid., II 374a–376c, III 414a–b.

25. Ibid., II 376c–III 413e.

26. Ibid., III 412d–414b, 416b–417b, IV 424a–425e, VII 525a–530d, 531d–539e.

27. Ibid., III 414 b–e, III 415 a–c, IV 423c–d, VII 540c.

28. Ibid., IV 428d–432b, 433a–434c.

29. Ibid., IV 435b–c, 437b–438a, 439e–440e, 441a–c, 441c–442b.

30. *Phaedrus* 246; *Republic* 443c–444e.

31. *Republic* VIII 545–549, 550–554, 555–560, 562–570, IX 571–580.

32. *Laws* V 739a–b; *Statesman* 293e–300c, 301b–c, and 303a–b; *Republic* VIII 544c, IX 576d.

33. *Statesman* 302b–303b.

34. *Statesman* 264c–285b; 303e–309e.

35. *Laws* X 884–886e, 886d, 889, and 907–910.

36. *Laws* I 631b–632c, 634d, 636a–d, 839a; X 909d–910d.

Chapter Ten. Aristotle: Metaphysics

(Unless otherwise stated, all works cited are by Aristotle.)

1. An early source of information on Aristotle's life is Diogenes Laertius, *Lives of Famous Philosophers* V, 1–3. David Ross, *Aristotle,* gives a good survey of his life and writings.

2. Aristotle, *Metaphysics* Alpha 1, 981a1–981b9, 982a1.

3. Ibid., Alpha 2, 982a5–30, 983a1–10.

4. Ibid., Alpha 1, 992a32–992b9. Quoted from *Metaphysics,* translated by Richard Hope, 32.

5. Ibid., Alpha 1, 980a1, 981b20, 982b10.

6. *Nicomachean Ethics* I 6, 1096a11–15. Quoted from *The Nichomachean Ethics,* translated by David Ross, 7–8.

7. *Metaphysics* Alpha 9, 990a34–991a8. This material is repeated in Mu 4, 1078b34–1079b3.

8. Ibid., Alpha 9, 991a8–992b13.

9. Ibid., Zeta 11, 1037a29 and 13, 1038b2, Eta 1, 1042a27; *De Anima* II 1, 412a6–10.

10. *Metaphysics* Zeta 13, 1038b9–10, 15 and 16, 1040b27.

11. Ibid., Beta 4, 99b1 and Zeta 15, 1096b29–1040a2; *Posterior Analytics* I 11, 77a5 and II 19, 99b20.

12. *Metaphysics* Eta 6, 1045a25–1045b18, Lambda 2, 1069b14–15; *Physics* Gamma 1, 200b25–201b15.

13. *Metaphysics* Alpha 3, 983a22–34 and Delta 2, 1013a24–35; *Physics* Beta 3, 194b16–195b30 and Beta 7, 198a12–198b9.

14. *Metaphysics* Theta 8, 1049b2–1051a; *De Partibus Animalium* I 6, 39b 11f.

15. *Physics* Beta 8, 198b10–200b10; *Politics* 1253a8.

16. *Physics* Beta 4, 196a1–6, 198a12.

17. Ibid., Beta 1, 193b12–20.

18. Werner Jaeger, *Aristotle,* 66–67, 158.

19. *Metaphysics* Alpha the Less 2, 941a–994b30, Lambda 6, 1071b4–11 and 7, 1072a25–1072b10; *Physics* Gamma 1, 200b31, Theta 7, 261a31, Theta 8, 263a3, and Theta 8, 264a7–265a12.

20. *Metaphysics* Lambda 6, 1071b12–22 and 7, 1072a24.

21. Ibid., 7, 1073b3–15; *Physics* Theta 6, 258b10–260a19.

22. *Metaphysics* Lambda 7, 1072a20–1072b30 and 8, 1073a26–1073b1.

23. Ibid., 7, 1072b10–30 and 9, 1074b15–35.

24. Simplicius, *De Caelo* 289, 1–15, in *The Works of Aristotle,* Vol. 12 (Selected Fragments), edited and translated by David Ross, 87–88.

25. Werner Jaeger, *Aristotle,* 158.

26. Aristotle, *Poetics* IX, 1451a23–1451b48.

27. Ibid., VI, 1449b10; *Nicomachean Ethics* II 6, 1106b15–24; see Leon Golden and O.B. Hardison, Jr. *Aristotle's Poetics,* 133–137.

28. *Poetics* IV, 1448b1–22.

29. *Metaphysics* Alpha 1, 981a1–981b9.

Chapter Eleven. Aristotle: Physics, Biology, and Psychology

(Unless otherwise stated, all works cited are by Aristotle.)

1. *Metaphysics* Zeta 10, 1036a9, Eta 6, 1045a25–35, Lambda 2, 1069b14–15; *Physics* Alpha 4–9, Gamma 1, 200b25–201b15. David Ross, *Aristotle,* 66, 168.

2. *Physics* Delta 2, 4, and 7.

3. *Physics* Delta 8 and 9.

4. *Physics* Delta 10, 219b9 (translated by Richard Hope). See also Delta 10, 218b11–19 and Delta 11, 219b1–10.

5. *Physics* Delta 11, 219b10–220a27.

6. Ibid., Theta 8, 261b27 and 9, 265a12–15; *Metaphysics* Lambda 8, 1073a30, 1073b18–1074a14.

7. *De Anima* II 1, 412a and 2, 414a.

8. Ibid., II 2, 413b; 3, 414a27–30; and 4, 415a20–25.

9. Ibid., II 4.

10. Ibid., II 2, 413b4; 3, 414b1–5; and 3, 414b, 15–20; *De Sensu et Sensibili* I, 436a9.

11. Werner Jaeger, *Aristotle,* 67.

12. *De Anima* II 5, 416b, 417a, and 418a; II 10, 422b; II 12, 424a19; and III 2, 425b–427a.

13. Ibid., II 6, 418a; 7, 419a; and III 3, 428b.

14. Ibid., II 6, 418a; III 1, 425a; *De sensu et Sensibili* I, 437a7–9.

15. *De Anima* III 2, 425b–427a.

16. Ibid., III 3, 427b–429a; III 7, 431a and b; III 8, 432a; *De Memoria et Reminiscentia* I, 449b31.

17. *Metaphysics* Alpha I, 980a21–981a1; *De Memoria* 450a15, 450b12–451a25, 451b16–20, and 451b24.

18. *De Anima* II 3,414b.
19. Ibid., III 4, 429a–430a and III 7, 431a.
20. Ibid., I 4, 408b18–19 and II 2, 413b25. Translated by J.A. Smith, in *Introduction to Aristotle,* edited by Richard McKeon.
21. Ibid., III 5, 430a.
22. Ibid.,
23. See David Ross, *Aristotle,* 152–153.
24. For a brief history of how Aristotle's writings reached the form in which we know them see David Ross, *Aristotle,* 7–19, or G.E.R. Lloyd, *Aristotle: The Growth and Structure of His Thought,* 9–18.

Chapter Twelve. Aristotle: Knowledge and Logic

(All works cited are by Aristotle)
1. *Posterior Analytics* I 2, 716b14, I 4, 73a20–24 and I 8, 75b20–24.
2. *Metaphysics* Beta 999a25–999b24; *Posterior Analytics* I 11, 77a5–9.
3. *Posterior Analytics* II 3, 90a35–91a12; II 10, 93b28–94a19; II 13, 97a22–38.
4. Ibid., I 22, 83a21–35.
5. See notes 1. and 2.
6. *Posterior Analytics* I 1, 71a1–I 2, 72a5.
7. Ibid., II 19, 99b33–100b17.
8. Ibid., I 4, 73b1–25.
9. Ibid., I 6, 75a27–36.
10. Ibid., I 6, 75a 12–15.
11. Ibid., I 14, 79a15–32.

Chapter Thirteen. Aristotle: Ethics and Politics

(Unless otherwise stated, all works cited are by Aristotle.)
1. *Nicomachean Ethics* I 3, 1094b11–28. Quotations are from the David Ross translation.
2. Ibid., I 1, 1094a1–2; 1094a15–20; 4, 1095a10–20.
3. Ibid., I 51095b15–1096a10.
4. Ibid., I 7, 1097b1–35 and 1098a7–18.
5. Ibid., I 8, 1099b1–10; I 9, 1100a1–5; X 7, 177a29–30; X 8, 1178a21–30.
6. Ibid., II 1–9; VI 1, 1138b35–2, 1139b15; VI 12, 1143b15–13 and 1144b30; X 7,1177a10–8, 1178b23.
7. Ibid., I 8, 1098b10–1099a30; X 2, 1173a1–X 5, 1176a30; X 6, 1176a30–1177a10.
8. Ibid., II 1, 1103a10–1103b1; III 5, 1114a1–25.
9. Ibid., II 2, 1104a10–35; II 7, 1107a32–1107b31.
10. Ibid., II 6, 1106a30–1106b8; II 7, 1107a26–30.
11. Ibid., II 8, 1109a1–19.
12. Ibid., II 6, 1107a8–25.
13. Ibid., II 9, 1109a20–29. See also II 6, 1106b 17–24 and II 6, 1107a 1–4.
14. Ibid., III 1, 1110a1; III 2, 1111a20–25; V 8, 1135a15–35.

15. Ibid., III 1, 1110b25–27.
16. Ibid., VII 1, 1145b5–30.
17. Ibid., V 1, 1129a6–10 and 1130a10–14.
18. Ibid., VIII 1, 1155a1–24.
19. Ibid., VIII 3, 1156a6–24; 4, 1157b1–4; 5, 1157b24–37.
20. Ibid., VIII 1, 1155a25; VIII 3, 1156b23–30.
21. Ibid., VIII 3, 1156a20–36.
22. Ibid., V 1, 1129a33–35 and 1129b11–24.
23. Ibid., V 6, 1134a29–30.
24. Thomas Hobbes, *The Leviathan,* Chapter XIII; David Hume, *Enguiry Concerning the Principles of Morals,* Appendix III.
25. *Nicomachean Ethics* V 2, 1130b29–34.
26. Ibid., V 3, 1131a10–1131b24.
27. Ibid., V 4, 1131b25–1132b200.
28. Ibid., V 5, 1132b21–1133a25.
29. Ibid., V 6, 1134b7–18.
30. *Politics* I 1, 1252a7–17; I 1, 1252a24–1252b16; I 3, 1253b1–13. Quotations from the *Politics* are from the translation of Ernest Barker.
31. Ibid., I 3, 1253b14–22.
32. Ibid., I 4, 1254a13–16; I 5, 1254b16–39.
33. Ibid., I 6, 1255a3–1255b15.
34. Ibid., I 7, 1255b16–39.
35. Ibid., I 5, 1254b14–15; I 13, 1260a4–33.
36. Ibid., I 2, 1252b27–1253a2.
37. Ibid., I 2, 1253a8 and 29. See also 1253a2–17 and 25–35.
38. Ibid., III 7, 1279a25–35; IV 11, 1295a25–33.
39. Ibid., III 7, 1279a25–1280a1.
40. Ibid., IV 11, 1295a25–1296b12.
41. Ibid., III 17, 1287b36–1288a14; IV 11, 1296b2–1297a13; IV 1–10.
42. Ibid., III 14, 1284b35–1285b32.
43. Ibid., III 15, 1285b33–1287a35.
44. Ibid., IIII 16, 1287b8–1287b35.

Chapter Fourteen. Hellenistic Cultural Background

1. Gilbert Murray, *Five Stages of Greek Religion,* 17.
2. Ibid., 155.

Chapter Fifteen. Epicureanism

1. Diogenes Laertius, *Lives* X.3–11. See R.D. Hicks, *Stoic and Epicurean,* 153–162, for information on the life and character of Epicurus. There are two convenient sources of the available works of Epicurus and Lucretius. *The Stoic and Epicurean Philosophers,* edited by Whitney J. Oates, provides translations of the extant works. A.A. Long and D.N. Sedley, *The Hellenistic Philosophers,* vol. 1,

provides translations of the principle works arranged topically. For specific passages use the Index of Sources beginning on page 492. All quotations of Epicurean and Stoic writers are from the Long and Sedley translations.

2. Porphyry, *To Marcella* 31.

3. Lucretius, *De rerum natura* 5, 1161–1225. All references to Lucretius are to this work.

4. Epicurus, *Letter to Menoeceus* 123–124.

5. Epicurus, *Letter to Herodotus* 76–77; Lucretius 5, 146–155 and 1161–1225; 6, 68–79.

6. Lucretius 3, 830–911 and 966–1023.

7. Epicurus, *Menoeceus* 124–127; *Principle Doctrines* 11–13.

8. Epicurus, *Menoeceus* 127–132; *Principle Doctrines* 8–10, 29; Vatican Collection Part A 71, 73, 81; Lucretius 2, 1–61.

9. Diogenes Laertius, *Lives* 10.136–137; Epicurus, *Principle Doctrines* 3–4, 8–13; Vatican Collection Part A 4; Lucretius 2, 1–61.

10. Epicurus, *Principle Doctrines* 7, 14, 15, 21; Vatican Collection Part A 23, 27, 34, 52, 58, 68.

11. Diogenes Laertius, *Lives* 10.118–20; *Epicurus Exhortation:* Vatican Collection Part A 51.(See translations in Whitney S. Oates, *The Stoic and Epicurean Philosophers.*

12. See for example Athenaeus 546f, Plutarch, *Against Epicurean Happiness* 1089D, and Cicero, *Tusculan Disputations* 3, 41–42.

13. Epicurus, *Letter to Herodotus* 38–40; Lucretius 1, 334–390, 419–482; Sextus Empiricus, *Adversus mathematicos* X.2.

14. *Herodotus* 68–73; Lucretius 1, 445–482; Sextus Empiricus, *Adversus mathematicos* X.219–227.

15. *Herodotus* 40–43, 54–59; Lucretius 1, 503–598 and 599–634; 2, 381–407, 478–531 and 730–833.

16. *Herodotus* 41–42; Lucretius 1, 958–997.

17. *Herodotus* 60.

18. Ibid., 43–44, 61–62; Lucretius 2, 80–124 and 142–164.

19. Lucretius 2, 216–250.

20. *Menoeceus* 133–134.

21. Epicurus, *On Nature* 34, 21–22.

22. Ibid., 34, 26–30.

23. Lucretius 2, 251–293.

24. Cicero, *On Fate* 21–25.

25. *Herodotus* 45, 73–74.

26. Lucretius 2, 1052–1104; 4, 823–857; 5, 156–234.

27. *Herodotus* 63–67; Lucretius 3, 136–176 and 417–462; 4, 877–891.

28. *Herodotus* 46–53.

29. Lucretius 4, 256–268.

30. Ibid., 4, 722–822.

31. Ibid., 4, 353–363, 379–386, and 469–521; Saint Augustine, *Contra academicos* 3, 11, 26.

32. Epicurus, *Principle Doctrines* 23.

33. *Herodotus* 37–38, 82; Lucretius 4, 379–386; Diogenes Laertius, *Lives* 10, 34.

34. Sextus Empiricus, *Adversus mathematicos* VIII.211–216.

35. *Principle Doctrines* 31–35; Vatican Collection Part A 70.
36. *Principle Doctrines* 36–38.
37. Lucretius 5, 1105–1157.
38. *Principle Doctrines* 17.

Chapter Sixteen. Stoicism

1. Diogenes Laertius, *Lives* VII.1–4; Cicero *Academica* 1, 43; 2, 16; 2, 76–78; Eusebius, *Praeparatio Evangelica* 14, 6, 12–13. See Hicks, *Stoic and Epicurean,* 4–6.
2. Diogenes Laertius, *Lives* VII.16–26; A.A. Long and D.N. Sedley, *The Hellenistic Philosophers,* Vol. 1, 189 and 504.
3. Diogenes Laertius, *Lives* VII.5.
4. Ibid., VII.6–12.
5. Ibid., VII.27–28, 31, and 36–38.
6. Ibid., VII.168–176.
7. Hicks, *Stoic and Epicurean* 16–17.
8. Diogenes Laertius, *Lives* VII.179–202.
9. Diogenes Laertius, *Lives* VI.81, VII.39, 55–56, and 71–74; Cicero *On the Orator* 2, 157–158; Long and Sedley, 504.
10. Stobaeus, *Anthologium* 2, 63, 25–64, 12; Clement, *Miscellanies* 2, 21, 129, 4–5; Long and Sedley, 506.
11. Cicero, *On the Nature of the Gods* 2, 88; Galen, *On Hippocrates' and Plato's doctrines* 4, 3, 2–5; 4, 7, 24–41; 5, 5, 8–16; Clement, *Miscellanies* 2, 21, 129, 4–5; Long and Sedley, 507.
12. Long and Sedley, *The Hellenistic Philosophers* 502, 504 and 507.
13. Diogenes Laertius, *Lives* VII.117.
14. Diogenes Laertius, *Lives* VII.101–103; Stobaeus 2, 96, 18–97, 5.
15. Epictetus, *Discourses* 2, 6, 9; Stobaeus 2, 76, 9–15; 2, 83, 10–84, 2; Sextus Empiricus, *Adversus mathematicos* XI.64–67; Diogenes Laertius, *Lives* VII.160.
16. Diogenes Laertius, *Lives* VII.107–109; Stobaeus 2, 85, 13–86, 4 and 2, 93, 14–18; Cicero, *On Ends* 3, 17, 20–22; Epictetus, *Discourses* 2, 10, 1–12.
17. Stobaeus 2, 75, 11–76, 8; Diogenes Laertius, *Lives* VII.87–89; Stobaeus 2, 77, 16–27.
18. Seneca, *Letters* 76, 9–10 and 92, 3; Epictetus, *Discourses* 1, 6, 12–22; Cicero, *Tusculan Disputations* 5, 81–82; Cicero, *On Ends* 3, 31.
19. Diogenes Laertius, *Lives* VII.89–103; Plutarch, *On Moral Virtues* 440e–441d; Stobaeus 2, 63, 6–24 and 2, 66, 14–67, 4; Seneca, *Letters* 113, 24; Plutarch, *On Stoic Self-contradictions* 1046e–f.
20. Diogenes Laertius, *Lives* VII.127; Plutarch, *On Moral Progress* 75c; Cicero, *On Duties* 1, 46; Seneca, *Letters* 116, 5.
21. Epictetus, *Discourses* 4, 12, 15–19.
22. Stobaeus 2, 88, 9–90, 6; 2, 90, 19–91, 9; Diogenes Laertius, *Lives* VII.110–115, 118–119.
23. Diogenes Laertius, *Lives* VII.115.

24. Stobaeus 2, 93, 1–13; Galen, *On Hippocrates' and Plato's Doctrines* 4, 6, 2–3; Epictetus, *Manual* 5.

25. Seneca, *On Anger* 2, 3, 1–2 and 4; Gellius, *Attic Nights* 19, 1, 17–18.

26. Cicero, *On Ends* 3, 60–61; Diogenes Laertius, *Lives* VII.130; Seneca, *Letters* 12.10, 65.22, 117.21, 120.14; Epictetus, *Discourses* I,24,20 and III, 24, 95. See also R. D. Hicks, *Stoic and Epicurean*, 98–101, also Eduard Zeller, *Stoics, Epicureans, and Sceptics*, 335–340.

27. Diogenes Laertius, *Lives* VII.39–41.

28. Ibid., VII.148.

29. Ibid., VII.134–136 and 148–149; Sextus Empiricus, *Adversus mathematicos* IX.75–76; Eusebius, *Praeparatio* 15, 14, 1; Aetius, *Opinions* 1, 7, 33; Cicero, *On the Nature of the Gods* 1, 39 and 2, 37–39 and 75–76; Cleanthes, *Hymn to Zeus;* Cicero, *On the Nature* 2, 16, 88, 93, and 133; Sextus Empiricus, *Adversus mathematicos* IX.133–136.

30. Sextus Empiricus, *Adversus mathematicos* VIII.263; Cicero, *Academica* 1, 39.

31. Diogenes Laertius, *Lives* VII.134; Calcidius 292–293 (see translation in Long and Sedley, *The Hellenistic Philosophers*); Stobaeus 1, 213, 15–21.

32. Diogenes Laertius, *Lives* VII.141; Eusebius, *Praeparatio* 15, 14, 2 and 15, 19, 1–2; Alexander, *On Aristotle's Prior Analytics* 180, 25–31 and 33–36; Lactantius, *Divine Institutes* 7, 23; Numesius, *De natura hominis* 309, 5–311, 2; Philo, *On the Indestructibility of the World* 52, 54, 76–77 and 90; Marcus Aurelius, *Meditations* 2, 14; Origen, *Against Celsus* 4, 68 and 5, 20.

33. Sextus Empiricus, *Adversus mathematicos* VII.234; Hierocles, *Elements of Ethics* 1, 5–33 and 4, 38–53; Plutarch, *On Stoic Self-contradictions* 1037f and 1053d; Galen, *On the Formation of the Foetus* 4, 698, 2–9; Aetius, *Opinions* 4, 21, 1–4; Stobaeus 2, 86, 17–87, 6; Diogenes Laertius, VII.143; Eusebius, *Praeparatio* 15, 20, 6.

34. Stobaeus 1, 161, 8–26; Sextus Empiricus, *Adversus mathematicos* IX.332 and X.3–4; Cleomedes, *De motu circulari corporum caelestrium* 8.10–14; Simplicius, *On Aristotle's On the Heavens* 284, 28–285, 2.

35. Simplicius, *On Aristotle's Categories* 350, 15–16; Stobaeus 1, 105, 17–106, 4 and 1, 106, 5–23; Diogenes Laertius, *Lives* VII.144.

36. Diogenes Laertius, *Lives* VII.142, 144–146, and 155.

37. Stobaeus I, 138, 14–I, 139, 4; Sextus Empiricus, *Adversus mathematicos* IX.211; Aetius, *Opinions* 1, 11, 5.

38. Aetius, *Opinions* 1, 28, 4; see also Gellius 7, 2, 3; Cicero, *On Divination* 1, 125–126.

39. Stobaeus 1, 79, 1–12.

40. Diogenes Laertius, *Lives* VII.149.

41. Cicero, *On fate* 28–30 and 39–43; Gellius 7, 2, 6–13; Eusebius, *Praeparatio* 6, 8, 25–29; Alexander, *On Fate* 181, 13–182, 20; Marcus Aurelius, *Meditations* 8, 14.

42. Diogenes Laertius, *Lives* VII.46–48 and 83.

43. Ibid., VII.43–45 and 57–58.

44. Ibid., VII. 49, 55–57, and 63–68. Also Sextus Empiricus, *Adversus mathematicos* VII.11–12 and 70.

45. Diogenes Laertius, *Lives* VII.65. Also Cicero, *On Fate* 38.

46. Sextus Empiricus, *Adversus mathematicos* VIII. 74 and 88–89.
47. Diogenes Laertius, *Lives* VII.65; Sextus Empiricus, *Outlines of Pyrrhonism* II.138–140.
48. Ibid., VII.69–70; Sextus Empiricus, *Adversus mathematicos* VIII.93–98.
49. Diogenes Laertius, *Lives* VII.71–74; Sextus Empiricus, *Outlines* II.104–106 and 110–113; Gellius 16, 10–14.
50. Diogenes Laertius, *Lives* VII.75–81; Benson Mates, *Stoic Logic* 32, 44.
51. Sextus Empiricus, *Adversus mathematicos* VIII.429–434.
52. Sextus Empiricus, *Outlines* II.229–235; Diogenes Laertius, *Lives* VII.82 and 189–198.
53. Eduard Zeller, *The Stoics, Epicureans, and Sceptics* 123–124.
54. Benson Mates, *Stoic Logic* 89–90.
55. Stobaeus I, 136, 21–137, 6; Aetius, *Opinions* I, 10, 5; Simplicius, *On Aristotle's Categories* 105, 8–16; Syrianus, *On Aristotle's Metaphysics* 104, 17–21.
56. Diogenes Laertius, *Lives* VII.46 and 49–51; Aetius 4, 11, 1–4.
57. Ibid., Sextus Empiricus, *Adversus mathematicos* VII.247–252.
58. Ibid., VII.53; Cicero, *Academica* 2, 21.
59. Cicero, *Academica* 1, 40–41; Epictetus, *Discourses* 1, 22, 1–3 and 9–10; Sextus Empiricus, *Adversus mathematicos* VIII.331a–332b.
60. Sextus Empiricus, *Adversus mathematicos* VII.253–260 and 424.
61. Cicero, *Academica* 2, 145.
62. Sextus Empiricus, *Adversus mathematicos* VII.151–155.
63. Stobaeus 2.111, 18–112, 8; anonymous Stoic treatise (Herculaneum papyrus 1020); Plutarch, *On Stoic Self-contradictions* 1056e–f.
64. Stobaeus 2.73, 16–74, 3.

Chapter Seventeen. Skepticism

1. Cicero, *Academica* 2.130; Diogenes Laertius, *Lives* IX.64–65. Diogenes Laertius, Sextus Empiricus, and Cicero provide most of our information on the Skeptics.
2. Diogenes Laertius, *Lives* IX.61 and 64–66; Sextus Empiricus, *Adversus mathematicos* VI.87–88 and XI.140.
3. Diogenes Laertius, *Lives* IX.68–71.
4. Diogenes Laertius, *Lives* IX.109–116; Eusebius, *Praeparatio* 14.18, 1–5.
5. Diogenes Laertius, *Lives* IV.28, 32–38, and 43.
6. Sextus Empiricus, *Adversus mathematicos* VII.158; Diogenes Laertius, *Lives* VII.171.
7. Cicero, *Academica* I.43 and II.16; Eusebius, *Praeparatio* 14.6.12–13; Sextus Empiricus, *Adversus mathematicos* VII.151–157.
8. Sextus Empiricus, *Adversus mathematicos* VII.159–165, 402–410 and IX.139–41; Cicero, *On the Nature of the Gods* 111.44; Cicero, *On Divination* II.9–10; Cicero, *On Fate* 26–33.
9. Sextus Empiricus, *Adversus mathematicos* VII.166–184; Diogenes Laertius, *Lives* IV.65.
10. Diogenes Laertius, *Lives* IV.67; Cicero, *Academica* 2.103–4.
11. Cicero, *Academica* 2.59 and 148; A.A. Long and D.N. Sedley, *The*

Hellenistic Philosophers 447–449, 470, 501, and 506; Sextus Empiricus, *Outlines* I.235.

12. Diogenes Laertius, *Lives* IX.78–88, 106–107; Photius, *Library* 169b18 and 170b3; Sextus Empiricus, *Outlines* I.36–166. Copleston, *A History of Philosophy*, vol. I, 442–43, outlines Anesidemus's ten modes and Agrippa's five modes.

13. *Outlines* I.8–10 and 25–29. Translations are by R.G. Bury in the Loeb Classical Library edition, *Sextus Empiricus*, edited by R.G. Bury.

14. Ibid., I.4 and 19–20.

15. Ibid., I.226.

16. Ibid., I.3.

17. Ibid., I.36–37 and 176–179 ; II.18–20.

18. Ibid., I.44–7 and 59.

19. Ibid., II.159–166 and 193–204.

20. Ibid., I.32; III.9–11.

Chapter Eighteen. Neo-Platonism

1. Gilbert Murray, *Five Stages of Greek Religion*, 155.

2. R.H. Barrow, *Plutarch and His Times*, 77–78, 82, 103–105; Frederick Copleston, *A History of Philosophy*, Vol. I, 452–453.

3. Barrow, *Plutarch*, 75–77, 82–83.

4. Plutarch, *Superstition* II.165B–C; *Isis and Osiris* 78.

5. Plutarch, *Isis and Osiris* V.376f–382D; *De E apud Delphos (The E at Delphi)* V.384D–394C; *The Oracles at Delphi* V.394D–409D; *The Obsolescence of Oracles* 409E–438E.

6. *Isis and Osiris* V.361A–E and 369A–F; Copleston, *History* I, 453–454.

7. *Isis and Osiris* V.371A–B.

8. Plutarch, *On the Delays of the Divine Vengeance* VII.18.259, 25.279–285, and 32.297–99; *Life of Romulus* I.28.181–183.

9. Philo, *Every Good Man Is Free* and *On the Contemplative Life.* See Samuel Sandmel, *Philo of Alexandria: An Introduction* 32–39.

10. Sandmel, *Philo,* 14–15, 28.

11. Ibid., Chapter 2.

12. Sandmel, *Philo,* Chapter 3; Philo, *Works* in Loeb Classical Library, Vol. X, 269–433.

13. Sandmel, Philo, 22–25.

14. Philo, *De agricultura* 31; *De confusione linguaram* 146–147; Sandmel, *Philo,* 14, 36, 54, 59, 60, 91–92, 95.

15. Sandmel, *Philo,* 59, 60–61, 92.

16. Copleston, *History* I, 452, 455. Plutarch, *Isis and Osiris* V.361A–E and 364E–367E.

17. Copleston, *History,* I, 446–449.

18. Porphyry, *Life of Plotinus* 1, 3, 8.

19. Ibid., 23.

20. Plotinus, *Enneads* I.iii.1 and 6.

21. Ibid., V.i.7; VI.ix.3 and 5–6.

22. Ibid., V.i.7; VI.ix.3.

23. Ibid., IV.viii.1 and 6; V.i.6 and 7; VI.ix.2–3, 6 and 9.
24. Ibid., V.i.6 and 7; V.vii.1; V.ix.5–10, 12, and 14.
25. Ibid., III.vii.11–12; V.1.2 and 7; V.ix.7.
26. Ibid., V.i.8.
27. Ibid., I.i.5; III.v.4; IV.ii.1, iii.5, and viii.8; VI.ix.1.
28. Ibid., II.ix.10–11; IV.viii.1–5; V.i.1 and 3; V.ix.2.
29. Ibid., V.i.7; VI.ix. 3 and 9.
30. Ibid., VI.ix.3–5 and 7.
31. Ibid., III.viii.6; VI.ix.9 and 11.
32. Ibid., III.iv.2; VI.ix.10; Grace Turnbull, *The Essence of Plotinus,* 89n.
33. Plotinus, *Enneads* II.iv.3; II.v.2–5; IV.iii.7.
34. Ibid., II.ix.8–11; III,1.1–4 and 8–10; IV.viii.1 and 5.
35. Ibid., V.ix.11.

Chapter Nineteen. Augustine

1. Augustine, *The Confessions* I.7–19, II.4–7, and VI.15.
2. Augustine, *De doctrina christiana* (On Christian Doctrine) II.18.28.
3. *Confessions* VII.1.3–21.
4. Augustine, *De trinitate* (On the Trinity) IV.1.3.
5. Frederick Copleston, *A History of Philosophy,* II, Chapter V.
6. Augustine, *De libero arbitrio* II.12.33, 13.36, and 15.39 (translated by Dom Mark Pontifex).
7. Paul Tillich, "Two Types of Philosophy of Religion," 3–13.
8. Augustine, *Confessions* I.1; *Third Discourse on Psalm 32,* Section 16.
9. *Confessions* XI.3–9, XII.7.
10. Ibid., XII.3–6, 9, 11–15, 19–25; *De civitate dei* (City of God) XI.21.
11. *Confessions* III.7, 1–15; VII.12.
12. Ibid., VII.13.
13. Ibid., II.4–8; VII.16; *Civitate* XI.17; *De libero arbitrio* I.15.31–35, II.20.54, and III.1.2 and 17.47–49.
14. *Civitate* XIV.12–15.
15. *De quantitate animae* (Of the Greatness of the Soul) 1.2 and 13, 22; Copleston, *History* II, 78–80.
16. *Trinitate* XV.12; *Civitate* II.26; *De libero arbitrio* II.3.7.
17. *De immortalitate animae* (On the Immortality of the Soul) I–IV, IX, and XIII; *Confessions* XX–XXIV.
18. *Civitate* XI.21; *De libero arbitrio* III.1–4.
19. *Confessions* XI.10–28.
20. Ibid., 20 and 28.
21. *Civitate* XII.13–14.
22. Ibid., XI and XV.1–2.
23. Ibid., I.35, XIX.28, and XXI.9–10.
24. Ibid., XIX.18; *Confessions* XIII.9; *Trinitate* XV.12.
25. *Trinitate* XII.13, XIV.22, and XV.12; *Contra academicos* 3, 11, 26.
26. *Confessions* X.14. Translated by Rex Warner.
27. Ibid., X.8–19.

28. *De libero arbitrio* 2, 3, 7; *Civitate* II.26; Augustine, *Contra academicos* III, 10, 23 and 11, 26; Augustine, *Soliloques* I.1, 8–10, 12, and 15.

29. Copleston, *History,* Vol. II, 60–67; *Soliloques* I.3 and 8; *Trinitate* XII.14–15.

30. *Confessions* XXII; *De libero arbitrio* II.9–10, 13, 16–17, 19.

31. *Civitate* XIV.7.

32. *Confessions* IX, XI–XII.

33. Ibid., X.30–34; *Civitate* XIV.16 and 26.

BIBLIOGRAPHY

Allen, Reginald E., editor. *Greek Philosophy: Thales to Aristotle*, third edition. New York: The Free Press, 1991.

Aristotle. *The Works of Aristotle,* edited and translated by David Ross. Twelve volumes. Oxford: The Clarendon Press, 1952.

————. *Introduction to Aristotle,* edited by Richard McKeon. New York: The Modern Library, 1947.

————. *Metaphysics,* translated by Richard Hope. Ann Arbor: The University of Michigan Press, 1968.

————. *Nicomachean Ethics,* translated by David Ross. Oxford and New York: Oxford University Press, 1980.

————. *The Politics,* translated by Ernest Barker. Oxford and New York: Oxford University Press, 1995.

————. *Physics,* translated by Richard Hope. Lincoln: University of Nebraska Press, 1961.

Augustine. *Arbitrario Libero,* translated by Dom Mark Pontifex. Westminster, MD: Newman Press, 1955.

————. *The City of God,* translated by Marcus Dods. New York: The Modern Library, 1950.

————. *Confessions of Saint Augustine,* translated by Rex Warner. New York: The New American Library, 1963.

————. *St. Augustine on the Psalms*, vol. 2, 211, translated by Dame Scholastica Hegbin and Dame Felicitas Corrigan. Westminster, MD: The Newman Press, 1961.

Barrow, R.H. *Plutarch and His Times.* Bloomington: Indiana University Press, 1969.

Benson, Hugh H. *Essays on the Philosophy of Socrates.* New York and Oxford: Oxford University Press, 1992.

Burnet, John. *Early Greek Philosophy.* Cleveland and New York: Meridian Books, 1957.

Copleston, Frederick. *A History of Philosophy.* Garden City: Doubleday, 1985.

Cornford, F.M. "Mystery Religions and Presocratic Philosophy." In *The Cambridge Ancient History.* Cambridge: The University Press, 1960.

Diels, Hermann. *Die Fragmenter der Vensokratiker,* 5th, 6th, 7th editions, edited by W. Kranz. Berlin, 1934–1954.

Diogenes Laertius. *Lives of Eminent Philosophers,* translated by R.D. Hicks. *Two volumes. Cambridge: Harvard University Press, 1958.*

Freeman, Kathleen. *Ancilla to the Pre-Socratic Philosophers.* Cambridge: Harvard University Press, 1962.

Fuller, B.A.G. *A History of Philosophy,* revised edition. New York: Henry Holt, 1945.

Golden, Leon and O.B. Hardison Jr. *Aristotle's Poetics: A Translation and Commentary.* Tallahassee: University Presses of Florida, 1981.

Grote, George. *A History of Greece from the Earliest Period to the Close of the Generation Contemporary with Alexander the Great.,* 6th edition, volume 7. New York: Harper, 1899.

Guthrie, W.K.C. *The Greeks and Their Gods.* Boston: Beacon Press, 1955.

————. *The Sophists.* Cambridge: Cambridge University Press, 1971.

Hicks, R. D. *Stoic and Epicurean.* New York: Russell and Russell, 1962.

Jaeger, Werner. *Aristotle.* New York, London, Oxford: Oxford University Press, 1934.

Kirk, G.S. and J.E. Raven. *The Presocratic Philosophers.* Cambridge: Cambridge University Press, 1969.

Kristeller, Paul Oskar. "The Modern System of the Arts." *Journal of the History of Ideas* 12, no. 4 (1951): 496–527 and 13, no. 1 (1952): 17–46.

Lacy, A.R. "Our Knowledge of Socrates." In *The Philosophy of Socrates,* edited by Gregory Vlastos. Garden City, NY: Doubleday, 1971, 22–49.

Long, A.A. *Hellenistic Philosophy.* New York: Charles Scribner's Sons, 1974.

Long, A.A. and D.N. Sedley. *The Hellenistic Philosophers: Volume I, Translations.* New York: Cambridge University Press, 1987.

Lloyd, G.E.R. *Aristotle: The Growth and Structure of His Thought.* Cambridge: Cambridge University Press, 1968.

Mates, Benson. *Stoic Logic.* Berkeley: University of California Press, 1961.

McLean, George F. and Patrick J. Aspell, editors. *Readings in Ancient Western Philosophy.* New York: Appleton-Century-Crofts, 1970.

Murray, Gilbert. *Five Stages of Greek Religion.* New York: Columbia University Press, 1925.

Oates, Whitney J., editor. *The Stoic and Epicurean Philosophers.* New York: The Modern Library, 1940.

Philo. *Works,* translated by F.H. Colson and G.H. Whitaker. Ten volumes. Cambridge: Harvard University Press, 1958–1962.

Philostratus. *Lives of the Sophists,* translated by Wilmer Cave Wright. Cambridge: Harvard University Press, 1961.

Plato. *The Collected Dialogs of Plato,* edited by Edith Hamilton and Huntington Cairns. New York: The Bollingen Foundation, 1961.

Plutarch. *Lives,* translated by Bernadotte Perrin. Cambridge: Harvard University Press,

————. *Moralia,* translated by Frank Cole Babbit. Cambridge: Harvard University Press, 1960.

Rohde, Erwin. *Psyche: The Cult of Souls and Belief in Immortality Among the Greeks.* London: Routledge, 1925.

Ross, David. *Aristotle.* London: Methuen, 1964; New York: Barnes and Noble, 1964.

Sandmel, Samuel. *Philo of Alexandria: An Introduction.* New York: Oxford University Press, 1979.

Saunders, Jason L., editor. *Greek and Roman Philosophy After Aristotle.* New York: The Free Press, 1966.

Sextus Empiricus. *Against the Professors* (Adversus mathematicos), translated by R.G. Bury. Cambridge: Harvard University Press, 1959.

———. *Outlines of Pyrrhonism,* translated by R.G. Bury. Cambridge: Harvard University Press, 1960.

Sprague, Rosamond Kent. *The Older Sophists.* Columbia: University of South Carolina Press, 1972.

Taylor, A.E. *Plato: The Man and His Work.* Cleveland and New York: World Publishing, 1956.

Tillich, Paul. "Two Types of Philosophy of Religion." *Union Seminary Quarterly Review* (May 1946): 3–13.

Turnbull, Grace H. *The Essence of Plotinus.* Westport, CT: Greenwood Press, 1934.

Untersteiner, Mario. *The Sophists,* translated by Kathleen Freeman. Oxford: Basil Blackwell, 1954.

Vlastos, Gregory, editor. *Plato: A Collection of Critical Essays.* Two volumes. Garden City, NY: Doubleday, 1971.

———. *The Philosophy of Socrates.* Garden City, NY: Doubleday, 1971.

Willoughby, Harold. *Pagan Regeneration.* Chicago: University of Chicago Press, 1960.

Xenophon. *Memorabilia and oeconomicus,* translated by E. C. Merchant (The Loeb Classical Library). Cambridge: Harvard University Press, 1954.

Zeller, Eduard. *Outlines of the History of Greek Philosophy.* Cleveland and New York: Meridian Books, 1955.

———. *Stoics, Epicureans, and Sceptics.* New York: Russell and Russell, 1962.

INDEX

ABOUT THE AUTHOR

Don E. Marietta Jr. is the Snyder Distinguished Professor of Ethics and professor of philosophy at Florida Atlantic University. He is author of *For People and the Planet: Holism and Humanism in Environmental Ethics* (Temple, 1995) and *Philosophy of Sexuality* (M.E. Sharpe, 1996), and he is coeditor of *Environmental Philosophy and Environmental Activism* (Westview, 1995).